Edmd J Perez

ADULT LEARNING IN THE SOCIAL CONTEXT

ADULT LEARNING IN THE SOCIAL CONTEXT

PETER JARVIS

CROOM HELM
London • New York • Sydney

© 1987 Peter Jarvis

Croom Helm Ltd, Provident House,
Burrell Row, Beckenham, Kent BR3 1AT

Croom Helm Australia, 44-50 Waterloo Road,
North Ryde, 2113, New South Wales

British Library Cataloguing in Publication Data

Jarvis, Peter
    Adult learning in the social context.
    1. Learning, Sociology of
    I. Title
    153.1'5   BF318
    ISBN 0-7099-1483-0
    ISBN 0-7099-6012-3 Pbk

Published in the USA by
Croom Helm
in association with Methuen, Inc.
29 West 35th Street,
New York, NY 10001

Library of Congress Cataloging-in-Publication Data

Jarvis, Peter.
    Adult learning in the social context.

    Bibliography: p.
    Includes index.
    1. Adult education — Social aspects. 2. Learning.
3. Educational sociology. I. Title.
LC5225.S64J37 1987 374 87-20024
ISBN 0-7099-1483-0
ISBN 0-7099-6012-3 Pbk

Printed and bound in Great Britain
by Billing & Sons Limited, Worcester.

Contents

Figures

To
Maureen,
Frazer and Kierra,
In Gratitude

Preface

> There can be few intellectual quests that, for educators, and trainers of adults, assume so much significance and yet contain so little promise of successful completion as the search for a general theory of adult learning. Kidd (1973) has compared the quest to the search for Eldorado . . . Learning activities and learning styles vary so much with physiology, culture, and personality that generalized statements about the nature of adult learning have very low predictive power.   (Brookfield, 1986, p. 25)

The above was published at about the time this book was in an early draft and it also echoes the sentiments of this author. While the pursuit of Eldorado may be a never-ending task, it does not prevent some people embarking upon it. This study is no more than a very tentative attempt to plot one or two other possible approaches to the quest. It certainly does not seek to provide authoritative answers, indeed it might merely be regarded as an exercise in asking even more questions. Even so, it is hoped that the questions asked and some of the suggestions made might prove helpful to others who are seeking to understand more fully how adults learn.

This book was not written without considerable help from colleagues and fellow students. Dr Maureen Pope, from the University of Surrey, read an early draft of the first three chapters; Dr John Peters, from the University of Tennessee, also read the first three chapters; Dr Mark Tennant, from Sydney College of Advanced Education, read the second chapter; Dr Roy Ingham from Florida State University spent a great deal of time talking with me and also reading a paper which constitutes part of the fourth chapter. Other colleagues have heard some of the earlier parts of the book when they have been presented as seminar papers and they have also made helpful comments, which have been taken into consideration in the final draft. I am grateful to all of them for their time and consideration. Unfortunately, few of the later chapters have been exposed to such scrutiny, from which they would have no doubt benefited a great deal.

In addition, gratitude is expressed to David Boud, from the University of New South Wales, for permission to reproduce his model of the reflective process. Thanks must also be given to all of those people who participated in the workshops from which the model of the learning processes was devised and upon which this book is based and, in addition, to the many colleagues and students who have participated in seminars that have explored some of these issues since the model was produced and who have made insightful comments and suggestions about adult learning.

My family, to whom this book is dedicated, have suffered most during its preparation and to them I must extend my deep gratitude for their forebearance during the whole of the period.

The book itself is divided into four sections: the first two chapters constitute the basis of the work, examining the state of some of the learning theory and, thereafter, discussing the way that this model of learning was devised; the next four chapters discuss fairly fully the elements of the model; Chapters 7 to 9 examine the different forms of learning that emerged from the research and relate them to their social context; the last chapter relates some of the foregoing to the art of teaching adults. Finally, there is a bibliography containing full references to all the works cited in this study.

Many colleagues and friends have provided the ideas that have gone into the preparation of this book and without which it could not have been written, and to all of them I am extremely grateful, although none of them can take any blame for the finished product! I only hope that it might prove helpful to some in seeking to understand the process of adult learning a little better and, perhaps, to others to enable them to facilitate the adult learning process a little differently.

1

The Social Context of Adult Learning

The less complete and fixed the instinctual equipment of animals,
the more developed is the brain and therefore the ability to learn.
The emergence of man can be defined as occurring at the point
in the process of evolution where instinctive adaptation has reached its minimum. But he emerges with new qualities which differentiate him from the animal: his awareness of himself as a separate
entity, his ability to remember the past, to visualise the future, and
to denote objects and acts by symbols; his reason to conceive and
understand the world; and his imagination through which he reaches
far beyond the range of his senses. Man is the most helpless of
animals, but this very biological weakness is the basis of his
strength, the prime cause of his specifically human qualities.

(Fromm, 1949, p. 39)

At the heart of life itself is the process of learning. It would be easy
to assume that conscious living and learning are synonymous
processes, but it will be argued later that this is not so. Nevertheless, they are very close to each other and constantly overlap.
Learning occurs in a variety of modes: formal, informal, non-formal
directed, self-directed, open, distance, etc. With few exceptions,
e.g. Woodruff (1968), teaching rather than learning has occupied the
academic stage until recently and the central place in educational
theory, but in recent years learning has assumed a more prominent
role. Books about learning have begun to appear in initial education,
e.g. Entwistle (1981), higher education (Marton *et al.*, eds, 1984),
lifelong learning (Knapper and Cropley, 1985) and adult education,
which has emphasised learning for a longer period of time than
has most branches of education, e.g. Kidd (1973), Cross (1981).
However, some of these studies tend to restrict learning to that

which occurs within the traditional educational context.

Most learning theory in adult education has taken a predominantly psychological perspective, which is not surprising since adult education has been concerned with both adult development and traditional approaches to learning. This merely reflects the fact that education generally has emphasised the cognitive psychological approach to learning and, in addition, Piaget's studies of cognitive development have also played a significant role. This study, however, is more concerned to examine the learning processes from a social perspective. Such an approach is by no means a new one to learning theory, since some of the phenomenologists of the past, notably Schutz, and more recent writers on adult education, such as Freire, have produced implicit studies of human learning from this perspective. This approach is not to deny the significance of the psychological, indeed considerable reference is made to it here, but to complement it.

This analysis clearly draws upon the work of the above writers *inter alia* but also upon some of the author's own research. However, learning is a tremendously complex phenomenon, as the following pages illustrate, so that this study does not endeavour to be more than an initial attempt at understanding adult learning from this perspective. However, it is important from the outset to clarify a number of fundamental issues: three present themselves as being sufficiently significant to merit immediate attention: the concept of learning; adult learning within the context of this study: the social dimension of learning. These points constitute the discussion of this opening chapter.

INITIAL CONSIDERATION OF THE CONCEPT OF LEARNING

The concept of knowledge has been of greater significance to the philosophers than has been the process whereby that knowledge has been acquired, which is not really surprising, since there has often been greater interest in the product than the process in society as a whole. But it is significant that knowledge is being suggested here as at least a product of learning since some of the classical definitions of learning in psychology have omitted the process altogether. Borger and Seaborne (1966, p. 14), for example, define learning as 'any more or less permanent change in behaviour which is the result of experience'. In a similar vein, Hilgard and Atkinson (1967 ed, p. 270) define it as 'a relatively permanent change in behaviour that occurs as a result of practice'. There is only an apparent difference between these two definitions since 'experience' and 'practice' appear to be used synonymously, although they are entirely different phenomena as will become apparent throughout this study. That these definitions are similar is best demonstrated by pointing out that in a later edition of their book Hilgard, Atkinson and Atkinson (1979, p. 190) actually substitute experience for practice in their definition. The similarity of these definitions is to be found in their behavioural nature, both are concerned to note that a change in behaviour has occurred — a product. Now there is an obvious link between behaviourism and certain forms of empirical sociology that seek to measure phenomena quantitatively and objectively, but such an approach is not advocated here for a number of reasons. An initial criticism of the behavioural definitions is that they specify that learning is the product of a particular process, namely behaviour modification, whereas learning is both a process and a product. Secondly, as well as having a behavioural component it may also be a cognitive, or an affective, or a cognitive and affective, process and none of these need be identified with a behavioural outcome. Indeed, there can even be some situations where the learner knows (cognitive) and wishes (affective) to change a behaviour pattern as a result of some learning process, but is aware that the management of the occupational organisation, or the peer group, would frown upon such behaviour, so that the learner consciously does not act in accord with the learning that has occurred. But failure to act does not deny that learning has actually occurred, and in the case of this illustration learning has occurred in a number of ways, including that of recognising what would be regarded as acceptable behaviour within the social setting. Learning may result in, but cannot be identified with, behavioural change. Consequently, the behaviourist definitions contain too many logical fallacies to be accepted here. Borger and Seaborne (1966, p. 16) are not unaware of this problem but claim that 'our judgement of whether any learning has taken place must ultimately rest on making some sort of observations'. However, this attempt to defend the definition only compounds the problems, since learners may assess their own learning, which may actually be far more accurate than any of the present methods of assessment utilised in education. However, there is a far more damaging criticism of this defence since, ultimately, it is claiming that the conceptualisation of any phenomenon must be limited to the methods used to study it, which is totally illogical, since the logical outcome of such a position must be that phenomena only exist when they are discovered!

Borger and Seaborne (1966, p. 18) are aware, however, that cognitive processes do exist and that they are significant to learning:

> . . . it is important to remember that the organism does have an 'inside', and whatever explanations we put forward to account for change in behaviour will, in the long run, have to fit in with what we can discover, by different means, about the working of the inside.

However, Skinner (1971) would dispute this, since he argued that what is going on inside individuals is no more than a response to their environment. Even thought itself, which he (1971, p. 189) considered to be 'the last stronghold of autonomous man', is no more than a product of the environment, in his opinion. While this argument has certain attractions, there seem to be some crucial flaws to his position and three of these will be raised here. First, if a person can be taught to think critically and also to be autonomous, then it is difficult to maintain that what is going on within a person in subsequent situations is merely the result of the environment, or determined by previous experiences. Secondly, if Kohlberg's (1973) research on the stages of moral development has any substance, then that stage of being autonomous or acting on principles would seem to stand in contradistinction to Skinner's position. Thirdly, there are a number of methodological problems about behavioural research that will be examined in more detail here.

Watson, the founding father of behaviourism, studied both animals and children and came to the conclusion that 'stimulus-response (S-R) connections are more likely to be established the more frequently or recently an S-R bond occurs' (Child, 1981, pp. 84–5). However, and quite significantly, Watson also noted that children make many unsuccessful attempts before they arrive at a correct solution and that, having arrived at one, other attempts were not made. Hence, a logical outcome of this finding is that children actually learn that their attempts are not correct, so that they are experimenting all the time and, therefore, learning all the time. Such a conclusion would be in accord with Kelly's (1963) claim that the human being is ultimately a scientist seeking to predict and control through experimentation.

Perhaps the most well known of all psychological research into learning, although not now the most frequently utilised approach, is that of Pavlov (1927), who proposed the theory of classical conditioning. Briefly, this claims that the learner is conditioned (learns ?) to associate the presentation of a reward with a stimulus that occurs fractionally prior to it. Thus Pavlov's dogs salivated at the sound of a bell, since they had been fed on previous occasions when the bell sounded. This form of conditioning appears to be limited to reflex mechanisms and emotional reactions, but if there is a cognitive element then this must also be seen as part of the process. Hence, children learn to look forward to Mrs X teaching them because she has previously created a nice, warm friendly atmosphere in the classroom. While this might not have been the intention of the class teacher, the process has been similar. This is the same as Knowles' (1984, pp. 14–17) recognition of the importance of setting suitable climate in which adults may learn. By contrast, operant conditioning occurs when the response is actually shaped by the rewards so that after every occasion when the response approaches, approximates to or achieves the desired behaviour, the child receives a sweet, or the adult is praised for a very good attempt, etc. Operant conditioning was expounded by Skinner (1953), whose initial research was with rats and pigeons. Child (1981, p. 89) neatly summarises Skinner's conclusions about learning:

- each step in the learning process should be short and grow out of previously learned behaviour
- in the early stages, learning should be rewarded regularly and, thereafter, it should be controlled by a schedule of reinforcement
- reward should follow rapidly on feedback
- the learner should be given the opportunity to discover stimulus discriminations for the most likely path to success.

Obviously, Skinner and other behaviourists seem more concerned to discover the technology whereby a correct response can be learned rather than understanding the learning process *per se*. Additionally, they have done so with animals and children; with the former, no mechanisms exist to discover the content of their thought processes, if there are any, and with the latter little or no attempt was made to find out what they were thinking . Since the researchers were also adults, the child learners were placed in a controlled environment which thereby created the conditions to produce conformity. This is a similar point to the one that Yonge (1985) raised when he sought to distinguish andragogy from pedagogy on the grounds that a different form of teacher-learner relationship exists between adult learner-teacher and child learner-teacher and that the former may be more egalitarian than the latter.

Thus it may be concluded that behaviourism is based upon a number of suspect premises and that some of its conclusions about learning may be too sweeping for its own research design. Hence, the behaviourist definition of learning is rejected here. It would now

5

perhaps be possible, although rather tedious, to examine every other school of psychology in the same manner, seeking a definition that is acceptable. Such a procedure was decided against here, rather a perspective almost diametrically opposed to the behaviourist one was chosen to examine next; that of the experientialist writer, David Kolb (1984).

Kolb, like Borger and Seaborne, is interested in experience, but he highlights those forms of learning that begin with experience and those which begin with the cognitive and are then tested through experience. He discusses these two processes, which he calls apprehension and comprehension: the former he regards as the grasping of an experience while the latter is the cognitive mode that results from the transformation of experience into knowledge. Hence, he seeks to combine these into a single definition of learning, which is 'the process whereby knowledge is created through the transformation of experience' (Kolb, 1984, p. 41). Clearly, less empirical research evidence has been conducted from this perspective than that of behaviourism. Nevertheless, Kolb has sought to show through his learning style inventory and his learning cycle that human learning is both an experiential and a reflective process. In this he also finds support amongst many adult educators; both from the radical domain and from the more conservative, from Freire (1972a, 1972b) and from Knowles (1978, 1980). While Knowles discusses learning in the former of the publications mentioned, he does not actually produce his own definition. Rather he demonstrates that he supports a humanistic approach without the precision of an accepted definition. Kolb's definition, however, is clearly stated and, consequently, it is open for discussion. From this definition, Kolb proceeds to show how he believes that there are four forms of knowledge and that each of these relate to his learning cycle and to the learning style of the learners. Since considerable discusion is devoted to his learning cycle in the following chapter it is not considered necessary to explore it all here. However, the strength of his approach lies in the fact that he actually starts with human beings and he assumes that the process of thought is not a delusion nor completely controlled by the environment and, thereafter, he seeks to show what he considers learning to be. It is possible to criticise him on his existentialist assumptions. Indeed, empirical sociologists, amongst other scholars, might do just this, but the phenomenologists would not. Hence, it is important to recognise that there are fundamentally opposing perspectives in the social sciences about how phenomena should be analysed. Since these distinctions cannot be resolved here, it is necessary to recognise the philosophical foundations of Kolb's position, and indeed of that adopted here, and then return to an analysis of his definition.

Perhaps the major criticism of Kolb's definition is that it implies that learning is a singular process and that the outcome is always knowledge. Marton and Saljo (1984) report on a number of recent studies of learning and demonstrate that it is a very complex process but one in which individuals' strategies differ, with some students seeking holistic approaches to their learning and others being more atomistic. However, one significant aspect about their paper is that they record how Saljo's research demonstrated that adults have five qualitatively different approaches to learning:

- a quantitative increase in knowledge
- memorising
- the acquisition of facts, methods, etc, which can be retained and used when necessary
- the abstraction of meaning
- an interpretative process aimed at understanding reality (Marton and Saljo, 1984, p. 52)

One significant aspect of this research is that it suggests that there may be more than one type of learning process and that it does point to the fact that the level of cognition differs with different learners. These different approaches to learning are very important and will be referred to again in a subsequent chapter.

It was also implied above that learning may not only have a cognitive outcome. If, for instance, the climate has been set which is conducive to learning, in the way that Knowles (1984), among others, suggests, then the learner may learn to associate learning with 'feeling good', so that an affective outcome may also be learned. However, this does raise a major conceptual difficulty, since learning and conditioning may be regarded a fundamentally different. Perhaps the point at issue here is the level of conscious awareness being exercised by the learner during the process. But it is suggested that there is such a phenomenon as pre-conscious learning, which produces cognitive outcomes, and so it would be difficult to distinguish between preconscious cognitive and pre-conscious affective outcomes in the learning processes. The topic of the pre-conscious is one which will be returned to in the fifth chapter. Additionally, Kolb's definition omits the aspect of skills acquisition through practice, etc. implicit in the definition of Hilgard and Atkinson. Hence, it is considered necessary to widen Kolb's definition and suggest that learning is the transformation of experience into knowledge, skills and attitudes, and to recognise that this occurs through a variety of processes.

Knowledge itself is a difficult concept to define since it is clear that knowledge is no single phenomenon and people arrive at a state of knowing through different processes and have different methods of verification of what they hold to be knowledge. For the sake of clarity Berger's and Luckmann's (1967, p. 13) definition of knowledge as 'the certainty that phenomena are real and that they possess certain characteristics' is accepted here. In order to clarify the definition further it is now necessary to distinguish knowledge from attitude: the latter may be viewed as an enduring system 'of cognitions, feelings and action tendencies with respect to various objects' (Krech *et al.*, 1962, p. 139).

It should be noted here that a variety of processes are suggested rather than one single process, and it should be recognised from the outset that most people probably realise that many different learning processes exist. But if they were asked to explain what they meant by learning they would probably do so in terms of memorising information that was presented to them within the formal organisation of the school. This is a social definition of learning, a process that has been labelled as learning, so that it is essential to distinguish between the social and a conceptual definition.

Having thus examined the concept of learning and arrived at a definition which indicates something of the breadth of the phenomenon, it is now necessary to relate this to adult learning.

ADULT LEARNING

It is necessary from the outset to clarify a number of issues here, since adult educators have sometimes tended to confuse adult education and adult learning. It was easy to see how this could have occurred when learning was regarded as synonymous with enrolling on a course and attending formal education classes. However, since it is now recognised that self-directed learning is a common occurrence, it is important to regard education and learning as conceptually distinct phenomena. Indeed, it was claimed elsewhere (Jarvis, 1986, p. 8) that education may be regarded as the institutionalisation of learning. Hence, learning is a phenomenon in its own right and should be studied as such (see Merriam, 1986, for a full discussion of the literature relating to adult learning). It is now conceptually imprecise to confuse education and learning in the manner that it has been hitherto in some adult education literature. The focus of this study is upon learning: education will only be discussed as an adjunct to it.

However, there is a far more important reason for discussing the concept of adult learning here and that is because some adult educators have tended to regard the process of adult learning as being different to that of child learning. It is necessary to review the debate that has occurred within adult education in order to clarify the issues involved here.

The debate really began as a result of Knowles's (1970) seminal study *The Modern Practice of Adult Education: Andragogy versus Pedagogy* in which he contrasted adult learning (andragogy) to child learning (pedagogy). Andragogy may be defined as 'the art and science of helping adults learn' according to Knowles (1980, p. 43) and pedagogy as 'the art and science of teaching children' (ibid.). An immediate conceptual problem presents itself with these two definitions and that is that Knowles has not exhausted his possibilities, so that it might be asked what he would call 'the art and science of teaching adults' or 'the art and science of helping children learn'. However, it is not necessary to pursue this here, since these problems are implicit in the debate that followed. For Knowles, the theory of adult learning was based on four assumptions:

- the adult's self-concept is different to that of the child;
- adults have a reservoir of experience that they can bring to their learning and which acts as a rich resource;
- adults are ready to learn;
- adults have a problem-centred approach to learning whereas children are subject centred.

Obviously these assumptions are not grounded in rigorous empirical research nor based on a solid theoretical foundation. Indeed, more recently, Knowles (1984, p. 12) added a fifth assumption:

- adults are motivated to learn by internal factors rather than external ones.

Knowles is currently very clear that his model of andragogy is parallel to pedagogy and not antithetical to it, but the initial title to his book did suggest that they were opposing ideas. However, not all scholars actually accepted Knowles's original formulation. As

9

early as 1972, Houle was gently critical of the two terms, but the main debate did not begin until a few years later. It commenced when McKenzie (1977) sought to provide Knowles's rather pragmatic formulation about adult learning with a more solid philosophical foundation, by claiming that andragogy was existentially orientated. He suggested that since adults and children are existentially different, andragogy and pedagogy are logically different. However, Elias (1979, p. 254) responded to this by claiming that this distinction is not necessarily significant since men and women are existentially different but that nobody claimed that 'the art and science of teaching women differs from the art and science of teaching men'. Feminists may not make such a claim! This, however, was not McKenzie's response; rather he accepted Elias's point but claimed that that this existential difference was insignificant in relation to the lifespan, whereas there was a significant difference between adults and children in this respect. While there may be some foundation in this point, it may be more related to experience than to age *per se*, and this will be argued more forcefully in the succeeding chapters.

It is not necessary here to review the remainder of this debate. Suffice to note that in 1979 Knowles chose to re-enter it, and this time he acknowledged that andragogy and pedagogy were not two discrete processes based upon age but that 'some pedagogic assumptions are realistic for adults and some andragogical assumptions are realistic for children in some situations' (Knowles, 1979, p. 53). Since then there have been few writers who have sought to distinguish andragogy from pedagogy on the grounds of age. Some writers, however, have been concerned to criticise Knowles's formulation of andragogy, in some cases on the grounds of its ideological rather than its psychological character, but since this is not really the concern of this section of the chapter it will not be pursued here. One writer, however, has raised an interesting point that does require consideration. Yonge (1985) has suggested that a difference between andragogy and pedagogy lies in the manner by which the learner is accompanied through the learning process by the teacher; with the child there is a relationship of trust, understanding and authority, but when the child matures the relationship changes. For Yonge, pedagogy highlights the childlike elements in the relationship whereas andragogy focuses upon the adult ones. Thus the way that the learner defines the total teaching and learning process may affect the process significantly: a child defining it in a dependent and 'obedience'-giving manner may seek to memorise the content of what is being taught but an adult, defining it differently, may question the validity, or the relevance, of that content. Now this is an important point since it does not suggest that there is an intrinsic difference in the learning processes, only that there is a difference in the external processes that accompany the teaching and learning process. In short, there is a social difference rather than a psychological one. However, this social difference may actually result in a different learning process occurring; this will be discussed in a subsequent chapter. Even so, it is possible, briefly, to illustrate this point here. If a teacher expects a learner to reproduce the information that has been presented, then the learning process may merely be rote learning, whether the learner be a child or an adult. But if a teacher expects the learner to solve a problem, then the learning process may involve both reasoning and reflecting, irrespective of the age of the learner. However, there might be more likelihood of children being expected to reproduce and adults being expected to problem solve because of their respective statuses. Teachers may be less likely to expect conformity from adults, or even to encourage it. Hence, it is possible to see how the social conditions in which the learning occurs may be a constituent causal factor in different learning processes occurring which relates to Yonge's position. Thus it is recognised here that adult learning may be no different from child learning, given the same social situation, so that the sub-title of this section, 'Adult Learning', relates only to the social status of the learner and not to intrinsically different forms of learning.

Finally, it must be recognised that for the purpose of this discussion the term *adult* refers to a social status rather than a biological age, since in some countries in the world adulthood is achieved at younger biological ages than in others. This point does demonstrate the significance of recognising that learning does not occur in social isolation and that the occurrence of different forms of learning may be the result of social and cultural pressures rather than biological differences alone.

THE SOCIAL DIMENSION OF LEARNING

It will be clear from the above discussion that the position adopted here is that learning is not just a psychological process that happens in splendid isolation from the world in which the learner lives, but that it is intimately related to that world and affected by it. Indeed, Woodruff (1968, p. 197) made this point clearly in 1968 when he wrote that 'learning of all kinds begins with direct perception of something in life'. This is a position that is adopted throughout this book. Hence, it is as important to examine the social dimension of adult learning as it is to understand the psychological mechanisms of the learning process. It is considered necessary here to spend a little time justifying this position, although it is not necessary to prolong the debate.

Every person is born into a society that has already established its own culture; a concept which may be regarded as the sum total of knowledge, values, beliefs, attitudes of the society, etc. This culture appears to be objective to the individual and is, in part, acquired by everyone in society through their socialisation process, and through other similar processes such as formal education. Because of the commonality of this phenomenon, culture appears to be objective but it is better recognised as objectified. The process of acquiring culture may be depicted simply by Figure 1.1.

Figure 1.1 The process of internalisation of 'objectified culture'

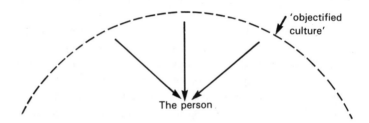

That no person is a total social isolate is a truism and it is through interaction with other people that the individual actually acquires this culture. The arrows in Figure 1.1 indicate the direction of the transmission in an interaction between an individual, who may be described as a learner, and any other person, who may be regarded as a teacher. But in other interactions, or even at another moment in the same interaction, the learner may become the teacher. Hence, it may be seen that every interaction may be regarded as a potential process of teaching and learning and in that interaction each participant may play both roles of teacher and learner, so that Figure 1.1 may be regarded as a little over-simple.

Additionally there are other processes through which a person learns about the culture of the society, such as exposure to the media and the reading of books, etc. Much of the discussion of socialisation tends to suggest that it is something that occurs only in childhood, but sociologists regard this initial process as primarily socialisation.

Secondary socialisation is any subsequent process that inducts an already socialized individual into new sectors of the objective world of his society' (Berger and Luckmann, 1967, p. 150), so that learning may be regarded as something that occurs throughout the lifespan, whenever new experiences occur and new interactions take place.

As the individual grows and matures within the context of social living, the person becomes, in part, a reflection of the sum total of experiences that the individual has in society. But that culture is not a single undifferentiated phenomenon, it varies by socio-economic class, by ethnic community, by region and even by gender. Each of these differences may be treated as sub-cultures and so Figure 1.1 may be applied to each situation and the resulting acquisition will vary in accord with the objectified sub-culture that the individual internalises. Hence, every aspect of the person is social; even the language a person acquires is social. Bernstein (1971), for instance, showed how linguistic codes differed between children of different social class. He claimed (1971, p. 110) that his research showed that the two codes, elaborated and restricted, are 'functions of different social structures'. While his work has been criticised on methodological grounds, he has still highlighted the fact that there are different codes of speech related to different socio-economic groups in society. The extent to which language constrains thought, however, is of concern to this study. It will be discussed in the fifth chapter, and it will be shown that there is some relationship between the two, but that thought is not totally bound by one linguistic cultural mode of communication.

From the above discussion it is quite easy to understand why Lawton (1973, p. 21) regarded the curriculum as a selection from culture, since education is one of the means whereby that culture is transmitted to the individual learner. Obviously, Lawton's work has been undertaken within children's education, but his ideas are as relevant for adult education as they are for children's. For instance, culture need not only be class based but occupationally orientated as well, so that the curriculum in professional preparation is that selection of the professional sub-culture that is generally accepted as being worth transmitting to new recruits to that occupation by those who have power and responsibility in the profession.

However, the individual does not only inhabit a socio-cultural milieu. One other important dimension must be recognised; the temporal dimension. Not only is the person changing as a result of the experiences of social living, the socio-cultural milieu is also undergoing change. Hence, that over-arching depiction of objectified culture is itself an ever-changing phenomenon and therefore the objectified culture that is being transmitted is always undergoing change. Change is in fact endemic to social living and stasis is the rarity rather than the reverse.

Thus it may be seen that all aspects of the individual are, to some degree, a reflection of the social structure. But this is not merely an acquisition, or receptive process, since this social self affects the manner in which persons perceive and interpret their experiences in social living. Individuals do not merely receive these impressions from culture and have them imprinted; rather there is a process of thought and then, also, one of externalisation. Hence, individuals actually modify what is received and it is the changed version that is subsequently transmitted to other people in social interaction. It is the failure to recognise this that is one of the major criticisms of the behaviourist position.

Figure 1.2 The nature of the individual in relation to 'objectified' culture

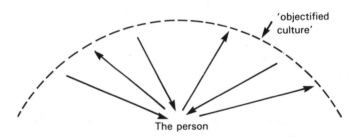

In Figure 1.2, the arrows indicate both the process of internalisation and that of externalisation. The person is both teacher and learner in any social interaction and, as learners, individuals process those experiences and only accept those perceived aspects of them that for various reasons they wish, or are forced, to accept.

But the significant feature of this discussion is that throughout it has been recognised that learning is occurring. Interaction is, however, social and the content with which the learner is presented is also social. Hence, there is a social dimension to learning, which is the focus of this study.

It is for these reasons that it is maintained here that the study of learning is as much the prerogative of the sociologist as it is of the psychologist. Learning is a rich social process and to restrict it to the individualistic processes of some psychological research is to render it a disservice.

CONCLUSION

The main focus of this opening chapter has been to highlight the fact that learning always occurs within a social context and that the learner is also to some extent a social construct, so that learning should be regarded as a social phenomenon as well as an individualistic one. As yet, however, the actual process of adult learning has not been examined in this study and this constitutes the focus of the following chapter.

2

Adult Learning Processes

The opening chapter sought to demonstrate that learning is a legitimate field of study for social sciences, in addition to psychology, and it demonstrated that micro-sociology, especially interactionism and phenomenology, has a great deal to contribute to the understanding of the adult's learning processes. Additionally, it defined learning as the process of transforming experience into knowledge, skills and attitudes. The purpose of this chapter is to highlight the actual processes of learning and it contains four main sections: the first examines one clear attempt to demonstrate the human learning processes — Kolb's learning cycle; the second records the methodology whereby a new model of adult learning processes was constructed; the third section discusses the model that evolved as a result of the research; the fourth examines the different responses to a potential learning experience that emerged in this research. However, this latter section is only a brief introduction to the model, since the remainder of the book endeavours to expound some of the issues that the model raises.

KOLB'S LEARNING CYCLE

Dewey (1938, p. 25) recognised that: '. . . all genuine education comes about through experience, [although this] does not mean that all experiences are genuinely or equally educative . . . For some experiences are miseducative.' It is this insight to which return will be made several times in the ensuing pages, since it is claimed here that even miseducative experiences may be regarded as learning experiences and that *all* learning begins with experience. Experience is something that happens to a person, in which the person is involved usually as a result of conscious living and the reaction to such may result in learning. Learning and experience are not synonymous, neither are learning and education, but there is a considerable overlap between them and these points will become clearer as the argument proceeds.

However, some writers have tended to regard experience as something that is concrete, and even affective rather than cognitive. This is certainly true of those thinkers whose main educative concern is often termed 'experiential education', where they actually mean affective education. However, to restrict experience to the affective domain is to limit it far too greatly, since it is possible to experience the world through a number of different senses: Merleau-Ponty (Mallin, 1979, p. 15), for instance, claims that people relate to the world in a combination of the cognitive, the perceptual, the affective and the practical. Hence, experience is not limited here to concrete nor to affective experiences only. Indeed, a similar criticism may be levelled at those scholars who limit learning to the cognitive domain, since this assumes that the individual only responds to experiences in the life world in a cognitive manner. Such is not the case, since every response to a social situation may contain an emotive as well as a cognitive element. These points are also implicit criticisms of Kolb's model of learning, since he limits the breadth of the learning experience, but before any other discussion takes place it will be wise to examine Kolb's own position.

Figure 2.1 Kolb's learning cycle

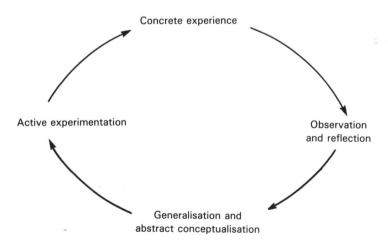

In his work Kolb has sought to incorporate three very distinct phenomena within the same model; there are, first of all, the actual learning processes, then there is the relationship of these to knowledge and, finally, there is the style by which the learning occurs or the knowledge is acquired. It is one of the strengths of this approach that Kolb draws the types of relationship that he does, since it is obvious that these three ideas are intimately connected. This model is extremely clear in this way and it has attempted to incorporate a wide variety of perspectives, including psychology, philosophy and some semiotics. It has provided a clear foundation upon which future researchers can build in order to achieve an even greater understanding of learning *per se*. Hence, this study is a very important one for the advance of learning theory but it does appear rather too neat and perhaps oversimple, so that it is necessary to examine it in greater depth. This will be undertaken by looking at each of his three elements in turn, starting with the learning cycle itself.

Kolb (1984, p. 30) claims that there are four elements in learning: concrete experiences (CE), reflective observation (RO), abstract conceptualisation (AC) and active experimentation (AE). These are placed in sequence in his model, which he then regards as being cyclical, so that it is possible to begin the learning process anywhere in the cycle. Clearly, it is possible to consider having a sense experience and reflecting upon it, perhaps drawing lessons from it and then trying them out in a similar situation so it fits the pattern perfectly. However, what has happened to the learner in the process? How does that learning experience affect the next time that the individual encounters a similar situation? These are questions that the model does not answer in its present form. However, consider the situation where a person is reading a complex mathematical tome and is involved in abstract conceptualisation from the outset: the next stage of the learning process might be reflection rather than active experimentation and so the arrows would need to point in both directions. In addition, Schon (1983, pp. 49–69) discusses the idea of reflection-in-action in which the active experimentation is followed directly by the reflection, or they occur almost simultaneously. Hence, there may be stages of Kolb's cycle that are not sequential.

It will be seen from the above criticism that the example that is the 'best fit' to the model is the one that begins with the concrete experience, and this reflects the fact that Kolb is concerned with a very specific form of experience in devising this model. Therefore, the model does provide a perspective upon reality for that form of experience, but it does not actually relate too precisely to other forms of experiencing and learning.

18

This leads nicely to the second aspect of the discussion. Kolb wisely demonstrates that learning and knowledge are intimately related. This is another of the very important aspects of his work, but for adult educators it is perhaps important to relate this to Yonge's (1985) argument about how the learner is accompanied through the learning process. If the learner is a child who thinks that the teacher wishes the knowledge to be learned in the way that it is presented, i.e. as if it were an empirical fact, then the learning may result in a form of memorisation. If the learner is an adult in an art appreciation class, seeking to understand and interpret a piece of abstract art or sculpture, the knowledge/learning that the learner gains from it may be regarded as the creation of new knowledge as a result of undergoing a process of reflection. It is, therefore, important to see that different approaches to knowledge might produce different learning processes. Indeed, it might be useful to pursue this argument into the different types of knowledge, i.e. rational, empirical and pragmatic knowledge. It might be possible to learn rational/logical knowledge without reference to active experimentation, to learn empirical facts with reference only to memorisation and pragmatic knowledge by experimentation upon experience. Since these are conceivable, it does suggest that Kolb's excellent model might be a little over-simple.

Additionally, it is necessary from the outset to distinguish learning style from cognitive style, since learning and cognition are not synonymous. This distinction requires further consideration later in this book. There are also learning styles other than the ones that Kolb discusses (see Knox, 1977, pp. 477–8) and he would need perhaps to account for these. Finally, on a number of occasions when using Kolb's learning style inventory it has been discovered that individuals who have been replicating their assessment of their own learning style have not achieved consistent results. While this is to be expected, it does suggest that the approach is questionable, since it is most unlikely that actual learning styles would change so drastically as some people have observed to this writer when this method has been employed.

From the above discussion it will be seen that these three aspects that Kolb linked together, — learning, knowledge and learning style — are intimately related. But the above analysis also appears to be very critical of Kolb's learning cycle, although this must be seen in context, since his work has made a very important contribution to the advance of learning theory in that he attempted to produce a clear model of learning and he has highlighted a number of very important aspects within it. Indeed, he acknowledges that his approach is experiential and consequentially limited, as was shown earlier. Hence,

19

this examination has endeavoured to widen the discussion and, as such, it has sought to focus upon learning from a broader perspective. The model has been discussed at length here simply because it was one of the starting points for the research that is described in the next two sections of this chapter, when his cycle was actually employed and became the basis for a new model that is described later in the chapter. Hence, while this is a criticism of Kolb's model, it is also an acknowledgement that it was one of the stimuli that led to this study.

Indeed, not only was Kolb's work a stimulus in this study, his cycle was actually used as part of the research process, and it is for this reason that his work has been so fully discussed at the outset to this chapter. The remainder of this chapter, however, demonstrates how Kolb's work was used in this research, and then reports upon the research findings.

RESEARCH METHODOLOGY

It will be recalled that one of the major criticisms of the behaviourist approach to learning was that it did not seek to discover the thought processes that the learner went through in the process of learning; Kolb, by contrast, has highlighted the fact that learners reflect upon their experience and thereby learn. Other writers have also concentrated upon the process of reflection, notably Boud *et al*. (1985), in which they also produce a model of learning which will be discussed in the fifth chapter, when the reflective process constitutes the focus of analysis. However, the crucial point is the significance of trying to investigate the variety of thought and action processes that constitute learning. It was not regarded as feasible to try to get people to discuss their learning processes in the abstract, which ruled out any attempt to interview people in order to study how they learned.

Eventually a method was devised that enabled individuals to discuss their learning processes, and this grew out of a workshop situation. The author was invited to conduct a number of workshops for educators of adults about adult learning and its relation to teaching. In order to get adult educators to think about the learning process, which was for them so closely associated with teaching and learning, an exercise was devised that started from a concrete learning situation and moved to an abstraction. Indeed, the research methodology followed Kolb's learning cycle precisely!

Before this happened, the workshop participants were given a brief introduction to the day and it was indicated to them that learning theory was rather child based and behaviourist in many situations. Some of the weaknesses of traditional approaches were mentioned and discussed and then all the participants in the workshop were asked to think about any learning experience that they had had and to record what started the process, how they learned from the experience and what completed the process. Most people who undertook this exercise found it very difficult, which illustrates the fact that isolating learning in this manner in order to discuss it is something that occurs irregularly in educational circles.

Having got each member of the group to isolate a learning process in this way, the members of the workshop were then invited to move into pairs and to compare and contrast their experiences of learning. At this stage it was suggested that they may wish to begin to build a simple model of the learning processes that they had recorded. Since there were only two learning experiences to discuss, the models tended to be rather simple; indeed, in some instances they were not more than two descriptions! However, the pairs were then invited to snowball into larger groups of four by combining two pairs and to undertake the same exercise with their learning models. By this time some of the models that were being constructed were much more abstract, quite complex and were demonstrating very insightful analyses. The groups were often invited to share their ideas after the snowball, so that there was a period of feedback and more general discussion, during which time members of different groups sometimes modified their own models of learning slightly.

Thereafter, the groups of four were reconvened and this time they were given Kolb's learning cycle and were told that the leader did not necessarily accept that the model that they had been given was correct, and so they were then invited to change it in the light of their own discussions. Because they knew that the leader did not necessarily accept the model, they might have felt freer to adapt it, but it was recognised that at this stage, whatever position the leader adopted might have influenced the outcome of this discussion. Nevertheless, it was considered wiser to give the groups opportunity to feel free to disagree from the outset. After a considerable period of discussion the groups were invited to share their new models with the whole workshop and general discussion followed once again.

The final element in this research was then enacted; each group of four was given another model and they were then asked to modify that in the light of their previous discussion. At the first of these workshops, this stage was different since there was no other model to discuss. What actually occurred in this instance was that the group devised a model in open session that was to become the one used in the subsequent workshops. Thereafter, the second model produced was the one that emerged out of the previous workshops, so that each final stage modified the model with which the previous workshop concluded. This modification was undertaken in the light of the discussion and feedback each time. Obviously, there were fewer modifications as the number of workshops conducted increased.

Initially, groups who participated in these workshops were not told that there was a research project being conducted with their work, because at that stage there was still considerable doubt about how the investigation would proceed. Additionally, each of the stages, as described above, were not followed so rigorously that the procedure did not vary to suit the conditions of the workshop since, after all, the purpose of the workshop was always other than the research being recorded here. Indeed, with only one exception, all of the workshops were conducted with educators in order to help them think about their role of teacher a little more clearly and so, in these cases, having arrived at a model of learning, it constituted the basis for discussion about teaching. The one group in which the basis of discussion was not teaching was a group following an award-bearing course in adult development and in this instance the model formed the basis for discussion about human growth and development. However, it is quite significant to note that when the procedure was established and the groups were told that the outcome of the workshop was being incorporated into a piece of research about how adults learn, more of the participants discussed the final model with the author at the end of a session and made other suggestions about the structures of learning that were beginning to appear.

The actual process took over a year to complete, the first of the workshops being conducted with a group of adult educators in the Spring of 1985 and the final one in April 1986. In all, there were initially nine workshops conducted: four with groups of professional adult educators in the United Kingdom; two with educators undertaking part-time taught degrees in adult education, including doctorates, at the University of Tennessee; one with a group of Open University part-time tutors; one with a group of nurse educators; one with an in-service half-day for school teachers who taught children from eight to eighteen years of age. In addition, a number of other groups and individuals saw the model at various stages of its construction and were invited to comment upon it, since it was employed in a number of other group sessions. The total number of people who participated in these workshops were approximately 200, with about another 200 seeing the model and being asked to comment upon it at various stages in its construction. Two earlier versions of the model were published prior to this one, and at that time little reference was made to the manner in which the models were being constructed (Jarvis, 1986, 1987a).

It is perhaps significant that independently another approach to the study of adult learning was being undertaken by Ingham and Nelson (1984), who sought to understand the process through the use of life history. In this study they attempted to get respondents to talk about significant events in their lives and to highlight the learning processes that occurred. The objective of this research was to highlight significant elements in learning, rather than to devise a model of learning like the one constructed here. This approach reflects that of Houle (1984), who examined biographies of well-known people in order to understand their patterns of learning.

It might be claimed that this sample was not very accurately constructed and this would be a just criticism, since there was no way that the sample could be controlled. However, there were a variety of different age groups, from young adults to retired people, of both sexes, but since they were nearly all adult educators or university students they were predominantly from the middle classes. In addition, while the sample spanned both American and British groups, with one or two from other cultural backgrounds, there was a predominance of white English-speaking people in the various workshops that were conducted.

Another criticism that might be levelled at this research methodology is that it pre-supposed Tough's (1979, pp. 7–8) very deliberate learning and precludes any unintentional learning that occurs through the socialisation process, etc. This criticism would be totally justified and Niebuhr's (1984) approach in considering all the learning that has occurred within a person's life since birth might have focused upon this unintentional, or pre-conscious, learning. However, such an approach would not have enabled the research to highlight the processes in human learning that this research has produced. Therefore, reference will be made below to this factor when discussing the various forms of learning.

The final stage in constructing the model was to build into it, once again, the different learning routes that had been discussed throughout many of the workshops. None of these routes necessarily reflects any of the initial descriptions of learning that each of the participants in the workshops thought about, since it was not expected that any of them would necessarily devise a complete pattern of the learning

23

experience upon which they were concentrating. At the same time, many of the participants have subsequently informed the leader that they could fit the learning experience that they initially wrote down within the framework of the model.

The research methodology is recorded here so that it is possible to see how the model that is presented in the following section was constructed. It is also important to recognise that one of the strengths in such a model is that it emerged in the naturalistic conditions of the classroom, rather than through the more precise conditions of the research laboratory. Yet this naturalistic approach may have given rise to a much more insightful way of viewing the learning processes than the laboratory would have produced and, indeed, might have highlighted learning routes that the laboratory research would have failed to reveal.

A MODEL OF THE LEARNING PROCESSES

Having thus far offered a criticism of Kolb's model and then discussed the research methodology undertaken in this research, it is now necessary to present and discuss the model that has been devised here. It will be seen that the model in Figure 2.2 is much more complex than that produced by Kolb, although there is a very similar baseline. Additionally, it may be seen that some of the initial criticisms of Kolb's model have been overcome here.

Any model is bound to be an over-simplification of the reality, and learning is a very complex set of processes, so that this model probably only begins to illustrate some of them. The model connects the process of human learning to the person, who may grow and develop as a result of a learning experience, may remain virtually unaltered, or may actually be harmed as a result of the experience of learning. This latter outcome of learning is similar to Dewey's miseducative experiences. The significance of the idea that the self may be harmed in some way as a result of a learning experience cannot be over-estimated, although it has not been examined sufficiently in adult education literature. Further discussion will ensue on this point later in the study.

It will also be noted that one of the outcomes of learning is a more experienced person, who might have new knowledge, a new skill, a different attitude, a changed self-concept, or any combination of these, which illustrates the complexity of human learning. However this reference to a more experienced person does relate to Knowles's

Figure 2.2 A model of the learning processes

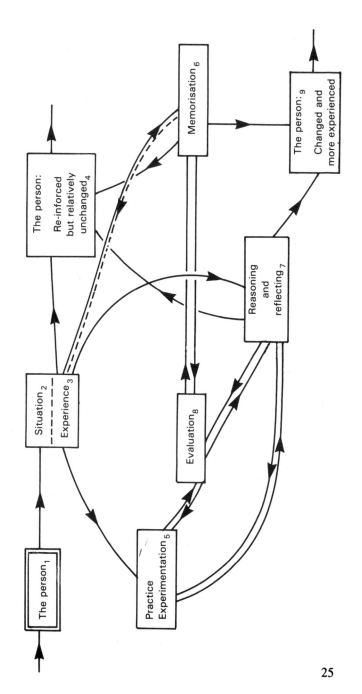

(1980) idea, discussed in the last chapter, that the adult's experiences can form a rich reservoir for future learning. It is the utilisation of this experience that Knowles claims is a basis for further adult learning, but such experience may only be used if the learner is enabled to capitalise upon it and this may depend upon the situation in which a new potential learning experience occurs. Hence, the social situation in which the learning experience is provided may determine the extent to which previous learning is used, and this is a significant factor in teaching, whether it be teaching adults or children; the difference between the two being that in many instances adults will have a larger reservoir of experience than a child. However, it must be pointed out that this is not inevitable, since experience is not completely age-related. It is quite easy to envisage an adult who has led a very sheltered life having a very limited experience of the world, whereas a child who has been forced to lead a very hard but varied life might have a larger reservoir of experience upon which to draw. It is also possible to envisage children in specific but familiar situations having wider reservoirs of experience in those situations than some adults for whom the situations are completely foreign.

The final feature of the model that requires comment at this stage is the fact that nine different routes from an experience that might, or might not, result in learning are mapped out in the diagram. These routes are not specified in the model because of the difficulty in isolating those that cover similar routes, but a brief pen-picture is provided so that it is possible to see how these relate to the model. Additionally, it must be recognised that since experience in the real world is a very complex phenomenon, it is possible to conceive of some situations in which learning follows more than one of the routes at the same time, focusing upon the same, or different, features of the same experience. For the purposes of identification, these nine responses to a potential learning experience have been given different names: presumption, non-consideration, rejection, pre-conscious, practice, memorisation, contemplation, reflective practice and experimental learning. It should be noted that the six actual learning responses to a potential learning situation are actually different types of learning and not different learning styles. It will be recognised that each of the learning processes recorded here is accorded differential status by society, with practice being given lower status than contemplation, etc, which relates closely to Young's (1971) argument that certain forms of knowledge are given higher status than others depending upon whether it is acceptable to the school curriculum. Each of these forms of learning will be discussed briefly later in this chapter.

Indeed, it is suggested here that these nine forms of response to a potential learning situation do form a hierarchy, with the first three types being non-learning responses, the second three, which includes pre-conscious learning, being non-reflective learning and the final three being reflective learning. These latter three are regarded as the higher forms of learning, although it will be shown later that non-learning responses are important to the stability of both the individual and society.

Other theorists have suggested different types of learning and it is important at this stage to relate this formulation to at least four previous approaches; those of Gagné, Saljo, Habermas and Argyris.

Gagné (1977) highlighted eight types of learning: the first seven of which he considered to be hierarchical, while the other he thought might occur at any level; these are: signal learning, stimulus-response, motor and verbal chaining, multiple discrimination, concept learning, rule learning and problem-solving. Signal learning, he thought, could occur at any level and this may be understood as a form of classical conditioning. The remaining seven stages form the hierarchy: stimulus-response learning he considered to be a form of operant conditioning, similar to the taken-for-granted situation that will be discussed later; his next two types are similar to the two forms of non-reflective learning in this model; whilst his remaining types are similar to, but not the same as, the reflective learning forms that emerge in this study.

Saljo (Marton and Saljo, 1984), it will be recalled from the opening chapter, suggested that there were five approaches to learning: a quantitative increase in knowledge, memorisation, instrumentality, abstraction of meaning and interpretation. Saljo's approach is somewhat different to that adopted here but, nevertheless, it is possible to detect similarities between his memorisation and abstraction of meaning and interpretation to those of memorisation and contemplation in the model constructed here. The differences can all be accounted for by reason of different research methodologies which were employed for different purposes.

Habermas (1971, 1972) discussed three primary learning domains, those of the technical, the practical and the emancipatory. The first two of Habermas's types do appear to relate to the more traditional learning forms, and are similar to the non-reflective types of learning referred to in this study. The third is similar to one of the potential outcomes of reflective learning, innovation, and in this it is similar to the outcome of Freire's problem-solving learning.

The distinction between non-reflective and reflective learning in this study appears similar, in the first instance, to Argyris's (1982) single and double loop learning, but on closer examination there is a difference. Argyris (1982, p. 88) suggests that single loop learning is learning within the confines of the theory-in-use, whereas double loop learning (1982, p. 106) is recognition that there is incompatibility of the espoused theory with the theory in use — in other words, it is a form of learning that recognises that the prevailing culture is open to question within the context of the experience of, or the problem experienced by, the learner. Argyris's distinction is very similar to that suggested by Botkin *et al.* (1979) who discuss the ideas of maintenance and innovative learning; the former being that form of learning that reacts to situations and problems in such a manner as to ensure the perpetuation of the current system while the latter is designed to bring about change and restructuring. Certainly, all of the reflective forms of learning can be double loop learning, according to Argyris's definition, although they need not be if the reflection leads only to acquiescence with the prevailing culture. The same conclusion can be drawn from Botkin's analysis. However, it will be argued later that reflective learning is potentially an agent of change, or what Habermas (1972, p. 310) refers to as 'an emancipatory cognitive interest'.

It is now necessary to discuss each of these responses briefly, although they will be discussed in greater detail later in this book.

RESPONSES TO THE POTENTIAL LEARNING SITUATION

In this brief section the nine types of response to the potential learning situation analysed above are discussed, starting first with the non-learning responses, thereafter moving to the three non-reflective learning responses and, finally, to the three reflective learning processes.

Type 1 — presumption

(The route that this takes is usually from boxes 1–4.)

This is the normal situation of a great deal of social interaction, since it presupposes that most people interact much of the time through patterned behaviour. However, these patterns are learned through the socialisation process from birth, not innate. Socialisation itself is not a process that occurs only in childhood. Indeed, sociologists recognise two very distinct forms of socialisation; primary and secondary. Berger and Luckmann (1967, p. 150) define these two in the following manner:

> Primary socialization is the first socialization process an individual undergoes in childhood, through which he becomes a member of society. Secondary socialization is any subsequent process that inducts an already socialized individual into new sectors of the objective world of his society.

This is a clear definition of the socialisation process, although it tends to assume that the society is a homogeneous whole having only one culture into which the individual is socialised. Later in this study it will be argued that it is necessary to recognise that there are a variety of sub-cultures that comprise the society's culture and it is into a configuration of these that each individual is socialised.

Clearly the use of the term 'socialisation' conveys specific meanings to sociologists, but it does perhaps hide the fact that this is a learning process, one already discussed in the opening chapter. Having learned and internalised these cultural expectations, then individuals behave in the manner that they have discovered to be acceptable both to themselves and to the people with whom they interact. The more that they repeat such behaviour in similar situations, the more they internalise it, so that it becomes second nature to them. Hence, each time that they enter another familiar situation they tend to enact the same pattern; in other words, the situation acts as a stimulus and their behaviour pattern is the response. The process is one that reinforces the established patterns of behaviour but does little else for the self. Underlying the pattern of behaviour is the taken-for-granted presumption that the current situation is the same as previous ones and therefore no variation in behaviour is necessary. Schutz and Luckmann (1974, p. 7) typify this situation:

> I trust that the world as it is known by me up until now will continue further and that consequently the stock of knowledge obtained from my fellow-men and formed from my own experiences will continue to preserve its fundamental validity . . . From this assumption follows the further and fundamental one: that I can repeat my past successful acts. So long as the structure of the world can be taken to be constant, so long as my previous experience

is valid, my ability to operate upon the world in this and that manner remains in principle preserved.

While this appears to be very mechanical, almost thoughtless, it is the basis of all social living. It would be quite intolerable for people to have to consider every word they were going to use in everyday speech, to consider every response to every social situation and not be able to presume some form of habituation of behaviour. Hence, the first response to a potential learning situation discussed here is the one that underlies all social living, called here, for the sake of convenience, presumption. It is one that pervades all behaviour irrespective of age, although the fact that it is a lifelong process does highlight that fact that social living, especially in complex, urban, industrial society, is always undergoing change, so that the familiar is not unchanging. Hence, learning through the process of socialisation must be lifelong, but this is another response to the social situation and will be discussed in great detail at a later stage in this study.

Type 2 — Non-consideration

(The route of this response is usually from boxes 1–4.)

There are a variety of reasons why people do not respond to a potential learning experience. Many will be aware of simply being too busy to respond to the opportunity. Others will be aware of being in a traditional teaching situation, where a lecturer is expounding a set of very interesting ideas and whilst the learner is thinking about one point the speaker raises another that appears interesting to the listener, but because of pre-occupation no time is spent upon that point and then it is forgotten in its original form, and so a learning opportunity has been missed. Situations like this indicate why some adult educators use the lecture method so sparingly, and even when they use it it is done in the form of dialogue or lecture discussion, so that it is possible for the learners to think about ideas that arise during the session.

Type 3 — Rejection

(The route for this response is usually boxes 1–3 to 7 to 9.)

Not every situation is a learning experience, nor does everyone provide opportunity for growth. Dewey (1938, p. 25) suggested that some experiences are miseducative and that it is possible to isolate such situations. For instance, when elderly or not so elderly people exclaim, 'I don't know what this world is coming to these days', there is an implicit statement that those persons are unable to comprehend certain situations in which they find themselves, so that they are unable to learn from them. In this type of response to a potential learning situation, i.e. 'I can't learn', the experience may be damaging to the elderly people's self-image, whereas in the last type of response there may be no effect at all. Later in this study these responses to a potential learning situation will be expanded sociologically and related both to Durkheim's concept of anomie and Marx's discussion of alienation.

The following three are non-reflective learning responses to a potential learning situation.

Type 4 — Pre-conscious

(The route for this response is usually boxes 1–3 to 6 to either 4 or 9.)

This is a form of learning that occurs to every person as a result of having experiences in daily living that are not really thought about but merely experienced. It is the form of learning that Beard (1976, pp. 93–5) calls incidental learning, through which she suggests people develop such phenomena as schemas of perception and action, etc. By contrast to this use of incidental learning by Beard, Mannings (1986, p. 4 — although no date is given on the research report) employs the term to refer to 'learning which occurs in any educational setting other than as a result of the main curricular content concerned'. This usage limits 'incidentality' to an educational setting as it is not used in the same manner as Beard employed the term, nor is it precisely the same concept as that utilised here. This research has not concentrated upon how the person internalises some of these experiences within the lifelong process of socialisation, as is Beard's concern, nor is it related to Mannings' perspective, although it is recognised that there is certainly some overlap in the ideas contained in these authors' work.

Another writer who has recently turned his attention to this form of learning is Reischmann (1986), who called this learning *en passant*, which he does not define but describes (1986, p. 3) as including:

short learning situations;
situations where less than half the person's total activation is on

the learning;

contents that are not 'clear' in the sense that the learner knows in advance what and how to use it or whether it will produce lasting changes in himself.

It is suggested here that Reischmann has actually included more than one type of learning in this description. For instance, the first type might be memorisation of a quite conscious nature while the third type is unclear. However, his second type does appear to be very similar to the pre-conscious learning that is being discussed here. In a sense Reischmann is discussing forms of unintended learning and these can also be regarded as reactive, within the typology employed here.

It is maintained here that a great deal of the acquisition of human culture occurs through this pre-conscious process of learning and that the routes taken through the learning process may be similar to that of rote learning. It is, perhaps, significant that so many researchers are examining this type of learning at this time. But since the objectives of this research did not really include this aspect of learning, it is included because subjects of the research discussed it with the researcher during the informal feedback sessions that followed a number of the workshops within which the research was conducted. Its significance, however, should not be minimised since this is a major part of the process whereby people learn and acquire their culture and by which it is maintained through taken-for-granted behaviour.

Type 5 — Practice

(The route for this learning response is boxes 1–3 to 5 to 8 to 6 to either 4 or 9.)

It will be recalled that one of the behavioural definitions of learning discussed in the first chapter highlighted the fact that practice constitutes a major element in some learning. Practice certainly forms a basis for one form of learning, skills learning. Traditionally, this form of learning has been restricted to such phenomena as training for a manual occupation or the acquisition of a high level of performance in a specific physical exercise, such as getting fit, playing a sport, etc. However, practice may also refer to the acquisition of social skills and even to the acquisition of language itself. These skills are often acquired through a process of conscious imitation, a form of learning that is often attributed to children but rarely discussed with adults, although such ideas as role-modelling are employed. Hence, there is no intention here to equate this form of learning with just one type of skills learning but rather to widen it and to recognise its significance within the context of both the socialisation process in particular and social living in general.

Type 6 — Memorisation

(The route for this learning response is boxes 1–3 to 6 and possibly to 8 to 6 and then to either 4 or 9.)

This response to a potential learning situation is perhaps the most commonly discussed of all, especially in children's education. Here the learners are expected to acquire the information with which they have been presented and learn it, so that they can reproduce it at a later stage. It relates to the type of research described by some behaviourists in which the reproduction of the 'correct' knowledge is regarded as the logical outcome of learning. This may well be the type of experience that some children are expected to have and this reflects Yonge's (1985) argument, discussed earlier, in which he suggests that pedagogy differs from andragogy in the manner by which the learners are accompanied through the learning process, with children being guided much more than some adults. Additionally, this approach to learning presupposes a specific form of knowledge, i.e. that the knowledge being acquired is empirical fact and that it is the only correct formulation of that knowledge. Often, habitualised knowledge is presented as if it were empirical factual knowledge rather than subjective presumed responses to familiar learning situations, and if these are learned by other learners then the habitualised knowledge assumes an authority to which it is not entitled.

The final three forms of learning are reflective learning responses to a potential learning situation, and it must be pointed out from the outset that reflective learning does not pre-suppose innovation since the reflective learner may as easily decide to accept the *status quo* as to reject it.

Type 7 — Contemplation

(The route for this type of learning is boxes 1–3 to 7 to 8 to 6 to 9.)

The seventh route through the learning process model produced above is one which the behaviourist definition omitted completely,

33

that of pure thought. It is suggested here their one response to a potential learning situation is merely to consider it and make an intellectual decision about it. This decision may be stored in the mind until a future social situation stimulates its recall. However, the actual learning route assumes no behavioural outcome during the process, so that the only way that the learning may be measured is through introspection or by the learner articulating, or communicating by some other method, the outcome of the learning experience. It is, therefore, important to recognise the significance of self-evaluation in learning when this type of learning occurs. It is obviously related to certain forms of knowledge — both logical knowledge and belief may be acquired through the contemplative method of learning — but it is also important to note that this approach to learning does not preclude teaching, nor does it exclude the possibility of applying that knowledge to a practical situation at a later date.

Type 8 — Reflective practice

(The route for this form of learning response is boxes 1–3 (to 5) to 7 to 5 to 8 to 6 to 9.)

It will be noted that in the above route it is possible to go in both directions from the experience, since if the experience is practical the learner might move immediately to think about it, but if there is a cognitive experience, the learner might experiment first.

One of the crucial elements in Schon's (1983) argument about professional practice is that many professional people 'think on their feet' and that they therefore learn from their own practice. This is clearly a form of learning that occurs not only in professional practice but in life itself. Indeed, this is the basis of a great deal of pragmatic knowledge. Many skills are learned, thought about and experimented with in practice. But situations are rarely so precisely the same that people perform all their actions mindlessly, although often the thought processes may be accelerated so that the action appears to have been immediate and without thought. Therefore, there is a relationship between this type of learning and taken-for-granted behaviour, on the one hand, and practice learning, on the other hand.

This form of learning clearly relates to the problem-solving situation, which Knowles considers to be the basis of adult learning. While such an assertion is not accepted here, since many children are also expected to problem solve in a variety of social situations, it is recognised that there are many situations in adult life where problem-solving is quite fundamental and so it is not surprising that Knowles made this distinction. Indeed, it will be suggested later in this book that the gap between biography and experience lies at the foundation of human learning, in other words the inability to cope with the situation unthinkingly, or instinctively, is at the heart of all learning.

Type 9 — Experimental learning

(The route for this final form of learning is boxes 1–3 to 7 to 5 to 7 to 8 to 6 to 9.)

The final form of learning that is isolated in this model is experimental learning and this is another way in which pragmatic knowledge may be learned. Unlike the reflective practice, the end product is not an advanced skill but knowledge that has been shown to relate to reality through experimentation. This approach to learning relates very closely to Kelly's (1963) understanding of human beings as scientists, seeking always to experiment upon their environment. Some forms of scientific and social scientific knowledge are certainly acquired by this method.

The complexities of this type of learning occupy the whole of the ninth chapter of this book.

CONCLUSIONS

This chapter has sought to demonstrate the learning processes of the human being; it is suggested that they are as applicable to children as they are to adults, although it is recognised that some forms may occur more frequently with one age group than another. However, it is not maintained here that this is a function of age but of the social situation in which each age group of learners finds itself, and in which age is but one variable in the whole process.

It might be asked why this book claims to be about adult learning when such a statement as the above is made: the response must be simple. The research upon which the model of the learning processes was constructed came from work with adult learners and it was tested with adults, rather than with children. Hence, the only claims that can be made for this model are with adults, although it is suspected that it is as valid for children as it is with adults. There may be a relationship between the frequency of use of these different types of learning and the age of the learner, but no evidence exists at present that might verify this.

Figure 2.2 has isolated each of the elements of the learning process in order to demonstrate that there are different routes through the process and that they all relate to different social situations, different forms of knowledge and have different purposes. However, it is recognised that these sequences may be either prolonged or immediate, depending upon the social situations of the learners.

Additionally, it will be noted in Figure 2.2 that there is a dotted line between memorisation and experience, and the reason for this is to record the fact that sometimes it is a memory of a past event that creates a new potential learning situation. Schon (1983) claims that the time interval between the original experience and the thought processes is not relevant, but it is maintained here that in some instances the original experience is a discrete phenomenon and the memory constitutes another discrete experience at another moment in time.

Finally, the learning processes start with the person and affect the person in some way or other, so that it is now necessary to examine the concept of the person. This constitutes the basis of the following chapter.

3

The Social Construction of the Person

The model of the learning processes discussed in the previous chapter commences and concludes with the person of the learner, which highlights the fact that learning and personhood are inextricably intertwined. However, few educators of adults have actually concentrated upon the idea of personhood, preferring to employ the concept of the self. While it might be argued that the self is at the heart of the 'mental component' of the human being, as indeed have Kidd (1973), Knowles (1980) and Rogers (1969), *inter alia*. However, it is suggested here that person is more than self and it is recognised that the emphasis upon self has resulted in an emphasis being placed upon factors other than knowledge and learning, such as that of the humanity of the learner. This is a position that was tentatively adopted elsewhere (Jarvis, 1983b), but one which has subsequently been slightly modified here, without loss of emphasis upon the aspect of humanity. It is maintained that the ideological orientations of the first three writers mentioned above are such that they lead to unnecessary emphasis being placed upon the feelings and emotions of the person and insufficient concentration being given to the actual process of acquiring knowledge through learning.

One adult educator who has consistently employed the concept of person is Paterson (1979), and his position must now be analysed in order to ascertain precisely how he employs the term. He suggests (1979, p. 15) that persons are:

> conscious selves, moving centres of action and awareness, whose being is the radically finite being of individuals conscious of the shifting but ever-present limits placed upon their being by time, space, and matter, but conscious also that these limits exist to be surpassed.

Elsewhere, he writes (1979, p. 32) that:

> The concept of 'person', however, is an open-ended concept. It is conscious selves who evolve as persons, and as a conscious self a man is always conscious of himself over and against his present circumstances, behaviour and identity; as a conscious self, he is always capable of surpassing his present level of personal existence, and of transcending himself. We can never say that of a man that he has exhausted his potentialities as a person, or that he has fully and finally realized in himself a perfect completeness of personal being. Thus we can never say that a man's education is complete.

In the light of the model of the learning processes discussed in the previous chapter it might be more accurate to claim, not that a person's education is never complete but that a person's learning is never complete as long as that person is alive. However, it is significant to note that in both of these quotations Paterson equates person with conscious self. Elsewhere in his study, Paterson (1979, p. 68) suggests that:

> Consciousness or awareness engages itself with its objects in various different modes — vision, hearing, and the modes of sense experience, feeling and emotion, memory, imagination, conceptualization, inference, judgment, and so on — but in any given conscious act . . . we find that several different faculties are brought into synthesis to form what is always a single, indivisible operation of consciousness. This unity of the single, instantaneous act of consciousness . . . is reproduced in the unity of the multiple, successive acts of consciousness, which intermerge to form a single continuous identity across time, the kind of identity to which we give the name of 'self'. Consciousness as we know it or can conceive of it does not occur in discrete flashes, but is always *individualized*, that is bound tightly up within the vital unity of a unique, on-going self. (Paterson's italics)

It is important to note that for Paterson 'self' exists within personhood, but that he is concerned to specify one condition of self, that of consciousness or awareness. It is this element that Mead (in Strauss, 1959) regarded as 'mind'. The concept of mind has a certain advantage over that of conscious self in that it emphasises the cognitive component but it also has a disadvantage of suggesting that that cognitive element can actually be located somewhere. Nevertheless, it is important to recognise that there is no actual physical entity in an individual which may be called the mind. Ryle (1963) was also keen to dispel the notion that mind could be located within the body, although his position may be construed as being closer to the behaviourist one than that adopted here. However, it cannot be emphasised sufficiently that whatever constitution of the person is adopted it is generally recognised that the person is more than just the human body. The position assumed here is that the person is body, mind and self and that the latter two components have a social constitution.

Paterson, however, made little or no reference to the physical body or to the central nervous system. Yet it has to be acknowledged that the body's physical organism is itself a constituent factor in the process of consciousness and, therefore, it would be unwise to omit it from all consideration. Indeed, for many years, there was in the social sciences a debate about the relative merits of nature and nurture. During this some sociologists turned to Freud for a more complete analysis (Wrong, 1961), while more recently socio-biology has emerged (Barash, 1980), in which it is argued that evolution is occurring in humankind by the survival of the fittest genes. While it would be true to state that the claims of socio-biologists still require further analysis and research, they do account for some of the similarities, etc. between succeeding generations. Yet socio-biology is a young discipline, even younger than adult education, and its claims still require refinement. Concentration upon the biological element of the person is really beyond the scope of this study, but while its effect is acknowledged, no attempt is made to discuss it here. However, it is foreseen that some of the greatest advances in learning theory in future might well emerge from biology and its associated disciplines.

Mind and self, then, are additions to the body, acquired through the process of social living and are major factors in the learning process, because they themselves have developed as a result of social learning. Both are social constructs so that the person may be regarded as a social construct. Mead (all references below are as in Strauss), above all social psychologists, focused his analysis upon these two factors in relation to society and so it is to his work that a great deal of reference is made below. The chapter has three main sections: the first examines the concept of mind; the second analyses the idea of the self as a social construct; finally, the social construct of the person and its relation to learning is discussed.

THE CONCEPT OF MIND

The title of this sub-section is that of a well-known book by Gilbert Ryle (1963) in which he attacked the idea that the mind, which he (1963, p. 61) regarded as the same thing as the soul in metaphysical literature, is a phenomenon with which individuals are born and which transcends them at death. He regarded this as 'the ghost of the machine' which he considered could not be proved to have a separate existence. Indeed, he argued that there is not a separate mind. Clearly his position is very similar to that of the behaviourists, a position that was not accepted in the opening chapter of this study. However, there are some points in this present analysis in which there is an agreement with Ryle. For instance, it is maintained here that the mind is a product of social forces, so that it is better regarded as a changing and developing phenomenon rather than an attribute with which persons are born and which remains unchanged throughout life. However, the mind is separated from the self here, a distinction which Ryle does not make, although Ryle does discuss issues of self-knowledge and introspection. It is recognised that the self in this present discussion comes closer to the metaphysical understanding of the soul, but that the self is a product of experience rather than an attribute of birth. This is especially true in Luckmann's (1967) analysis, which is referred to below. Unlike Ryle, however, it is maintained here that once the mind and the self have emerged as a result of experience, they assume something of a separate existence, interdependent with the body, but that they may not exist as distinct metaphysical entities. However, there is a reservoir of experience that relates to mind and self and allows for such individual processes as introspection etc. It is at this point that there is some difference with Ryle, since it is maintained that reflection is a learned human ability and is at the foundation of certain forms of learning. It is now necessary to explore the concept of mind further.

It will be noted throughout the following pages that references will be made to the several different factors in the learning process, even to those which constitute the subject of subsequent chapters. This is because the learning process does not constitute discrete processes and that mind and self are themselves learned phenomena. However, each of the elements of the process also constitute separate discussion in this study.

As was pointed out above, mind is not a physical entity with which persons are born. Mead (ibid., p. 127), for instance, suggests that:

it is important to recognise that that to which the word refers is something that lies in the experience of the individual without the use of language. Language does pick out and organize the content of experience. It is an implement for that purpose.

Obviously there is a physiological/neurological basis upon which mind develops, and for the purpose of this discussion it is recognised that there are certainly bodily drives that interact with the mental processes in specific ways, but it is also suggested here that omission of this discussion does not weaken the argument being formulated, since once mind is formed thought may occur as a result of a variety of stimuli. But it is important to see how mind is formed and begins to develop.

Mead argued that consciousness emerges as a result of social behaviour. Indeed, the social act is the precondition of consciousness. Hence, small children develop awareness only through the process of social interaction. Mead (ibid., p. 162) wrote:

. . . if . . . you regard the social process of experience as prior (in rudimentary terms) to the existence of mind and explain the origin of minds in terms of interaction among individuals within that process, then not only the origin of minds . . . cease to seem mysterious or miraculous. Mind arises through communication by a conversation of gestures in the social process or context of experience.

For Mead, then, the significant factor in the emergence of mind is gesture. Gesture (ibid., pp. 157–8) is 'that phase of the individual act to which adjustment takes place on the part of other individuals in the social process of behaviour'. Without gesture or interaction, there could be no mind. It is through the acquisition of language that people gain the necessary tools to develop the ability to think, but this does not mean that thought and language are synonymous. Their relationship is explored in Chapter 5. But it should be recognised that Ryle's 'ghost of the machine' is one that co-exists with body, rather than one that emeges as a result of experience. Mind can function independently of action, even though it requires experience to stimulate it.

Language, however, is neither an unchanging nor an unchangeable phenomenon. It reflects both historical time and social culture, so that the language that people use becomes one of the signs by which others can locate them both in history and in the social structure. Bernstein (1971, p. 78), for instance, suggested that 'associated with the organization of social groups are distinct forms of social language'. He went on to demonstrate that children from a non-manual socio-economic class background have usually acquired an elaborated speech code as well as a restricted code, whilst those from a manual class background have only a restricted code. Freire also focused upon the significance of language and he showed how language was used to reinforce the political domination of the elite and how educators sometimes have spoken to others while their language has not been attuned to the situation in which their addressees exist. Indeed, the dominant language locates the dominated and helps them locate themselves. It may be claimed that it defines their social situation for them, so that this is the 'knowledge' that is presented to them to be learned.

> The inherited colonial education had as one of its principal objectives the de-Africanization of nationals. It was discriminatory, mediocre and based on verbalism. It could not contribute anything to national reconstruction because it was not constituted for this purpose . . . Divorced from the reality of the country, it was, for this very reason, a school for the minority, and thus against the majority. It selected out only a very few who had access to it, excluding most of them after a few years and, due to continued selective filtering, the number rejected constantly increased. A sense of inferiority and inadequacy was fostered by this 'failure'.
>
> This system could not help but reproduce in children and in youth the profile that colonial ideology itself had created for them, namely, that of inferior beings lacking all ability; their only salvation lay in becoming 'white' or 'black' with white souls'. The system, then, was not concerned with anything related closely to nationals (called 'natives'). Worse than the lack of concern was the actual negation of every authentic representation of national peoples — their history, their culture, their language. The history of those colonized was thought to have begun with the civilizing presence of the colonizers . . . Culture belonged only to the colonizers . . . (Freire, 1978, pp. 13–14)

Later, Freire goes on to recommend that all the reading texts should be changed in order to rid the school texts of the ideology of the colonisers. Hence, for Freire, the oppressed had to learn a language that would free them from the structures of the world as they had experienced it and would, consequently, change their understanding of the world.

It was, perhaps, Mannheim (1936, pp. 1–11) above all scholars who highlighted the social nature of thought and, therefore, the social nature of mind. Mannheim (ibid., p. 22) specified that:

> Only in a quite limited sense does a single individual create out of himself the mode of speech and of thought we attribute to him. He speaks the language of his group; he thinks in the manner in which his group thinks. He finds at his disposal only certain words and meanings. These not only determine to a large extent the avenues of approach to the surrounding world, but they also show at the same time from which angle and in which context of activity objects have hitherto been perceptible and accessible to the group or the individual.

It will also be recalled from the first chapter that individuals are socialised into their sub-cultures. But at the same time the dominant culture of any society is not a free-floating phenomenon, but is created and maintained by those who have power in that society. It will be recalled that Marx and Engels claimed that:

> The ideas of the ruling class are, in every age, the ruling ideas; i.e. the class which is the dominant material force in society is at the same time its dominant intellectual force. The class which has the means of material production at its disposal, has control at the same time over the means of mental production, so that in consequence the ideas of those who lack the means of mental production are, in general, subject to it. (Cited in Bottomore and Rubel, 1966, p. 93)

Hence, the similarities of language lead to similarities of thought, and thought is 'the essential condition within the social process for the development of mind' (Mead, ibid., pp. 195–6). These similarities are not necessarily natural, but are manufactured and controlled by social forces such as power, and they may be similarities of class, gender, ethnicity, sub-culture, etc. rather than of society alone. Not only are their initial experiences constrained to some extent by social class, etc.: it would be true to claim that many people in similar social conditions have the majority of their experiences, especially if they are 'real' and meaningful to them, constrained by similar sets of social structures. Hence, the development of mind is related to the social structure within which people live. Thus, people's minds relate to their biographies. People from similar social backgrounds are likely to have had similar experiences, to have developed a similar language and therefore have similar minds. Consequently, they may appear to think similar thoughts and act in similar ways. This similarity allows for inter-subjectivity and empathy to be exercised more easily within the sub-cultural parameters than beyond them. By contrast, people from a different social background, even though they are of the same society, may have developed minds that are different from those of other social backgrounds, even though there will be similarities that reflect the nature of the wider society in which they all live.

But is mind merely the reflection of the social background? Is there no independence of thought? Obviously this is an important point and clearly people are not perfect reflections of their sub-culture, they do have an individuality. This individuality starts with the physical differences at birth and continues to develop as they respond to the wide variety of experiences that people in a modern technological society have. Yet minds become independent when they have developed 'an organized set of attitudes' (Mead, ibid., p. 192) — or universe of meaning, and this clearly does relate to the social structures within which the mind has developed. Hence, the position of the behaviourists, and of Ryle, is refuted here.

A significant factor in this discussion is that since gesture only has relevance when it actually does communicate meaning from one person to another, it is not always certain that people from different social backgrounds will communicate precisely with each other because the words that they employ may not signify exactly the same meaning. Meaning, therefore, is a social construction and relates to the sub-culture, or sub-cultures, within which people live:

> Gestures become significant symbols when they implicitly arouse in an individual making them the same responses which they explicitly arouse, or are supposed to arouse, in the other individuals, the individuals to whom they are addressed. In all conversations of gestures within the social processes . . . the individual's consciousness of the content and flow of meaning involved depends on his thus taking the gestures of the other toward his own gestures . . . Only in terms of gestures as significant symbols is the existence of mind or intelligence possible; for only in terms of gestures which are significant symbols can thinking — which is simply an internalized or implicit conversation of the individual with himself by means of such gestures — take place. (Mead, ibid., pp. 158–9)

Hence, mind is a social construct. People's minds, then, and the language through which they are developed, are constrained within the social parameters. But another feature that should perhaps concern adult educators is that Mead suggests here that intelligence is related to the same social constraints. Elsewhere, he wrote (ibid., p. 163):

We are partially concerned with intelligence on the human level, that is, with the adjustment to one another of different human individuals within the human social process. This adjustment takes place through communication — by gestures on the lower planes of human evolution and by significant symbols . . . on the higher planes of human evolution.

This does not mean that higher intelligence is necessarily related to the upper classes or that lower intelligence is related to the lower socio-economic classes. It does mean, however, that since communication patterns, and consequently minds, are related to the social position, the type of intelligence that people acquire is related to their previous experiences and to their position in the social structure. Indeed, it is possible to argue that intelligence is the ability to respond to experience, so that different types of intelligence relate in part to the ability to respond to different experiences. It has been recognised, for instance, that so-called intelligence tests have a middle-class bias and so it is hardly surprising that people from these classes score more highly when completing them. Additionally, it has also been recognised that certain forms of intelligence increase with age (Cross, 1981, pp. 157–64), which also suggests that intelligence may be based upon the ability to respond to life's experiences. Cattell (1963), for instance, has distinguished between fluid and crystallised intelligence; the former refers to that intelligence that has a biological basis, whereas the latter relates to experience, and this may well point to intelligence being social as well as biological.

Mind, therefore, is not a static phenomenon, but:

We must regard mind, then, as arising and developing within the social process, within the empirical matrix of social interactions. We must, that is, get an inner individual experience from the standpoint of the social acts which include the experiences of separate individuals in a social context wherein the individuals interact. (Mead, ibid., p. 195)

Hence, mind and intelligence can and do change and develop throughout life. This is not to deny that there is not a biological brain nor a neurological system, but it is to deny that mind, or intelligence, is something with which a person is born and which does not change throughout life. It is also to recognise the significant place that language plays in the development of the mind and in the social processes of thought. It is to claim that these processes that help to constitute personhood are social in origin and in nature and that the person is, therefore, a social construct. But the person is more than merely body and mind, the person also has a self. Much of the same argument about the formation of mind can and will be applied to the formation and development of the self, for as Mead (ibid., p. 161) claims: 'The body is not a self as such; it becomes a self when it has developed a mind within the context of social experience.'

THE SELF AS A SOCIAL CONSTRUCT

The third element in the person is the self, a concept that has been quite central to a great deal of adult education literature, even though the emphasis has not been upon the formation of the self so much as upon its development. Hence, this section seeks to cover both the broad sweep of adult education ideas about the self and also to examine its formation and development. This latter aspect follows the work of Mead again and, consequently, it is a development of the first section of this chapter, but towards the end of the section there is a significant reference to the work of Luckmann, who related the self to the personal universe of meaning.

The self in adult education literature. Since the dominant ideology in adult education has been liberal-humanistic it is hardly surprising that the literature has concentrated upon the manner in which the self can be developed through education. Perhaps the work of Maslow has been most pertinent here and his famous hierarchy of needs has been used with a great deal of frequency. Maslow (1968) presented this hierarchy as shown in Figure 3.1.

However, it was argued elsewhere (Jarvis, 1983b, pp. 14–19) that Maslow's hierarchy is actually a taxonomy and that he omitted a quite fundamental aspect; the need to learn. Indeed, it was argued in the last section that mind only develops through the learning processes that occur as a result of interaction, and it will be argued later in this present chapter that selfhood actually develops out of the need to

Figure 3.1 Maslow's hierarchy of human needs

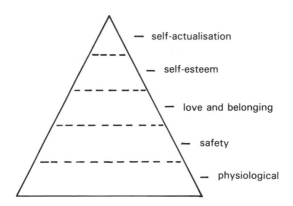

relate to the immediate society and environment. Hence, the need to learn was inserted in this taxonomy prior to the references to the self. It was placed at that point to show that the need to learn preceded the development of the self.

Maslow's work has caught the mood of adult education and, consequently, it has been very influential. Among those who have been influenced by it are both Kidd and Knowles, while the other theorist of similar persuasion who has been influential is Carl Rogers. Rogers (1969, p. 295), illustrating his model of the person, claimed that the individual:

. . . who emerges from therapy or from the best of education, the individual who has experienced optimal psychological growth — a person functioning freely in all the fullness of his organismic potentialities; a person who is dependable in being realistic, self-enhancing, socialized and appropriate in his behaviour; a creative person, whose specific formings of behaviour are not easily predictable; a person who is ever changing, ever developing, always discovering himself and the newness in himself in each succeeding moment of time.

While such a person may not be everybody's ideal individual, it is significant that Rogers has been influential in adult education. Yet, as the above quotation suggests, he has not really conceptually distinguished education from therapy, a confusion that is apparent elsewhere in his writing.

Even so, it is to these two thinkers that, in different ways, Kidd and Knowles have referred in their writing about adult learning. Kidd (1973, pp. 127–31) suggests a number of factors about adult learning, some of which relate to the self:

> gradually within the individual there is a development of the self, and this development is essential to all learning;
>
> all new experiences for the learner are symbolized and organized into some relationship to the self, or are ignored because there is no perceived relationship, or are denied organization, or are given a distorted meaning because the experience seems inconsistent with the structure of the self;
>
> perhaps the most important task in learning is the development of a self that can deal with reality.

The above points do reflect some elements of the model of the learning processes that was presented in the previous chapter. At the same time, it is possible to detect the humanistic ideology of growth here which, while it is accepted, need not play such a prominent part in learning theory *per se*. Additionally, it is important to note, in the light of the discussion in the previous section, that Kidd related learning directly to the structure of self without reference to mind.

Knowles, also, has placed a considerable emphasis on the self in his theory of andragogy, discussed in the first chapter. The basic tenets of this position, according to Knowles (1980, pp. 44–5), are as follows:

> . . . four crucial assumptions about the characteristics of the learners that are different from the assumptions upon which traditional pedagogy is premised. These are the assumptions that as individuals mature: 1) their self-concept moves from one of being a dependent personality toward being a self-directed human being; 2) they accumulate a growing reservoir of experience that becomes an increasing rich resource for learning; 3) their readiness to learn becomes orientated increasingly to the developmental tasks of their social roles; and 4) their time perspective changes from one of postponed application of knowledge to immediacy of application, and accordingly, their orientation towards learning shifts from one of subject-centredness to one of performance-centredness.

Knowles's work has obviously been very influential in adult education, but each of these four assumptions, and the fifth one that he

(1984, p. 12) added later about motivation to learn do require considerable research and appraisal prior to their being accepted — as was pointed out in the opening chapter of this book. Yet it must be noted here that Knowles not only regards the self as an important element in learning, something to be developed, but he also thinks that it will develop in a specific direction as a result of learning. But Reisman (1950) showed that some adults were other-directed, while some were tradition-directed and others inner-directed. If Reisman's classical research is correct, then Knowles would be forced into a position of claiming that those who were other-directed were not in fact adults. Indeed, this is precisely the position that he (1984, p. 9) is forced into by his definition of an adult as: 'One who has arrived at a self-concept of being responsible for one's own life, of being self-directing.' Thus it may be seen that Knowles is actually discussing a certain form of maturity rather than adulthood and that this has an ideological overtone rather than a philosophical perspective. Indeed, research in the United States, amongst other places, has shown this to be the case. Kohn (1969), for instance, found that manual workers in America were committed to a value system that stressed conformity to external authority while non-manual workers were committed to being more self-directing. Hence, Kohn's research demonstrates the non-manual bias in Knowles's assumptions.

While it would be perfectly possible to review other writers on adult learning theory, it would detract from the main purpose of this study. Therefore, in order to illustrate further the centrality of the self-concept to traditional adult learning theory, the points made by Brundage and Mackeracher (1980, pp. 23–6) that are relevant to this section are recorded below:

Adults are more concerned with whether they are changing in the direction of their own idealized self-concept than whether they are meeting objectives established by others;

Adults learn best when they are involved in developing learning objectives for themselves which are congruent with their current and idealized self-concept;

Adults with higher self-esteem and a more positive self-concept are more ready to accept change;

There is a positive correlation between flexibility, ego-differentiation and self-esteem;

The learner reacts to the learning experience out of an organized whole self-concept and perceives the experience as an integrated whole;

> The self is affected by each new role taken by the learner;
> Adults learn best when they perceive themselves as learners.

Brundage and Mackeracher (1980, p. 23) suggest that the self may be 'characterized as being an organized and consistent whole unit of perception' and they suggest that individuals seek to integrate all their experiences in it. What is also clear from the above points is that there is considerable concern in adult education for the self of the individual learner and this is accepted here as a fundamental underlying ideological position about education. Learning, however, is an amoral element in the process of social living. Indeed, it was claimed in the previous section that mind is one of the results of learning and that self emerges out of the development of mind. Adult educators have tended to look forward to the development of self rather then backwards to its emergence and this may be one of the reasons why there has been a greater emphasis placed upon self than there has upon mind. However, it is now important to look backwards to see how self emerges with mind in order to understand more fully the learning process.

The emerging self. No person is born with a self, only with the potentiality of developing one through social interaction. Berger (1966, p. 117) summarises this point nicely:

> Identity is not something 'given', but is bestowed in acts of social recognition. We become that as we are addressed [*sic*]. The same idea is expressed in Cooley's well-known description of the self as a reflection in the looking glass.

While not wishing to embrace a determinist position here, it is maintained that the self is influenced and shaped by social interaction, although it is clear that after its formation it can also play an active part in social interaction and so participate in the outcome of any social situation. But the significant aspect is that the self is actually formed in the context of social interaction. Mead (op. cit., p. 42) wrote:

> A self can arise only where there is a social process within which this self had its initiative. It arises in that process. For the process, the communication and the participation . . . is essential. That is the way that selves have arisen. That is where the individual is in the social process in which he is part, where he does influence himself as he does others.

Mead is clear that no self can develop prior to the development of language, since it is only through the use and recognition of arbitrary symbols (language), as well as other forms of communication, that individuals can become conscious of themselves as social human beings. Only when this consciousness exists can the self become an object to itself, which makes it distinct from other living things that may have no self-consciousness. In this instance self is both subject and object. This is quite a significant point in Mead's analysis and he tries to illustrate it by employing an example of a person being chased by another. He claims that during the chase the person being pursued is so pre-occupied with running away that he has no consciousness of his action at all. Yet a person being chased may be very conscious of himself and his action, since both the chase and the desired escape present him with problems. However, there are situations where the self is not self-conscious, that is in taken-for-granted situations. For instance, people driving a car along an open, empty road, listening to the radio, may be so engrossed either in the radio programme or in the journey that they are not conscious of the process of driving. This is the type of situation which Bergson (1920) described as *durée*, which is depicted in the learning processes model in the previous chapter as a taken-for-granted response to a potential learning situation. Naturally, this response will be discussed in much greater detail later in this book, but the point here is that there are situations in which action can occur without self-consciousness.

The self arises in social interaction, rather in the individualistic type of situation used in the above example, and there are two stages in its development, according to Mead: the first is through interaction with significant others and the second is through learning about the generalised other. In the first stage, the child interacts with significant others, e.g. parents and others who have especial attitudes towards it, and these attitudes are internalised. However, the child's world soon becomes wider than that of interaction with significant others alone. Through play, children learn to extend their world and their self-image. Mead points out that children first play by themselves, then there is side-by-side play and, finally, there is interactive play. Through play children learn about the phenomena of the world about them and through role play they begin to learn about the experience of others. Later, play turns into games and then 'the rules are a set of responses which a particular attitude calls out. You can demand a certain response in others if you make a certain attitude. These responses are all in yourself as well' (ibid., p. 216). Thus the role of others in play is an essential

51

precondition of the development of the self:

> At this stage we speak of a child as not yet having a fully developed self. The child responds in a fairly intelligent fashion to the immediate stimuli that come to him, but they are not yet organized, he does not organize his life as we would like to have him do, namely, as a whole. There is just a set of responses to the type of play. The child reacts to a certain stimulus and the reaction in himself is called out in others, but he is not a whole self. In his game he has to have an organization of roles, otherwise he cannot play the game. The game represents the passage in the life of the child from the taking of the role of others in play to the organized part that is essential to self-consciousness in the full sense of the term. (ibid., p. 216)

Eventually, however, the wider organised society provides the backcloth against which the self develops fully. Mead regarded the organised society, or community, as the generalised other; the attitude of the generalized other is the attitude of the whole community' (ibid., p. 218) He possibly assumed a greater homogeneity and cohesion in the wider society than there is in reality — society is more pluralist than totalitarian — but nevertheless this is an important feature in Mead's analysis. He was certainly aware that there are sub-cultural differences:

> If the given individual is to develop a self in the fullest sense, it is not sufficient for him merely to take the attitudes of other human individuals towards himself and towards one another within the human social process and to bring that social process as a whole into his individual experience merely in these terms, he must also, in the same way as he takes the attitudes of other individuals towards himself and towards one another, take their attitudes towards the various phases or aspects of the common social activity or set of social undertakings in which, as members of an organized society or social group, they are all engaged. He must, then, by generalizing these individual attitudes of that organized society or social group itself as a whole, act towards different social objects . . . (ibid., p. 219)

This stage can only occur when the individual has developed gesture and language so that the individual can both communicate to and receive communication from other people. Mead (ibid., pp. 213–14) used the example of Helen Keller and claimed that:

> As she recognized, it was not until she could get into communication with other persons through symbols which could arouse in herself the responses they arouse in other people that she could get what we term a mental content, or a self.

Hence, the second stage in the full development of the individual's self is when:

> that self is constituted not only by an organization of these particular individual attitudes but also by an organization of the social attitudes of the generalized other or the social group as a whole to which he belongs. (ibid., p. 222)

For Mead, the self comprises two elements — the 'I' and the 'Me'. The former is the response of the organism to the attitudes of others, while the latter is the organised set of attitudes of others which the self assumes. There is a certian similarity between Mead's position and that of Freud. Freud regarded the self as consisting of the id, the ego and the super-ego. In this case the id is the reflex action for the fulfilment of bodily drives, an element that Mead does not discuss, the ego is the reality principle in which the mental processes such as discrimination, memory, judgement and reasoning emerge and the super-ego is the attitudes of others, often significant others, that have been internalised (Hall, 1954, p. 41). The strength of Freud's position is that he emphasised the bodily drives, whereas the strength of Mead's is the emphasis he placed upon the social interaction and especially in the use of gesture in the formation of both mind and self.

Mead (ibid., pp. 224–5) regarded language as the key element in the process, for:

> language in its significant sense is that vocal gesture which tends to arouse in the individual the attitude which it arouses in others, and it is this perfecting of the self by the gesture which mediates the social activities that gives rise to the process of taking the role of the other.

Hence, the self like the mind is essentially cognitive in Mead's thinking. Like the mind it is not present with the individual at birth and arises out of interaction. Mead recognised that there is a certain similarity in his thinking about self to the theological concept of the soul, which some theologians might argue is within an individual at birth, although he (ibid., p. 115) was anxious that there should be no confusion between the two ideas:

> If we abandon the conception of a substantive soul endowed with the self of the individual at birth, then we may regard the development of the individual's self, and of his self-consciousness within the field of his experience, as the social psychologist's special interest.

It will be recalled that Ryle (1963, p. 61) was keen to refute the idea that the person has a soul, 'the ghost of the machine', although he equated it with the mind, rather than distinguishing self and mind in the manner that Mead did, a distinction which is accepted here. Luckmann, however, regarded the development of the self as a profoundly religious phenomenon in itself, although his conceptualisation of religion is far wider than the way in which it is usually understood.

Self, like mind, emerges through social interaction, through the use of language. Hence, people's self-concepts and self identities emerge through the same process of interaction. People perform a variety of roles and are expected to become the role player, so that they acquire several social identities depending upon the social situation in which they perform their role. There is a danger in this approach to understanding the self, that the self is seen as 'protean', that is as having no inner core but merely responding to every social situation. But Mead would claim that there is a constant in the self in as much as it reflects the constancy of the socialisation process. Hence, while individuals may have several selves, all of which reflect their position in the social structure, the 'I' is a consistent experience which may actually be the amalgam of the several experiences which constitute it. Therefore, Figures 1.1 and 1.2 may be further refined, showing that the person is open to the influence of several sub-cultures and may have several role identities although only one self identity.

Figure 3.2 seeks to depict the individual within a variety of different sub-cultures; in some the individual is at the centre and receiving the full pressure of that sub-culture, whereas in others the individual is only partially exposed to its social forces. Figure 3.2 is a much more realistic picture of pluralistic society and recognises that in some instances the individual merely 'receives' certain social impressions, while in other instances they are much more fully

Figure 3.2 The individual within a variety of sub-cultures

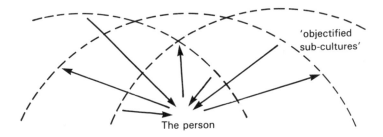

'objectified sub-cultures'

The person

processed. This demonstrates the extent to which there can be different forms of learning within any social experience, and also the importance of understanding the place of pre-conscious learning in the formation of the person.

People identify themselves and are identified by others by the roles that they assume within the process of social living; people learn to be themselves and, as Mead so clearly pointed out, language plays a significant part in that process. People acquire the language of their sub-culture, as Bernstein (1971, p. 78) showed, so that whenever they speak they reflect their background. Consequently, some people have elocution lessons in order to hide their social origins! But they initially think in the language of that background. But even more significantly, those with whom they interact use language which locates them in their position in the social structure. Freire (1972a, pp. 38–9) demonstrates this very clearly:

> Self-deprecation is another characteristic of the oppressed which derives from their internalization of the opinion of the oppressors hold of them. So often do they hear that they are good for nothing, know nothing, and are incapable of learning anything — that they are sick, lazy, unproductive — that in the end they become convinced of their own unfitness.

Both mind and self emerge in the same social process, both are social constructs. Hence, the person is a social construct and this conclusion has several important implications for adult education.

From the above discussion there are clear implications for any understanding of learning, but since the time of Mead there have been other theorists who have expanded upon this idea in different ways and some of their work is also significant. For instance, Luckmann

(1967) sought to illustrate how the process of the formation of the self was valuable to an understanding of what he called 'the invisible religion'. It is, however, even more significant in developing an understanding of learning, since he starts from an individualistic perspective in a complex but perceptive analysis of the formation of the self. He suggests (1967, p. 47) that as the human organism transcends its biological nature, a religious phenomenon has occurred. However, the significant thing about Luckmann's analysis is that he suggests (1967, p. 50) that an organism becomes, or acquires, a 'self' by constructing with others an 'objective and moral universe of meaning'. This is significant because it has to be recognised that before an individual is able to construct a universe of meaning the person has to pose questions of meaning. The process of focusing upon the unknowns of human existence, and asking questions about them, begins in childhood and continues intermittently throughout life. This ability to ask questions of meaning and to construct systems of meaning appears fundamental to humanity. Piaget (1929) recognised this in one of his early studies of children and now his work has been widely accepted by theorists of initial education. However, as children grow, so their universes of experience expand and their questions change accordingly. Many of the answers to the questions of meaning have an empirical basis, so that the learning of various disciplines begins with the questioning process. Some aspects of human experience are such that there are no empirical answers and in these cases belief knowledge emerges, systems of meaning that may be viewed as religious, theological etc.

The significance of this position is that for so long as people's systems of meaning are congruous with their experience, they feel no need to pose questions of meaning. When they experience an 'unknown', then they are forced into a questioning position and this disjuncture is the start of the learning process. Its fundamental significance, if this argument is to be accepted, is that both mind and self are learned through the self-same process from exactly the same impetus as all other learning. Wherever there is disjuncture between people's biography and their experience they are in a situation where they can pose questions, but this was precisely the same situation with very young children which led to the formation of both mind and self.

It is, therefore, necessary to expand this discussion even further in relation to learning, which constitutes the focus of the next section of this chapter.

THE IMPLICATIONS FOR LEARNING

From the above discussion it may be seen that both mind and self are regarded as social constructs, both emerge from the experiences of everyday life through social interaction. They are both learned and both reflect the biography of the learner. Learning, it will be recalled, was defined earlier in this study as the transformation of experience into knowledge, skills and attitudes. Experience constitutes the subject of the next chapter, so that this aspect will not be pursued further here. Nevertheless, it is important to assess the implications of the foregoing discussion a little further and so this section has three sections; mind, self and meaning.

Mind. There is a sense in which mind may be regarded as the stock of knowledge that individuals acquire as a result of lived experience in the world, but as this stock of knowledge is changing with every experience, mind should not be regarded as a static phenomenon. But not all experiences, as will be seen from the subsequent discussion, produce new knowledge. Indeed, some experiences do no more than reinforce the already existing knowledge, and this is to be expected since it would be impossible for society to exist at all unless people actually had similar experiences and made similar responses to them at different times of their lifespan. Even so, there are other experiences that produce situations in which people are unable to respond in a taken-for-granted manner and these are potential learning situations.

The stock of knowledge that people acquire which is based upon their biography is continually being tested by the rigours of social living and, consequently, it is continually being revised in the light of new social experiences. Each person's stock of knowledge is both common and unique. It is common to people of the same social class, gender and ethnic background, but it is also unique, because people do respond to social situations slightly differently. It would be totally impossible for two people to have the same biography and therefore totally impossible for them to have exactly the same stock of knowledge. Hence, some people may take for granted what other people have to think about.

Throughout the process of social living, people are continually adding new knowledge to their stock of knowledge, since they are frequently having to think about things prior to action. Learning is, therefore, something that occurs all the time, even though the learner is not always in a classroom, but in lifelong learning the world is everyone's classroom. It is a disservice to the concept of learning to limit it to a formal educational mode. However, it has to be recognised that some of the resources for learning from everyday life, e.g. the media, are controlled in such a manner as to ensure that the information provided is not value free. Hence, the significance of creating people with critical minds, able to respond to their experiences in life in a critically aware manner (Jarvis, 1985a).

Since each person's biography is hidden from every other person it is impossible to know precisely what knowledge other people have acquired, or even how other people interpret a common social situation, unless they are prepared to communicate openly about their knowledge and understanding. This they are often unprepared to do and it is significant that in Freire's method of adult teaching he first seeks to understand the position of the potential learners; they become the teachers in the first instance, so that they can then set the agenda for the literacy programme that follows.

Thus it may be seen that most learning occurs in a social situation and, hence, the significance of the self to this discussion. Once the self has begun to develop it affects the way in which people interact and the way in which they respond to social experiences. Ultimately, therefore, the self-concept affects the way in which they learn and even what they learn from these social experiences. The literature on the self in social psychology is voluminous, but beyond the scope of this study. Even so, it must be recognised that adult educators have also placed tremendous emphasis upon this aspect of the person because they have recognised the effect of the self upon adult learning.

The self. The self, like the mind, appears to have a separate existence once it has developed, since it appears capable of resisting some of the forces that would change it. This does not mean that it necessarily becomes entrenched and is unable to change. Indeed it is still likely to change and develop with significant subsequent experiences, although it is recognised that there are times when it will resist opportunities to learn, e.g. prejudice, bigotry, which are discussed below. There appear to be three main elements in this developing phenomenon; self-image, self-esteem and the ideal self. The last of these is the image that people have of themselves to which they think that they should conform, whereas the self-image is the impression that they have of themselves and self-esteem is the feelings that people have about themselves. Clearly, the self-concept depends to a great extent upon the understanding that people gain fron others about themselves and this, in turn, depends upon the extent to which the people concerned value the others' appraisal of them. Lovell (1980, pp. 115–16), for instance, claims:

> If others who are important to us make it clear that they see us
> as intelligent, helpful and caring, in time we will come to see
> ourselves in this way and come to behave appropriately. If we are
> fortunate the self image that we develop will be one which is
> positive and which facilitates successful learning. We will feel
> encouraged to expand, extend, develop, mature and express these
> capacities which will lead towards a fulfilment of our potentialities
> . . . On the other hand, if the self image that we are encouraged
> to adopt is a poor one we may be inhibited from attempting to
> realize our full potential for the rest of our lives.

It is this latter aspect that Freire stresses with the colonised. They
were treated as if they and their culture were of little worth and they
learned to believe it. Hence, they saw themselves in this manner. By
contrast, the oppressors regarded themselves as dominant and so they
reinforced their own positive self-image.

However, it is important to note that in urban industrial society,
individuals live and move in a number of different social groups and
acquire different social identities within each. Hence, in one social
setting people may have a positive self-image and in another have
a negative one. Unfortunately, schooling is one of the social institutions which plays a significant role in learning. Many children,
especially those from working-class backgrounds, acquire a negative
self-image in relation to education and learning, as Willis (1977,
p. 91) shows in this address from a careers teacher to a fifth form
of school-leavers.

> Some of you think that you can just walk in and get an appren-
> ticeship with your standards. Your standards! Some of you can
> hardly write and read and add up and you think you've got a right
> to an apprenticeship . . . let me tell you, you have no right at all,
> not by a long shot, you don't have a right to anything and the sooner
> you appreciate that, the better you'll do.

Clearly this might have been an exasperated moment, but what do
the fifth formers learn from this? How does this help their self-image
about formal education? These were working-class boys and this would
help reinforce their image of themselves as unable to cope with the
formal learning situation. Yet in among the class there were no doubt
boys who in their own group had a very positive self-image, so that

their low self-image in respect of education may well affect their attitude towards learning formally for much of their lives. Belbin and Belbin (1972, p. 168) showed the truth of this:

> . . . one of 'the most intelligent personnel' who was offered day release from a chemical firm to prepare for a City and Guilds examination. This man passed his first year examination and towards the end of the second year left — not the classes, but the firm. His explanation was '. . . I am just scared of not passing the second year examination or of falling behind the others. You see, I've been a leading hand and I've got a reputation to keep up, I might fail to do so'.

A positive self-image in the world of work and a low self-image in the world of education resulted not in failure, but resignation from work in order to retain the high self-image.

In a similar manner Cross (1981, p. 123), summarising the research on why some adults do not participate in adult education, makes the following point:

> Ruberson and Boshier are quite explicit about the hypothesis that certain personality types will be difficult to attract to education because of their low self-esteem. The hypothesis that people with low self-esteem do not do well in achievement-orientated situations (which education is thought to be) has been a kingpin of psychological theories of motivation for some years. The hypothesis is also implicit in Miller's social class analysis, where he considers lack of achievement motivation a deterrent to the participation of the lower socioeconomic classes.

In precisely the same way it might be argued that those people with a low self-image are more likely to learn what they are told to learn, while those with more positive self-images may be more likely to question what they are told.

By contrast to these findings, it is significant that people with high status in a social group will actually estimate their own achievement potential:

> The higher an individual's status in his group, the more he will over-estimate his future performance; the lower his status, the less he will tend to over-estimate. Indeed, three of the ten lowest-ranking subjects *under*estimated their future performance. None

of the leaders or middle-ranking members gave underestimates. Harvey also found that the higher-status members not only set higher goals for themselves but were *expected* by their clique mates to perform a a higher level. The performance of the lowest status members was, on the average, underestimated by both the leaders and the middle-ranking members. The lowest-status members were expected to perform more poorly than they actually did. (Krech *et al.*, 1962, p. 81)

Self-image and social image both affect the way that performance is anticipated. Indeed, this might well raise significant questions about how people actually perform in an educational setting and the way in which they are expected to perform. This also raises questions about assessment, but these lie beyond the scope of this study.

Meaning. The concept of meaning plays an important part throughout this study, since people define the situations in which they find themselves and ascribe meaning or lack of meaning to them. Where they can ascribe meaning easily, they find it easy to respond in the manner which they have previously learned. Hence, there are non-learning responses to some potential learning situations. By contrast, where the situation is less meaningful, that is where there is a disjuncture between their experience and their biography people pose questions about their situation, which might restart the learning process.

But how they learn and what they learn must relate to both the situation in which they are and also to their own biography. Their biography is a social phenomenon and reflects in some manner their previous experiences and their situation. Certainly their experience of that situation must also be social. Hence the start of any learning process must necessarily be a social phenomenon, so that it now becomes necessary to explore the concept of the situation before any theory of learning can be propounded.

CONCLUSIONS

This chapter has sought to show that the person is a social construct and that those aspects of the person that are learned in the process of social living actually affect future learning. Some emphasis was placed in the final section of this chapter on the place of experience in the learning process and that constitutes one aspect of the following chapter, a chapter that recognises quite fully that learning occurs in the social situation.

4

Experiencing the Social Situation

From the previous chapter it is clear that both mind and self are learned within the context of social experience, which is itself related to the social structures so that it is now important to begin to explore the idea of individual experience that constitutes the basis from which learning emerges. However, what the individual actually experiences is itself contained within a social situation and to discuss the experience without reference to the social situation is to omit one of the more significant elements of the learning process. However, it will be noted from Figure 2.2 that the arrow from the person enters the dual box at the point of the situation and leaves from the experience, since it is the way in which the person experiences the social situation that affects the learning process. Since experience occurs within the context of the social situation, it is necessry first to explore that concept. The social situation may be understood to be the objective dimension of experience. Having analysed this dimension, the subjective concept of experience can be explored, and this discussion incorporates the idea of experience, as included within Knowles's (1980, p. 44) discussion of andragogy. In this analysis, it is recognised that the internalisation of all previous experiences which can readily be recalled to mind, which is approximately how Knowles employs the term, does affect the manner in which any new experience is perceived and from which learning might consequently occur. Perhaps more significantly, however, the concepts of meaningfulness and meaninglessness are analysed within the framework of experience and this is also placed in the wider perspective of the person being a meaning-seeking being. Finally, there is the recognition that some experiences occur so frequently, because of the nature of social living, that they cease to be meaningful and become taken-for-granted, while others call for a response, which lies at the start of the learning process.

THE SOCIAL SITUATION

Life may be conceptualised as an on-going phenomenon located within a socio-cultural milieu which is bounded by the temporality of birth and death. Throughout life, people are moving from social situation to social situation; sometimes in conscious awareness but on other occasions in a taken-for-granted manner. Life, then, is a temporal phenomenon which is rather like a piece of cord threaded between numerous social situations and in order to analyse the idea of the social situation, it is necessary to isolate one artificially from all of the others and remove it from the duration of time. Bergson (1920) called the thread of time in the former situation *durée*, while he called the latter *temps vécu*, which is the subjective element of experience that will be discussed in the next section. However, for the purpose of analysis only, the social situation that constitutes the basis of this exploration is a discrete phenomenon, a social situation that is bounded by time.

Since people live within a socio-cultural-temporal milieu, it is possible to begin to isolate the elements of the social situation in terms of the social and the cultural. However, it is important to recognise that because of the nature of social life, social interaction for the majority of people spans more than one sub-culture, so that a social situation may occur within a sub-cultural setting with which an individual is unfamiliar or within a sub-cultural setting within which the person has had previously unpleasant experiences. Hence, a person's response to such social situations will differ from those of another person who is either familiar with, or happy within, that sub-cultural setting.

Thus it may be seen that one person's response to a social situation may be totally different to another person's, and that this will depend to a considerable extent upon how the actor defines the situation. Hence, learning takes on an individualistic overtone even though people may share an apparently common social situation. This, then, constitutes a measure of the discussion in the forthcoming section of this chapter. However, this present section confines itself to the nature of the social situation within which people interact and experience. Any situation has a number of dimensions and these require further exploration. It is suggested that there are at least two dimensions to any social situation; pro-action/reaction and individual/group. Within the context of learning, the former dimension has an implicit point about intention in a similar manner to Tough's (1979) notion of deliberate learning, to which reference has been made previously in this study. The latter dimension is made more complicated because social interaction can occur in at least three different types of social group; informal, non-formal and formal. Hence, it is possible to construct a model of a situation within which learning may occur and this shows that there are at least eight different types of situation from which learning may stem (see Figure 4.1).

Figure 4.1 Types of situation

	Individual	Informal	Non-formal	Formal
Pro-active				
Reactive				

For the sake of simplicity, these eight situations may be termed:

- pro-active individual
- pro-active informal
- pro-active non-formal
- pro-active formal
- reactive individual
- reactive informal
- reactive non-formal
- reactive formal

Each of these now requires some elaboration, but for the sake of clarity this will be undertaken by examining the three main elements.

Pro-activity/Reactivity. At first sight this dimension appears to be no more than a re-wording of the psychological research about motivation and, indeed, adult education literature is full of research reports, etc. about this topic (see, for instance, Wlodkowski, 1985). However, there is a subtle difference between that discussion and the issues that are raised here. The significance of the debate about motivation is that it refers in some manner to the personalities of the persons under discussion. Some people may be highly motivated to join an adult class while others may be less inclined to do so and, naturally, adult educators seeking class enrolments wish to understand something about these differing motivations. In contrast to this, the pro-active/reactive dimension refers to the extent to which individuals have 'created' the situations in which they are or whether they are reacting to a situation which has been created by others. In a sense, there is a similarity between the pro-active element here and Tough's (1979, p. 7) 'very deliberate act of learning', but it is not intended to restrict the time of the learning episode in the manner that he does.

Pro-activity assumes that the actor is an agent, in some ways free to act upon the social structures and even to change them, free to seek out things and discover and free to think. Hence, people in leadership positions tend to be pro-active; people from the upper social classes are more likely to be pro-active than are those lower down the social hierarchy; people who have impulsive personalities may well be regarded by others as pro-active; those who hold strong religious/ideological views may be pro-active at certain times and in specific social situations. Hence, a normally reticent and retiring person, who is usually other-directed, may feel obliged to be pro-active in situations which contravene specific and strongly-held beliefs. In contrast, reactivity occurs in a number of different ways; a person who is in a dominated position may react to the pro-activity of those who dominate, the more so when that domination leads to an overt oppression. Reactivity, in this sense, may be seen to be a response to oppressive social structures, but it may be called revolutionary. Another form of reactivity occurs when people are out of harmony with their socio-cultural milieu. Elsewhere (Jarvis, 1983b) it was argued that people endeavour to live in a state of equilibrium with that milieu but when disharmony occurs people react to seek to recreate the state of equilibrium. The work of Aslanian and Brickell (1980) is indicative of the manner in which people do this in life transition situations. This is effectively when they are freed of the constraints of social structures because they are in the process of being changed from one set of constraints to another. They suggest that changes in the life situation act as a trigger for learning; learning may precede, accompany or follow a transition and need not necessarily be directly related to that transition.

Clearly this discussion relates closely to aspects of motivation but the concern here is slightly more sociological, it relates to the extent to which individuals are the agents in creating the social situations or whether they are reacting to the pressures created by the social structures. People may be agents in some situations and reactors in others and their motivation to learn in any situation may differ according to the role that they have played in creating it. But it should not be assumed that people will learn more when they are pro-active since they may only be pro-active in situations with which they are familiar, so that they take for granted a great deal that occurs. In contrast, the unfamiliarity of specific situations may act as a spur to learning and so reactive situations may result in people learning a great deal.

In addition, there is clearly a relationship between pro-activity and self-direction and since self-directed learning is a significant concept in the study of the education of adults it is necessary to examine the similarities and differences between them. Self-direction might mean that a person can join a group and learn in a reactive manner within the group, whereas pro-action here means that the learner takes the initiative in creating a potential learning situation. Self-direction is a feature of the person *per se* rather than the person in relation to the specific social situation. This difference must be borne in mind in the subsequent discussion so that the two concepts are not confused.

Individual/Group. Immediately it must be noted that coupled with the previous discussion, four possible types of situation occur; those individual ones in which people are either pro- or reactive and this also occurs in relation to group situations. However, it has to be recognised that many learning situations do occur when an individual is totally alone: for instance, a person who trips over a doorstep recognises that the doorstep is there and so internalises the act and stores it for future reference. This is a reactive individual type of situation and one in which considerable learning occurs, although it often goes unrecogniseed as a learning experience because it is a common form of experience in everyday living. In a similar manner a person may have an experience in a group, pleasant or unpleasant, and having left the group think about it and subsequently modify ideas or behaviour. Some people may specifically be self-directed learners and, wishing to learn about something, they simply purchase a book and read about it. This is a pro-active individual and, claims Mezirow (1981, p. 17), this is the goal of andragogy. Mezirow recognises that the felt need to learn might also lead a person into dialogue and that this is also self-directed. Indeed, this is a pro-active group situation. By contrast, people participating in a group discussion may be faced with a debate in which their own views are challenged, so that in the course of the discussion they either modify their position or adduce additional reasons for holding the position that they do. This final situation is a reactive group one and clearly it is one through which such learning occurs in adult education, since group discussion is a common teaching/learning technique employed by adult educators (see

Jaques, 1984). One of the significant factors of many of the situations that have been suggested here is that they encourage interaction and, it will be recalled from the previous chapter, that both mind and self emerge in the interactive learning situation. However, all social interaction does not occur in the same type of group and so the third sub-section here examines this dimension.

Informal/Non-formal/Formal. Coombs and Ahmed (1974, pp. 16–21) suggested that people learn within three different types of social environment, informal, non-formal and formal, and this distinction has given rise to some discussion in educational circles about different forms of social environment in which learning occurs. They suggested that informal situations occur when people learn from the media, etc. but within the typology adopted here this is probably an individualistic situation. By contrast, informal situations, as employed here, occur in social interaction between friends or acquaintances, etc. This is the process of much social living, such as living within the family, and is a source of a great deal of learning from both pro-active and reactive situations. However, it is important to note that it is one of the types of social situation which is also bounded to a considerable extent by social class, ethnicity, gender, interest, etc. Hence, the learning that occurs within this type of social situation may be considered to be bounded by certain social parameters that lead to differentiation between people by class, etc. in respect of both mind and self. This is an important element within learning, because it does mean that people's stock of knowledge must be influenced by their class position, etc. This is one of the factors that lead to certain forms of social continuity between generations.

Formal education, suggest Coombs and Ahmed, occurs within the school and the classroom. Since their concern is with education *per se* they concentrate upon the school. However, learning may occur in any formal situation and many formal educational settings are no longer in the typical school. Formal, within the context of this discussion, relates to any bureaucratic or 'official' situation in which people play roles within organisations. Obviously, one element within the context of the formal organisation is power and the teaching and learning that occur usually emanate from the hierarchy of the organisation downwards and are perhaps traditionally instruction-orientated, although in certain educational situations this is undergoing change (Knowles, 1984). It is perhaps significant to note here that many organisations of this nature assume what may be called a middle-class sub-culture, simply because leaders in formal settings tend to come from the middle and upper classes. This makes such situations total-ly different to the informal ones because they tend to reflect the social origins of the participants and are, consequently, variable according to who is interacting. However, people can choose to enrol in a formal educational class or they may be sent, so that they may be either pro-active or reactive in the situation.

Coombes and Ahmed (1974, p. 8) define non-formal education as 'any organized, systematic, educational activity carried on outside the framework of the formal system to provide selected types of learn-ing to particular sub-groups of the population, adults as well as children'. They suggest that such activities as agricultural extension may be included within this categorisation. They are clearly trying to differentiate between the informality of normal social living, the group experience of the formal classroom and this third category in which education is provided for individuals outside of the formal school system. Non-formal is regarded here as organised and systematic interaction between people outside of a formal organisa-tional setting so that, for instance, a teacher practitioner in nursing may be regarded as providing non-formal education (see Jarvis and Gibson, 1985). However, the interaction between an employee and a supervisor may be regarded as a non-formal situation in which lear-ning might occur. It would be wrong to claim that these situations are not affected by the participants' social origins, etc. but they are less variable than the informal situations.

LaBelle (1982) has sought to clarify these terms and he also recognises that in third world societies non-formal education has lower status than formal education, because high status education is related to the school in people's minds. However, both he and Coombs and Ahmed are more concerned about education than they are about learning *per se*.

By contrast, Mocker and Spear (1981) do employ these terms dif-ferently; for them, formal learning occurs where learners have no control over the objectives nor the means of learning; non-formal learning occurs where learners control the objectives but not the means; informal learning where learners control the means but not the objectives. While this is a nice distinction, it is not employed here because it relates more closely to the learning process than it does to the social situation as a whole. Because they have related it to the learning process they are able to go on to specify that in self-directed learning the learners control both the means and the objectives of learning. However, it is clear from the discussion above that since learners can voluntarily give up the control of the direction of the learning, and still be regarded as self-directed, this distinction is one that cannot be accepted here. Nevertheless, Mocker and Spear have raised the important issue of the different types of learning, even though they have not actually placed them within the social context, so that it is important to note the differences in the use of terminology.

From the above discussion it is important to highlight the fact that formal, non-formal and informal are used here to refer to situations, not to types of learning nor types of education. Formal situations are bureaucratic, non-formal are organised but not necessarily in a bureaucratic environment and informal situations are ones where there are no pre-specified, although there are always covert, procedures of interaction.

Thus it may be seen that a situation has a number of parameters and people interacting within any social situation may not perceive the situation in the same way, may not define it in the same manner and may not experience it in the same way. In other words, experience of a social situation is subjective rather than objective, and it is the subjective definition of the situation which creates the experience and potentially leads to learning. Hence, it is now necessary to focus upon experience.

THE SUBJECTIVITY OF EXPERIENCE

No social situation has meaning in itself or for itself. Indeed there is a genuine sense that the experiences that actors have in a situation are socially constructed and the meaning imposed upon them, and this is important when seeking to understand adult learning. It will be recalled that Dewey (1938) recognised the significance of the inter-relationship between experience and education and he actually claimed (1938, p. 25) that 'all genuine education comes about through experience'. It is the sum total of all previous experiences that people bring to a situation, that is their body, mind and self, and it is this which Knowles (1980, p. 44) refers to as a rich reservoir of experience in his formulation of andragogy. But his claim is clearly one that requires additional elaboration. People bring their cognitions, their emotions, their physical abilities and their self-concept. These are then utilised by the actors in a social situation both in order to understand the situation and to help determine how they may act as a result of their understanding. Therefore, in order to understand the basis of experience it is necessary to unravel this interplay between the persons and their social reality a little deeper, that is between two sets of conditions — both subjective and objective. Perhaps this might be clarified a little by Figure 4.2.

Figure 4.2 Towards an understanding of experience

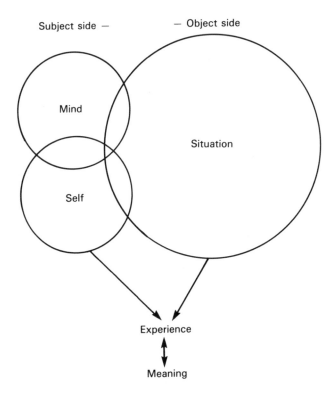

The terms subject side and object side in Figure 4.2 are borrowed from Merleau-Ponty's ontology of a situation, since they clearly specify the two major aspects of this process, although it is not considered necessary to pursue all the elements of his analysis here.

The overlapping circles in Figure 4.2 seek to demonstrate that in every experience there is an interplay of mind and self, on the one hand, and of both with the situation on the other. This may be further understood from Figure 4.3.

Dewey (1938, p. 39) argued that every genuine experience has an active side which changes to some degree the objective conditions under which people's experience is had. They seek to impose upon the situation in which they find themselves certain expectations

Figure 4.3 The interplay of subject and object sides

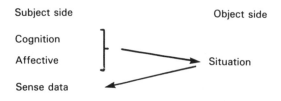

which they bring to it, so that perception is always selective, but at the same time they are recipients of sense data. These data are received through each of the senses: visual, aural, tactile, taste and smell. Obviously, in the majority of situations the aural, visual and tactile are the means through which the stimuli that are the most significant in the process of adult learning are received, but the other two must not be ruled out, especially in pre-conscious learning. It must also be recalled that Brundage and Mackeracher (1980, p. 31) claim that adults learn best when they 'can process information through multiple channels' and 'when novel information is presented through a variety of sensory modes and experiences'. At the same time it must be recognised that because experience is multi-faceted, people tend to focus upon, or be aware of, certain dimensions of it only. The aural dimension is among the most powerful, but most people can recall being bored in a lecture and turning their attention to some other aspect of the environment and the stimuli upon which attention is focused are received through different senses. Another reaction to such a boring situation is to endeavour to re-create an experience by seeking to recall other pleasant memories and then perhaps to reflect on these and even to learn from them. Hence, it is not only 'turning the mind off' but focusing it upon other facets of the current situation. Attention, then, is a major part of the process whereby the situation is changed into an experience.

In addition, it should be noted that in contemporary society people are exposed to a variety of experiences, i.e. the media, on which they do not place the initial interpretation; that is, provide it with its initial meaning. These experiences may be regarded as secondary experiences rather than primary ones. The point of the primary experiences is that actors are actually in the social situation and impose their own meanings upon them, whereas they are not present in secondary situations and the meanings that they receive are presented to them as if they were part of the actual happenings. However, these meanings are only a selection of the facts, they are the selection made by other people are a result of their own biographical experiences: the extent to which the reporters are able to disassociate themselves from their own biographies, or even wish to do so, is open to considerable debate. However, many secondary experiences tend to be treated by people as if they were primary ones, so that it is important to recognise one of the features of modernity and to recognise the significance of the more reflective types of learning within such a society in order to ensure the possibility of democracy.

Another important factor is that it is easy not to regard secondary experiences as learning experiences, since the information is not presented in the normal teaching and learning situation. But this is important; learning is given a social definition rather than a conceptual one, and this affects individual responses to different situations.

People do not receive sense data like a camera receiving and recording the light impressions on a negative but rather their awareness is selective and relates to their knowledge, etc. and the motivation that they bring to a situation. Child (1981, p. 77) notes that perception always depends upon previous experience. Additionally, there is a considerable body of research that shows that the mind also interprets the sense data received in order to make sense of it. Perhaps a couple of examples will demonstrate this point clearly. Kelley (1950) recorded how two groups of students were given different descriptions of a lecturer; one was told that he was a 'very warm person' while the other was told that he was rather 'cold'. They then listened to him lecture and were later asked to rate the lecturer. Those who were told that he was warm rated him as more considerate, more informed, more sociable, more popular, better natured, more humourous and more humane than did the group who were told that he was cold. Kelley also found that there was a greater tendency for the students who were told that the guest lecturer was a warm person to interact with him. Hence, perception of persons is a phenomenon that affects the way in which interaction occurs thereafter. In addition, there are many studies that show how people perceive objects and patterns in a way that demonstrates that they have imposed an interpretation upon the object or picture that they are observing. A significant conclusion that might be drawn from this discussion is that it is possible for individuals to perceive what are apparently the same facts from a situation and experience them differently, even to experience them in such a manner as to confer diametrically opposing meanings upon them. Initially this conclusion might appear to be far-fetched, but the above evidence points in this direction and, in addition, Lukes (1981) has argued that it is possible in the social sciences for theories to conflict with each other and yet to be compatible with all the data that exist about the facts. This is an important conclusion in seeking to understand the process of adult learning because it points to the fact that no observer, or teacher, can necessarily or automatically understand the experience that any person is having at any moment in a learning situation and nor can that observer or teacher automatically understand the meaning that the learner is placing upon that experience. But is this not contradicting the point that in social interaction there is a degree of commonality that enables such assumptions to be made? No, because inter-subjectivity is perfectly normal and possible, but in a great deal of normal social interaction there is either a degree of commonality of social background or a common reason for the meeting. Even in the latter there is sometimes misunderstanding or awkwardness in the social interaction by less confident actors.

It is important in understanding the process of adult learning to begin to isolate some of the variables that consistently affect the manner in which people perceive their situations. A number are suggested here; socio-economic class, position in a group, ethnicity, sex and age. While not all of these examples are taken from the field of adult education, they are taken from human interaction situations and it is suggested here that whatever the situation, the finding is relevant for the purposes of this study. MacKenzie (1975) has argued clearly that people's position within the social class hierarchy is related to the manner in which they perceive society: those people who are objectively in the lower social classes see society as having two classes ('them and us'), with their own class as the larger of the two. By contrast those people who are objectively in the middle classes in society regard society as having three tiers, with their own class (the middle class) as being the largest. Asch (1955) showed that in some group relationships the pressure of the group actually caused individual member's perceptions to be distorted. Freire (1972a, pp. 38–7 claimed that the oppressed

> so often . . . hear that they are good for nothing, know nothing and are incapable of learning anything — that they are sick, lazy, and unproductive — that in the end they become convinced of their own unfitness. 'The peasant feels inferior to the boss because the boss seems to be the only one who knows things and able to run things.'

In a similar manner, Thorson and Waskel (1985, p. 237) write:

> Some older people cease to grow. For a variety of reasons, many older people have lost confidence in their own ability to learn and have accepted the stereotype that they can no longer be effective learners. Society conspires with this acceptance of a negative self-image by excluding older people from situations, such as work, that act as continuing stimuli for growth.

Feminists point out how males have traditionally defined the social situation for women, so that they have learned to define it for themselves in precisely the same way as do men, but that they now have to free themselves of this approach and learn to define it from a woman's position.

It would be perfectly possible to continue listing the evidence that demonstrates that social situations have no intrisic meaning but that they are each defined by the actors according to their previous experience and according to their place within the specific situation. However, this is not regarded as necessary here. Perception, then, is itself socially constructed and even constrained, reflecting the socio-cultural milieu of those who define the situation. Consequently, it relates to the actual experience that they have. Whilst certain sociological variables have been listed here to show how perception is socially constructed and constrained, it would also be possible to extend this analysis to cover such other variables as relevance, motivation, etc. It is important to recognise that these also operate in this process, but these variables are themselves dependent to a considerable extent upon some of the social variables already discussed and so they are not pursued further at this stage.

While this discussion points to the fact that individuality in perception and social definition must occur to some extent, since each person lives within a unique constellation of sub-cultures, it must also be recognised that there is a certain commonness between people that allows for communication and inter-subjectivity. This occurs because certain groupings of people do share common dominant sub-cultures, such a social class, sex and even age.

It will be recalled from Figure 2.2 that there is a route into experience from memory and this has been put there since it is quite a common situation for people to re-create previous experiences in their mind and to seek to learn from them. During this thinking process the person may be detached from physical surroundings and even oblivious of them. Yet a cognitive experience occurs which may begin a learning process. It operates in precisely the same manner as do other experiences. Even if the mind recalls the original experience precisely as it was experienced, the memory has already undergone a process of perception. However, it must also be recognised that there is in addition a process of selective remembering and, consequently, one of selective forgetting. There is considerable research within psychology that demonstrates the process of suppression and much shows that it relates to aspects of the self. But it is not regarded as necessary to extend that discussion here. The point is that people do have cognitive experiences and the memories recalled are themselves social constructs.

From all of the above discussion in this section, two factors can be concluded: first, that the experience that the participants have is itself socially constructed and it is mediated through the channels of perception; secondly, that the experiences do not have meaning in themselves and that the participants seek to define their situations and to impose meaning upon them. Thus their situations are socially defined and the meanings that individuals impose upon them are socially constructed. Even so, it must be recognised that not every situation lends itself to being defined by the participants, although most pro-active situations can be so defined since very little pro-active behaviour occurs mindlessly. Hence some experiences are meaningless to the participants and so the eightfold diagram of different types of situation might now be reconstructed as in Figure 4.4, showing more of the different types of experience.

Figure 4.4 Different types of experience

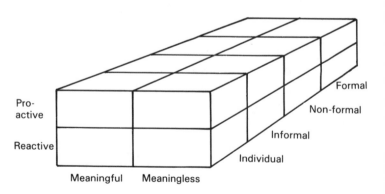

It is necessary to note that experience is used here in relation to the manner by which persons apprehend or comprehend the social situation. The memories of all of these experiences constitute their biography and the way that Knowles (1980) and Usher (1985, 1986) *inter alia* employ the term is much closer to the way in which biography is used here. Hence to use people's experience as a learning resource is to recognise that they bring their own biography to every situation that they experience.

At this stage it is necessary to consider the concept of meaning in relation to experience, and even more in relation to learning, so that the following section of this chapter discusses meaningfulness and meaninglessness.

MEANINGFUL AND MEANINGLESS EXPERIENCE

In everyday experience individuals may be barely conscious of the passing of time and they frequently respond to their experiences in a rather automatic manner. The fact is that as a result of previous learned experiences people build up a stock of knowledge and a positive self-concept that enables them to respond to such situations with a degree of confidence that almost appears to be mindless behaviour. Indeed, as Dahlgren (1984, pp. 23–4) points out, most learning is directed at striving for meaning; to have learned something is to have grasped its meaning, and then the person is almost able to take the situation for granted, as it appears to be self-evidently meaningful. For instance, an experienced car driver rarely considers the intricacies of driving a car when travelling to work each day. The response to the stimulus is almost automatic, it is what Schutz and Luckmann (1974, p. 8) refer to as 'taken-for-granted' behaviour and what some psychologists regard as over-learning. Schutz and Luckmann (1974, p. 7) write:

> I trust that the world as it has been known by me until now will continue further and consequently the stock of knowledge obtained from my fellow men and formed from my own experience will continue to preserve its fundamental validity . . . From this assumption follows the further and fundamental one: that I can repeat past successful acts. So long as the structure of the world can be taken as constant, as long as my previous experience is valid, my ability to operate upon the world in this and that manner remains in principle preserved.

This is a significant observation in terms of understanding both behaviour and learning. For so long as there is continuity between people's own personal stock of knowledge and their self-concept and the socio-cultural milieu that they experience, then they are enabled to perform in an almost unthinking manner. It might be claimed that these experiences are pre-reflectively meaningful to the persons who are having them. In this process of living people hardly separate out one experience from another; it is precisely what Bergson (1923) referred to as *durée*, a continuous coming-to-be and passing-away of phenomena. In this duration of time, experience in the socio-cultural situation of everyday life merely acts as a reinforcement of the stock of knowledge and of the self-concept that is already held. However, this reinforcement does not add to the stock of knowledge, nor does it dramatically change the self-concept, so that while it is subconsciously meaningful, it is not really a learning experience and little or no growth has occurred in the self. This is a process of habitualisation of behaviour and is quite natural, but there are dangers in this process if such self-confidence in the actor leads to role performance in a habitualised manner when the situation has actually changed slightly, but the actor's perception of it has not changed because the change has not been recognised. This is a form of response of which most people are aware and it is something of which professional practitioners and managers in the work place have to beware (Schon, 1983). Yet this is clearly an essential state for social living, since it would be quite impossible for society to exist and to function with any degree of normality if people had to think deeply about the majority of situations in social living, and perhaps devise innovative responses to those situations. In addition, it would be quite impossible for people to survive as people if there were no norm of human behaviour. Hence, the first type of meaningful experience is one in which there is a taken-for-granted response to a situation. Later in this chapter situations will be explored which are so familiar that they become meaningless and destructive of the self, but at the moment it is necessary to concentrate upon those situations which are much more normal.

A second type of response is one in which the situation is not quite so meaningful but sufficiently so for the actors to recognise that their stock of knowledge, or their self-confidence, is insufficient to enable them to cope with the experience in a taken-for-granted manner. Schutz and Luckmann (1974, p. 8) write: 'In the natural attitude, I only become aware of the deficient tone in my stock of knowledge if a novel experience does not fit into what has up until now been taken-for-granted valid reference schema.' That is, when persons have a new, but basically quite similar, experience to previous ones, then the stock of knowledge acquired and/or the self-confidence gained throughout the process of living is not sufficient to allow them to provide an automatic response. An awareness of a deficiency in that stock of knowledge or in that self-concept has occurred and in a sense they have experienced a need to learn. In other words, when there is a disjuncture between the individuals' stock of knowledge and/or their self-concept and the socio-cultural milieu in which the experience occurs, then there is a potential learning experience. This is a similar condition to the one described by Mezirow (1981, pp. 6–9) when he suggests that the first stage of perspective transformation is a 'disorientating dilemma' which leads to self-examination. It is important to recognise that this disorientating dilemma can occur both in the mind, or in the self-concept, or in both, and they demand different responses from the person, which might lead to different learning responses, or even to no response at all. This latter point is discussed briefly below, since it relates to anomic experience.

There was a suggestion in the above paragraph that need is a deficiency concept but this may not always be so in such a straightforward manner since the experience in which the disjuncture occurs may also be an idealised one, that is, an imagined situation, in which the actors might wish that certain competencies were theirs or certain conditions existed, so that they might perform in a more sophisticated manner. This is a significant point in considering the problem of the gap between biography and experience (the disorientating dilemma), since the human can project forward wants and desires, so that there is disjuncture between an imagined future experience and the present biography. It is at this point that needs and wants and interests converge, although all relate to this disjuncture, and it is a factor that is frequently omitted from discussion about these three concepts. Indeed, one difference between needs and wants that has not been discussed fully in the literature on needs is this temporal dimension, in which needs relate to a present experience and wants to an idealised future one. In addition, it may also be seen that the concept of disjuncture is an important factor in the quest to understand the social context of adult learning and it requires some elaboration here.

It is important to reiterate the fact that since people's biographies and their social situations are both socially constructed, that this disjuncture which potentially leads to learning is also socially constructed and thus it will necessarily be different for different people. When people become aware of this disjuncture and, consequently, of the need to learn, it is what Ingham and Nelson (1984, p. 18) refer to as 'the teachable moment'. The significant thing about these moments is that they relate to the biographies of people, so that the disjuncture is related to the social situation of individuals. This gives rise to certain questions about teaching groups of people since they may experience different points of disjuncture, or even no disorientating dilemma at all in the class situation.

Perhaps it is also important to note at this stage that there are some situations where the disjuncture might not be evident to the actors, but other interested persons — such as managers — consider that there is a need to learn and in these instances individuals are expected to learn. Alternatively, teachers merely produce information and expect that learners will learn, because that is what is expected of them. Both of these situations involve a power dimension, which is true to the reality of social living. However, they both also impinge upon the element of meaningfulness, since when the need to learn is recognised by the actors it often produces pro-active responses and these are often more highly motivated. By contrast, when a learning situation is imposed upon people from without, there is always the possibility that that which is provided is less than meaningful and that this will not result in effective learning, or that it will result in non-reflective learning.

Disjuncture, or discontinuity, between biography and experience of the wider world is a fundamental condition of human learning. Indeed, it might be argued that it is in fact the human condition itself (Fromm, 1949, pp. 38–50) in which humankind seeks to establish harmony between themselves and the world about them — or even mastery over that world. This is perhaps an ideal of utopian proportions but, as Freire (1972b, p. 40) maintained, education itself should be idealistic. The need to establish this harmony or mastery is at the start of the learning process: this continuity may be between biography and present experience or between biography and idealised experience. Where there is no harmony, this creates in human beings a state in which they might question their present situation, where they might seek to add to their skills, etc. so that they might achieve the desired state of equilibrium. Consequently, problem-solving learning seems to come closer to the human condition than memorisation, etc. When this disjuncture has been overcome and harmony has been established, then the human being habitualises the behaviour/knowledge and assumes a taken-for-granted response to situations. Thus it might be seen that taken-for-grantedness is, in fact, almost the fulfilment of the ideal, even though in a rapidly changing world it is a condition that may be achieved less frequently than in previous generations.

Yet the fundamental drawback of this position is that there is no human growth without learning and so the human condition must always be one in which there is the potential for disjuncture between biography and experience and growth occurs when the disjuncture is mastered and learning has occurred. Hence, the mixture of taken-for-grantedness and disjuncture is essential to human growth and development.

Both of the situations thus far discussed are pre-reflectively meaningful to the actors concerned and enable them either to act in a taken-for-granted manner or to commence learning about the situation, or idealised situation, in which they are. However, there are two other possibilities that require consideration here: the first is when the situation is such that it is so repetitive that the actors find it oppressive and the final one is when the situation is totally meaningless to the actors concerned. It is experiences like these that Dewey (1938, p. 25) referred to as miseducative' since they may arrest or distort the growth of the person undergoing the experience.

The idea of miseducative experience is important to understanding adult learning within the social context because it is often such an experience that inhibits adults from being pro-active about engaging in further formal learning situations. Adult educators are well aware of the problems that adults experience and the difficulties of the rectification process. However, these are also experiences that can and do occur in adulthood and old age.

In the taken-for-granted experience it will be recalled that there was such continuity between the people's stock of knowledge and their self-concept and the wider socio-cultural milieu that further reflection was unnecessary prior to action. However, if that milieu is unchanged and unchangeable, then the taken-for-grantedness becomes oppressive and eventually alienating. Experience in the workplace is not the only type of experience where this occurs, but it is the one in which much research has been carried out. This is also appropriate at the time of writing since there is considerable emphasis being placed upon the workplace as a place of learning and human resource development. Not all work is repetitive. Indeed, much of it is conducive to creative reflection, as Schon (1983) shows, so that this analysis is of only one particular type of experience and it is utilised here to demonstrate the effects of the relationship between the person and a particular type of socio-cultural milieu. The following is a description of assembly line work:

Try putting 13 little pins in 13 little holes 60 times an hour, eight hours a day. Spot weld 67 steelplates an hour and then find yourself one day facing a new assembly-line needing 110 an hour. Fit 100 coils into 100 cars an hour; tighten seven bolts three times a minute. Do your work in a noise 'at the safety limit', in a fine mist of oil, solvent and metal dust . . . Speed up to gain time to blow your nose or get a bit of grit out of your eye . . . (Bosquet, 1972, p. 23)

This is a description of life on an assembly line; consider the socio-cultural milieu in which these experiences occur. It is unchanging and unchangeable, so that people working within them can take — indeed are expected to take — their work behaviour for granted. The person is powerless to change the environment and so what can a person learn from such an experience? How meaningful can such experiences be? Beynon (1975, p. 118) reports interviews with people working on an assembly line.

It's the most boring job in the world. It's the same over and over again. There's no change in it. It wears you out. It makes you awful tired. It slows your thinking right down. There's no need to think. It's just a formality. You just carry on. You just endure it for the money. That's what we're paid for — to endure the boredom of it.
If I had a chance to move, I'd leave right away . . .

Unlike Schon's reflective practitioner, the socio-cultural environment does not provide experiences about which people can think and from which they can learn. It results in a slowing down of thought, even a closing of the mind. There is nothing in the experience upon which to reflect. The human being who is a meaning-seeking animal has to exist in an environment which eventually provides little or no stimulus for thought. Indeed, when life's experiences are enacted in a socio-cultural milieu that provides no stimulus, the experiences become means to other ends and so it might be better for the participants to be lost in the flow of time.

Nevertheless, in this type of experience people do close their minds to their immediate environment and create for themselves a cognitive environment, in which they can be lost in their thoughts. This is a cognitive experience, isolated from the socio-cultural milieu in which it occurs, but it may still be the start of one of the learning processes that are depicted in Figure 2.2. It is depicted by the dotted line going back from memorisation to experience. Another common experience of this type is when a child apparently turns off its attention from a school lesson that does not interest it and is lost in day dreams.

Being lost in thought may be a salvation from alienation, but the assembly line experience described here is always a potentially alienating one.

Alienation is a concept that was first used by Hegel and popularised by Marx. The latter is generally regarded as having developed the concept as a critique against capitalism, although Fromm (1966, p. 49) claims that it was primarily against the mode of production that Marx directed his criticism. Yet it is even wider than this, it is 'essentially experiencing the world and oneself passively, receptively, as a subject separated from the object' (Fromm, 1966, p. 44). It occurs whenever the individual is functioning within a socio-cultural milieu which provides no opportunity to reflect upon it and give it meaning, so that in the end the self is separated from the experience and action is separated from meaning. Self-estrangement occurs. There is nothing in the experience upon which the mind can reflect, there is little that can be meaningfully added to the mind's stock of knowledge and the self's development is stunted.

In contrast to this, when an experience can become a basis for learning and meaning there is, as has already been shown, a disjuncture between the socio-cultural milieu and the person's stock of knowledge and self-concept, but it is possible for the discontinuity to be too great and the reflection that occurs does not result in learning or meaning but in the realisation that the person cannot learn from the experience. For instance, people educated in the humanities might find the gap between their personal stock of knowledge and the socio-cultural milieu of a technological research institute too great to be bridged by reflection. Hence, if they wish to learn from the experience they have of spending time in such an institute, they would have to seek out additional learning opportunities first, in order to add to their stock of knowledge, so that they can impose meaning on the situation when they next enter such an institution.

Similarly, it has to be recognised that the socio-cultural milieu of everyday life does not remain static. As early as the 1920s, Scheler pointed out that some forms of cultural knowledge change faster than others. He (1980, p. 76) suggested, for instance, that the positive sciences change 'from hour to hour'. He went so far as to suggest that technological knowledge is artificial because it changes before it becomes embedded in the culture. It is not considered necessary to pursue Scheler's argument further here since it is almost self-evident in contemporary technological society that technological knowledge is changing at an ever-increasing speed and many people, especially the elderly, are finding it increasingly difficult to keep abreast with the rapid rate of change. They are, consequently, having experiences that are so divorced from their biography that they are unable to reflect meaningfully upon them. Such a state is sometimes apparent in the exclamation, 'I don't know what the world is coming to these days.' However, with the elderly there may be less motivation to seek an answer to that exclamation and they may well opt to remain in ignorance. This may be especially true if they do believe the stereotype about the elderly being unable to learn, etc. Being unable to learn new knowledge from their experiences is a debilitating experience, it is one in which those undergoing such an experience begin to lose confidence in themselves as people. It is a state to which Durkheim (1952) attached the label *anomie*, a state which he concluded led some people to commit suicide. It is not suggested here that the state of anomie described here results in suicide but it is recognised that when the gulf between the socio-cultural milieu and the person's stock of knowledge and self-concept is too great for learning to occur, it is a state of anomie and is both debilitating and not conducive to the development of the self.

In this analysis it is suggested that there are four broad responses that fall within the categories meaningfulness and meaningless; that neither of the extremes results in cognitive learning although they are both destructive of the self, whereas a taken-for-granted experience results in reinforcement for the self, but with little or no outlet for cognitive learning of a reflective nature. Only where there is a limited disjuncture between the biography and the experience is there the potentiality of reflective learning.

The conclusion to this chapter returns to Figure 2.2 and highlights the routes from experience in this process. Naturally enough, these relate very closely to the foregoing discussion.

CONCLUDING DISCUSSION

It will be recalled that Dewey (1938, p. 25) claimed that all education begins with experience. But it is maintained here that all learning begins with experience which is itself socially constructed and received through a variety of senses. Hence, those who claim the term experiential learning and relate it to only one form of learning, usually affective, or one type of experience, limit its connotation and in the process prevent learning being understood in its wider context. All experience offers the potential for learning but, as the foregoing discussion has tried to demonstrate, not every experience results in human growth and development, or even in learning. The latter point is one of the inevitable consequences of patterned human behaviour and a necessity for social human life.

There are three other routes from experience in the learning process model and these lead to memorisation, practice and thought, all of which relate to different learning processes. In at least some of these, the result of the learning is potentially a change in social behaviour but in other forms of learning there is no change in personal behaviour but there is in personal knowledge. In addition, there might be change in the self-concept. It is these that will be explored in later chapters of this book, but prior to that it is necessary to explore some of the ideas about thought and reflection that are currently prevalent in adult education literature.

5

Reflecting upon Experiences

> Consider thinking itself; you will find directions rather than states, and you will see that thinking is essentially a continual and continuous change in direction, incessantly tending to translate itself by changes of direction. I mean by actions and gestures capable of outlining in space and of expressing metaphorically, as it were, the comings and goings of the mind. (Bergson, 1920, p. 45)

In the previous chapters the fact that taken-for-granted responses to situations were not sufficient for every aspect of social living was seen to be at the heart and commencement of the learning processes. People are enabled in such situations to perceive the situation afresh and to have a new experience, one about which they can think. But experience is multi-faceted, as was pointed out earlier, and the mind usually focuses upon only a few aspects of a total experience, e.g. aspects of the cognitive, while other aspects of the experience may actually be internalised through less conscious means, referred to in this book as pre-conscious learning. The process of thought begins with the drawing together of these selective perceptions of experience with relevant memories of previous experiences and through this process new meaning, new understanding, new knowledge of the situation may, but not necessarily will, be generated. This latter point is a significant epistemological one to which further reference will be made below.

There are many studies in the field of psychology that explore the notion of thinking, but these lie slightly outside of the remit of this chapter. Even so, it is acknowledged that it is necessary for learning theorists to examine the research recorded in these studies in order to extend the general understanding of learning.

The thought process is referred to here, and by a number of other writers on this subject, as reflection. Reflection, in this context, means a process of deep thought, both a looking backwards to the situation being pondered upon and a projecting forward to the future, being a process both of recall and of reasoning. It will be noted that in the model of the learning processes, in Figure 2.2., this process is called reasoning and reflecting. In this latter situation, the relevant biographical knowledge/memory of previous experiences is brought together with the perception of the experience under review, so that analysis, synthesis and evaluation can occur. In this, it is recognised that learning might well be a process of change rather than one of merely reflecting previous experiences. This process is different to that of memorisation, as the model of the learning processes in the second chapter shows. Indeed, reflective learning may be the antithesis of the type of learning that involves only memorisation or rote learning.

Perhaps the most significant of all writers who have expressed their ideas on this subject is Dewey (1933), so that it is important to outline some of his ideas at the outset of this chapter. For Dewey, intelligence is not innate but related to the manner in which individuals respond to their experiences through the processes of thought. Indeed, it develops as the individual matures, and this is in line with the findings of Cattell, which were mentioned earlier, Dewey thought that individuals could create new knowledge and be emancipated from traditional situations because they had the ability to think reflectively upon their situation, and he wrote that reflective thinking can proceed with the intention 'to transform a situation in which there is experienced obscurity, doubt, conflict, disturbance of some sort, into a situation that is clear, settled, harmonious' (Dewey, 1933, pp. 100–1). Thus it may be seen that Dewey was advocating a similar perspective to that adopted here, where it is suggested that the disjuncture between biography and experience lies at the start of the learning process. He also suggested that there were a number of possible ways that the mind might approach this process and these included: hypotheses about possible solutions to problems; a comprehension of the problem to be solved; data collection; reasoning; experimentation to solve the problem. He did not expect these always to proceed consecutively, but it is possible to detect a problem-solving cycle in these processes. Additionally, Dewey suggested certain qualities of mind, such as sensitivity, imagination, the ability to analyse and synthesise and the power to reason, that should be among the qualities of an educated person.

In the light of the previous discussion about perceived differences between adult and child learning, it is perhaps increasingly important for educators of adults to examine the writings of those whose primary concerns in education have been with children's education, because they may have much to contribute to the growth of the theory of adult education.

Additionally, there have been a number of writers in the field of the education of adults who have concentrated upon the reflective process in learning and so it is necessary to explore their work at the outset of this chapter; the second part of the chapter discusses briefly the concept of unconscious reflection and relates this to the learning processes; the third section of this chapter concentrates especially upon the fact that thought is socially constructed, since it is recognised that a great deal of thought occurs through the use of language, which is itself a social construct; the final section of this chapter explores the extent to which thought is so socially constrained that it cannot be considered to be free. It concludes that while thought occurs within social parameters this does not prevent it from creating new knowledge, new meanings and new ideas, so that some forms of learning might be considered to produce new or innovative responses to the original potential learning situation.

TOWARDS AN UNDERSTANDING OF THE CONCEPT OF REFLECTION: A REVIEW OF THE LITERATURE

In recent years a number of thinkers on the education of adults have begun to consider the place of reflection in learning and it is therefore necessary to examine their work in order to see the way in which they have understood reflection. Additionally, it is necessary to test the model of adult learning processes against their findings. Some of these writers, such as Kolb, refer back to Dewey, while others have arrived at their conclusions independently of his work. Among those whose work is examined here are: Freire, Mezirow, Argyris, Schon, Kolb and Boud *et al*. This section commences with a brief analysis of the work of Freire.

Paulo Freire. The term 'reflection' occurs with frequency in Freire's writing and so it is appropriate that his use of the term should be fully understood. It is difficult to extract from Freire's writing a specific feature without distorting the comprehensive unity of his thinking, but readers are referred to more complete studies of Freire (Mackie, 1980, *inter alia*), in order to ensure that this analysis reflects his work accurately.

Freire was concerned that the oppressed people of Brazil had learned to take their oppression for granted and, consequently, act accordingly. He (1974, pp. 23–4) wrote:

> The excess of power which has characterised our culture from the start created on the one hand an almost masochistic desire to submit to that power and on the other hand a desire to be all-powerful. This habit of submission led men to *adapt* and *adjust* to their circumstances, instead of seeking to integrate themselves with reality. Integration, the behavior characteristic of flexibly democratic regimes, requires a maximum capacity for critical thought. In contrast, the adapted man, neither dialoguing nor participating, accommodates to conditions imposed upon him and thereby acquires an authoritarian and acritical frame of mind. (Freire's italics)

It might be asked immediately whether Freire regards reflective thought as necessarily critical and revolutionary and the response to this would have to be that critical thought does not necessarily mean that a revolutionary position is the automatic outcome of such thinking. However, the people with whom Freire worked when he first developed these ideas meant that to act back on the world and seek to change it was potentially a revolutionary situation. Criticism means the ability to think analytically or evaluatively as well as casting negative judgements, and it is with the former meaning that Freire employs the term. Elsewhere (1972a, p. 54) he attempted to show that reflective thought was an on-going process of dialogue through which there is a continuing re-creation of those individuals involved in the reflective process. For him, authentic reflection occurs in the challenge of living and thinking about life. However, the oppressed have lost that ability. Since they have accepted the power relations of their world, they no longer have the self-confidence to be independent thinkers and therefore they have first to achieve the state of conscientisation. The editor of Freire's book *Cultural Action for Freedom* (Freire, 1972b, p. 51) suggests that this might be defined as:

> the process in which men, not as recipients, but as knowing subjects, achieve a deepening awareness both of the socio-cultural reality which shapes their lives and of their capacity to transform that reality.

Hence, reflection need not be revolutionary but it does point to the fact that people can respond to the situation in more than one manner, as the variety of different types of learning being discussed in this book shows. Freire recognised that there is a non-reflective approach to learning and this he called the banking concept of education, which will be discussed in greater detail in a following chapter. He also recognised that there were more reflective approaches to learning and these he called problem-posing types of education. Only in problem-posing education can reflective thinkers be given the opportunity to utilise their human abilities to think creatively. However, Freire did not encourage armchair reflectivity, he expected that there would be action as a result of thought. Freire utilised the term praxis to refer to the relationship between reflection and action.

> The insistence that the oppressed engage in reflection on their concrete situation is not a call to armchair revolution. On the contrary, reflection — true reflection — leads to action. On the other hand, when a situation calls for action, that action will constitute an authentic praxis only if its consequences become the object of critical reflection. In this sense, the praxis is the new *raison d'être* of the oppressed; and the revolution, which inaugurates the historical moment of this *raison d'être*, is not viable apart from their concomitant involvement. Otherwise, action is pure activism. (Freire, 1972a, p. 41)

Thus it may be seen that for Freire action must follow the reflection, which may be regarded as the learning process, and then further reflection should occur as a result of the action. Freire's theory appears to be much more a theory of education rather than a theory of learning, in which he contrasts two types of learning, one that expects acquiescence to that which is presented to the learner and the other where there is both dialogue and reflective thought. Praxis is the relationship between thought and action where thought and learning appear to be used synonymously. No theory of reflectivity is to be found in Freire's writing, except the fact that people can be encouraged to think about their situation and that they learn most effectively when what they learn is relevant to this situation.

Freire (1974, p 47) shows the effect on the person who has engaged in dialogue which is a reflective type of learning when he writes of one person who said, 'I make shoes and now I see that I am worth as much as a Ph.D. who writes books' and another who was a streetsweeper who said, 'Tomorrow . . . I am going to work with my head high.' It is the effect of learning with which the final element in the learning process model in the second chapter is concerned in which the learning results in a changed person.

Jack Mezirow. Unlike Freire, Mezirow does produce a theory of reflectivity, and consideration must now be given to this.

Mezirow's studies of perspective transformation have led him to a position very similar to the one adopted here. He (1981, pp. 11–16) starts from the basis that perspectives are one of the constituent elements of human experience and that individuals reflect upon aspects of their experience, namely: their perceptions, their thoughts and their actions. All of these are to be found in the model of human learning in the second chapter and further reference will be made to some of these with later writers in this section and elsewhere in this study. Having postulated the basis of reflection, Mezirow (ibid., pp. 12–13) goes on to suggest that there are seven levels of reflectivity:

reflectivity: an awareness of a specific perception, meaning, behaviour, or habit;

affective reflectivity: awareness of how the individual feels about what is being perceived, thought or acted upon;

discriminant reflectivity: the assessment of the efficacy of perception, thought, action or habit;

judgmental reflectivity: making and becoming aware of value judgments about perception, thought, action or habit;

conceptual reflectivity: self-reflection which might lead to a questioning of whether good, bad or adequate concepts were employed for understanding or judgment;

psychic reflectivity: recognition of the habit of making percipient judgments on the basis of limited information;

theoretical reflectivity: awareness that the habit for percipient judgment or for conceptual inadequacy lies in a set of taken-for-granted cultural or psychological assumptions which explain personal experience less satisfactorily than another perspective with more functional criteria for seeing, thinking or acting.

Mezirow claims that the last three of these refer to critical reflectivity and that this is more likely to occur in an adult, rather than a child. The extent to which it is age related is, however, unproven. In addition, he has not included in this discussion anything about the social class, ethnicity, etc. of the learners and so the points raised earlier in this work about the mind and the self being social constructs and correlating, to some extent, with the socio-cultural background of the thinkers is not discussed. It is important that future research in adult learning include variables, other than age, in examining the thought processes. This will be discussed in greater detail later in this book, when the place of language, for instance, in the thought processes is assessed again. Mezirow claims that the final one of these seven is quite crucial to perspective transformation, which is an emancipatory process of learning. Indeed, this process is similar in outcome to Freire's problem-solving education and Argyris's double loop learning.

Mezirow's theory of reflectivity is an important stage in the development of adult learning theory, but it is not a theory of learning in itself. It is now necessary to relate it to the approach being adopted here.

There is a sense in which these levels of reflectivity do not correspond precisely to the model upon which this study is based, since it is possible to apply one or a combination, of the levels of reflectivity to any of the reflective learning processes. Mezirow also suggests that the lower levels of reflectivity are only relevant to non-reflective learning processes, and it is possible to relate the lowest two levels on his hierarchy to non-reflective learning, as it is employed here. That some forms of reflectivity do not lead to change in perspective is also one of the concerns of Argyris; in this sense Mezirow's analysis relates very significantly to the later analysis. It is also most important in the development of learning theory to relate Mezirow's ideas to Argyris's single and double loop learning.

In fact, Mezirow's formulation is the only one that has thus far attempted to discriminate different levels of thought in the learning process in this manner and it may also be related to Bloom's (1956) taxonomy of educational objectives (in all three domains, although Bloom was not directly responsible for the latter ones) in terms of levels of knowledge, affectivity and skill expected in the teaching and learning situation. Indeed, the manner in which Mezirow has combined both the cognitive and the affective is also important in this process of relating the work of different theorists. It is important to recognise that learning has both affective and cognitive aspects: this is an element that is insufficiently discussed in a great deal of learning theory.

Chris Argyris. Argyris's concepts of single and double loop learning have already been referred to in this study and therefore no further reference is made to them here. Suffice to note, however, that he recognised that reasoning plays a part in the learning process. Like many students of the learning process, Argyris notes that a great deal of human behaviour is of the taken-for-granted type:

> Everyday actions involve many premises, inferences, and conclusions. Most of them are performed at very high speed; indeed, many appear to be automatic responses. If they are automatic, it is probably because they are learned, highly skilled responses. If they are skilled responses, and if many people use them, then there is a strong probability that they have been learned through socialization. And if this is so, the responses are probably tacit; that is, they are performed without much conscious attention. (Argyris, 1982, p. 42)

Thus it may be seen that Argyris places a great deal of emphasis upon socialisation and while he does not develop this idea in terms of social class, etc., this is in accord with much of the previous argument produced here. However, it might be more accurate to claim only that some of the taken-for-granted behaviour is learned through socialisation since there are many other opportunities in social living to habitualise behavioural patterns.

Learning occurs, according to him (1982, p. 38) when people discover a problem, that is that they have a disjuncture between their biography and their experience and then 'they invent a solution to the problem, produce the solution, and evaluate the outcome'. Thus it may be seen that Argyris's approach to learning approximates to the problem-solving cycle. However, the process of inventing the solution is a little more complex than it appears here. People actually engage in the reasoning process by which he (ibid., p. 41) means that people create premises, make inferences from those premises and then draw conclusions from the inferences. Argyris does not, however, offer an analysis of the different reasoning processes, in the way that Mezirow analyses reflectivity.

Another strength of Argyris's work lies in the recognition that people do not always act directly in accord with their reasoning. He points out that they both distance and disconnect from that process and these two concepts do require additional analysis. Distancing is a feature which individuals are inclined to incorporate into their thinking, especially when they are employed in organisations, when they act to reduce their personal causal responsibility for the problems they are trying to solve. Disconnection is the process whereby people have programmes in mind that separate them from the processes of their own thought. Argyris's concern is to turn these two processes

93

around so that people can double loop learn, that is, so that they can become innovative and imaginative thinkers within their own sub-culture. A major significance of this finding is that action does not always follow the most well-constructed thought processes. Does this finding invalidate the model of the learning processes? Since Argyris is only claiming that there are more effective and efficient ways of thinking and learning than those that generally occur in organisations he is not really commenting upon the learning process as such. However, he is making a significant criticism of those learning theories that imply that there is a congruence between behaviour and thought. Hence, his finding suggests that not all behaviour is grounded upon the most logical thought processes and consequently he raises some questions about the relationship between learning and action that require further discussion.

Donald Schon. Donald Schon has written a number of books with Argyris (1974, 1978, *inter alia*), but his study *The Reflective Practitioner* (1983) provides the focus of this section. Schon, like Argyris, appears to come to this subject without a traditional theoretical educational background, so that a number of the classical studies in adult education are not referred to at all, which is a pity since studies such as Mazirow's would have enriched this significant piece of work.

Schon's concern is twofold; that professional practice is not the simple application of theory to practice but that practitioners actually think on the job. He recognises, however, that a great deal of professional practice can become taken-for-granted behaviour since there is a great deal of repetitiveness in practice situations, but there are novel situations. He writes (1983, p. 56) that:

> Much reflection-in-action hinges on the experience of surprise. When intuitive, spontaneous performance yields nothing more than the results expected for it, then we tend not to think about it. But when intuitive performance leads to surprises, pleasing and promising or unwanted, we may respond by reflection-in-action . . . In such processes, reflection tends to focus interactively on the outcomes of action, the action itself, and the intuitive knowing in the action.

There are tremendous similarities here with a number of the previous analyses, all of which point to a gulf between biography and experience which starts the process of learning. This process may be a reflection on the knowledge that the practitioner brings to the situation or upon the usual action by which the practitioner responds to the situation, and so Schon (1983, p. 62) suggests that there are different types of reflection:

> When a practitioner reflects in and on his practice, the possible objects of his reflection are as varied as the kinds of the phenomena before him and the systems of knowing-in-practice which he brings to them. He may reflect upon the tacit norms and appreciations which underlie a judgment, or on the strategies and theories implicit in a pattern of behavior. He may reflect on the feeling for the situation which has led him to adopt a particular course of action, on the way in which he has framed the problem he is trying to solve, or on the role he has constructed for himself within a larger institutional context.

Like Mezirow, Schon has outlined a number of different approaches to reflection, but unlike him he has not presented them within an hierarchical context, since any of the strategies may result in changed performance. This relates quite specifically to the model of learning discussed in Chapter 2. Any of a number of strategies of reflection can lead to a change in knowledge or a change in performance and none of the respondents in that research highlighted the different strategies in the same manner as Schon has attempted in the case studies which comprise the greater part of his book.

An important element in Schon's work is his recognition of the fact that the reflection may span a longer time period than the initial experience. Schon (ibid.) specifies this very clearly:

> A practitioner's reflection-in-action may not be very rapid. It is bounded by the 'action-present' — the zone of time in which action can still make a difference to the situation. The action-present may stretch over minutes, hours, days, or even weeks or months, depending on the pace of the activity and the situational boundaries that are characteristic of the practice.

He illustrates this from different forms of professional practice, such as the rapidity of the lawyers' interchange within a courtroom to the rehearsal period of an orchestra. Within the learning processes model, Schon's discussion can be located at three points: initially, the professional performance may be regarded as the experience upon which the reflection occurs; the lengthy time period relates to the process of recalling a memory and then re-creating a learning experience from it; but finally, it may also be located within the double arrows between thought processes and practical experimentation because once a taken-for-granted professional practice situation has been disturbed, all future behaviour resulting from similar situations is experimental until such time as a new behavioural pattern emerges and a new taken-for-granted is established. The extent to which such patterns should ever be established in professional practice is a debatable question, that they are is not doubted. Indeed, it is recognised that habitualising action is a most common and sometimes necessary feature of human action.

Schon appreciates that once this approach to professional practice is recognised then the traditional ideas of professional preparation, i.e. that new recruits learn the knowledge in the professional training school and then go out and practise it, no longer stands the test of observation. This has profound effects upon any understanding of knowledge, for no longer can it be held that there is a body of knowledge that is taught and then applied in practice. New knowledge is established in the learning situation when practitioners bring their knowledge to the situation and reflect upon their experience of the situation. Hence, it has been argued elsewhere (Jarvis and Gibson, 1985) that professional practice is at the interface of theory and procedure rather than the application of theory to it.   ✳

David Kolb. Kolb's diagram formed part of the research methodology of this study, so that it will be apparent that there are similarities and some differences in the two models. Further comparison is unnecessary for the purposes of this study. However, reflection does occur in his model and so it was considered appropriate to include his work here. However, he adds very little to the discussion about the concept, making such claims as learners should 'reflect on and observe their experiences from many perspectives' (Kolb, 1984, p. 30). He is concerned to demonstrate the fact that individuals have different cognitive styles and this is an important variable when analysing thinking. However, his own approach was quite fully discussed earlier in this work and so no further discussion is embarked upon here.

David Boud et al. Perhaps the fullest discussion upon reflection has occurred in the symposium edited by Boud and colleagues (1985). There are a number of points that they raise that are important and the model of learning that they produce is close to, but not as precise, as the model discussed in this study. Boud *et al.* note that reflection itself is something that is totally personal and individual, so that learning must ultimately be an individual process, a point with which there is considerable agreement here, although it is recognised that people can learn similar things if they have similar social backgrounds and are exposed to similar experiences. Since individuals reflect through the use of language, a social phenomenon, and utilise the memory of previous experiences, which are also social, there is a sense in which reflection, while it is individual, must also be a social process. They go on to make the point that reflection is a purposeful process and while there is considerable agreement with this point, it must be pointed out that most people experience an unconscious learning process when they actually stop concentrating upon a problem, maybe because they need to sleep or because they are required to undertake other things; and suddenly, intuitively as it were, a solution presents itself to their minds. This phenomenon is briefly discussed in the next section of this chapter, so that no further reference will be made to it here. The third point that they make is that reflection is a complex process that involves more than just thought: feelings also play a part. Boud and his colleagues rightly point out that emotive states may distort perception and they are also likely to influence the processes of thought. This is an important factor, since there may well be a significant but unconscious pressure upon learning that stems from emotions rather than the apparent rationality of thought. Their discussion leads them to a model of learning that is rather like that in Figure 5.1.

Figure 5.1 The process of reflection following Boud *et al.* (Boud, 1985, p. 36)

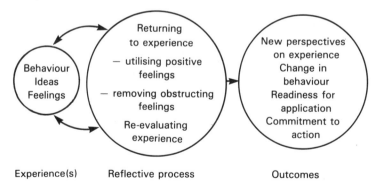

Source: Boud, 1985, p. 36

The model in Figure 5.1 is similar to, but not as full, as the model of the learning processes that has been presented here; like the model offered in this study, reflection plays a significant part and the emphasis that they place upon the emotions is something that has not emerged from this study, because the nature of the exercise was merely to discover the processes which people underwent during learning. However, this element is regarded as important, since emotions are themselves influenced by previous social experiences which might indicate that people from similar social backgrounds may have similar pro- and anti-feelings about similar things and experiences.

Later in the same symposium, Kemmis (1985, pp. 139 ff) produces a somewhat similar perspective on reflection to that adopted here. He notes that reflection has a social and ideological dimension, and he claims it also has a political dimension, since it is also action orientated. In this he would agree with Freire. However, there is another sense in which reflection might be political, and this is also implicit in Argyris's double loop learning and Botkin's innovative learning. Any reflection that assists in producing learning that is change orientated rather than merely a reflection of the socio-cultural milieu in which the learner lives is implicitly political. In as much as learning actually produces new knowledge that leads, or might lead, to new action, it has a 'subversive' dimension.

Summary. Before drawing this section to a close, it is important to draw together some of the main points that have emerged as a result of this review of the literature: this will form a foundation for some of the ensuing discussion about learning.

Perhaps the most significant factor in the above review in relation to this present study is that little attention has been paid to the social elements that play a significant part in the reflection process. For instance, there is an acknowledgement among some of the writers that socialisation is significant and that this may inhibit innovative thinking, but this is not developed to a great extent. There is little reference to the role of sex, socio-economic class or the social origins of language, apart from in the work of Paulo Freire. Mezirow raised the possibility that some forms of reflectivity may be age related but this was not developed very significantly. Hence, it would appear that, with the exception of Freire, many of the social constraints upon the reflective process have not been considered very extensively, and so this will form one of the major aspects of the ensuing analysis.

Reflection is seen here to be a very complex process involving both the cognitive and the affective dimensions; this recognition is very important indeed, because the affective dimension will itself affect the learning outcomes of any potential learning experience and this will in turn have been influenced by previous experiences. However, the cognitive dimension of thought involves the use of language and the use of language is also related to previous learning experiences. Hence, it will be necessary to refer to both of these factors again later in this chapter.

Intelligence is related to the manner in which people use their experiences and think about them. Hence, it does appear that ideas of static intelligence are suspect and that recognition that intelligence may be a much more dynamic phenomenon than intelligence tests usually imply. Indeed, Freire makes it clear that people see the world differently and learn differently when they become conscious of their social situation. What he regards as authentic reflection is when people respond to the challenge of their social situation and then have a perspective transformation. Indeed, there is considerable agreement between Freire and Mezirow at this point. However, it is also related to the double loop learning of Argyris and Schon, which they regard as a process of freeing people from their socialisation, which is less obviously different with their subjects than it is with Freire's. This is a phenomenon to which further reference will be made elsewhere in this book.

However, there is a clear difference between reflection and memorisation. Memorisation involves the internalisation of pre-established or apparently objective and empirical knowledge and already formulated procedures and skills, whereas reflection implies the possibility of the creation of new knowledge and different techniques. This epistemological point is significant to any theory of teaching and learning and will be referred to again in the final chapters of this study.

Another significant point that requires some elaboration is that where reflection occurs because there is a disjuncture between biography and experience, then it is possible to use the concept of felt or recognised need. But where the reflection occurs as a result of a disjuncture between idealised situation and biography, then it is much more significant to regard this as a felt or recognised want. However, one person's situation may be another person's ideal situation, so that the felt need and the felt want are themselves reflections of social situations and experiences and have no objectively valid manner of being tested or verified. This does not mean that they do not exist or that there may not be a moral imperative underlying at least need. However, it must be pointed out that both needs and wants may be conceived as derivatives of experience. This distinction does not do full justice to this complex debate between need and want, since it would be possible to argue that the idealised situation might also be regarded as a necessary situation for a person and, therefore, a need occurs. Hence, the point being made here seeks only to develop the discussion a little further, since the needs/wants question is one of quite crucial importance to the theory of the education of adults.

Finally, it must be pointed out here that while reflection is a significant factor in any theory of learning, theories of reflection are not in themselves learning theories. Hence, it is necessary to take some of the crucial issues that have been raised in this discussion and to use them to explore a little further the social theory of learning being developed here.

UNCONSCIOUS REFLECTION

In the previous section some of the main writers on reflection in adult learning have been reviewed and yet it is significant that few of them mention a fairly common occurrence in the process of learning; that is, the process whereby a person deliberately stops thinking about a problem, process, etc. for any number of reasons but later on a solution to the problem suddenly flashes into the mind. It is as if the brain had still been functioning quite specifically and independently of the conscious awareness of the process, which had itself been curtailed. This is a fairly common experience for most people and so it is of interest to students of learning. It is a process which Bruner (1977, pp. 55–68) refers to as intuitive thinking.

Bruner (1977, p. 60) defines intuitive thinking thus:

> For a working definition of intuition, we do well to begin with Webster: 'immediate apprehension or cognition'. 'Immediate' in this context is contrasted with 'mediated' — apprehension that depends on the intervention of formal methods of analysis and proof. Intuition implies the act of grasping the meaning, significance, or structure of a problem or situation without explicit reliance on the analytic apparatus of one's craft.

Bruner actually specifies two different types of what he calls intuitive thinking: first, that which occurs when an individual has been working for a long time on a problem and then rather suddenly discovers a solution without having the formal proof to justify the solution; and secondly, when an individual can respond to problems rapidly with good educated 'guesses'. However, Bruner does seem to be discussing two separate phenomena, the latter might be better regarded as akin to an holistic learning style (see Jarvis, 1983b, pp. 83–6) as opposed to a form of unconscious thought that follows conscious reflection. It is for this reason that Bruner's terminology is not adopted here. Even so, it is quite significant to note that adult education teaching and learning methods have for a long while recognised this *Gestalt* approach by adopting techniques such as brainstorming.

However, it is the first of Bruner's types which is the focus of this discussion, although some of the points that he raises about intuitive thinking in general do apply specifically to unconscious reflection. Bruner points out that there is not a great deal of research on the topic and that research should not be delayed until such time as the phenomenon is clearly delineated. At the same time, he does raise some pertinent points about the variables that may be related to it, including: copying intuitive thinking teachers, having the confidence to voice these intuitive ideas, familiarity with a breadth of topics in that field, the extent to which the integration of knowledge is taught. Bruner's emphasis upon self-confidence is perhaps significant in the light of the frequent references to it, and to status and authority relationships, elsewhere in this study. The relationship between self-image and intelligence and achievement is something that requires further research.

Since there does not seem to be a great deal of research upon this most common of phenomena, it is difficult to extend the argument greatly here about the social nature of adult learning, although it must be pointed out that many of the aspects that Bruner has raised point to the possibility of this skill being learned. Bruner does, however, recognise the possibility that some of this unconscious reflection may produce novel outcomes and, while he claims that whether this is so or not is of no significance to the psychologist, it is clearly of importance here. The fact that it may produce innovative ideas may be related to the fact that unconscious reflection is less constrained by the structures of analytic and deductive thought and by the burden of having to produce proof for the outcome of the thought: this may make it more likely to be innovative. Indeed, this may relate in some ways to Argyris's double loop learning and to Botkin's participative innovative learning.

Thus it may be seen that an important factor in the learning processes has for long been recognised but remains unresearched. In order to comprehend human learning better, it is important that more research be conducted in this area in order to investigate both how it functions, the extent to which it produces conformist or innovative responses to potential learning experiences and the extent to which it was inhibited by authoritarian teaching and learning situations but enhanced by egalitarian ones. That all thought is not innovative has been well documented and the next section of this chapter seeks to demonstrate the social nature of this process.

THE SOCIAL NATURE OF REFLECTION

That thought is social is almost self-evident, since an examination of any historical document reveals that the people of that historical time thought in the patterns and imposed the meanings upon situations that were common to their period. Indeed, Figure 3.2 indicates how the person is the recipient of a selection of the sub-cultures of the social group and is therefore constrained to think within certain parameters imposed by that experience. It was Mannheim (1936, p. 2) who wrote:

> Only in a quite limited sense does the single individual create out of himself the mode of speech and of thought we attribute to him. He speaks the language of his group; he thinks in the manner in which his group thinks. He finds at his disposal only certain words and their meaning. These not only determine to a large extent the avenues of approach to the surrounding world, but they also show at the same time from which angle and in which context of activity objects have hitherto been perceptible and accessible to the group or the individual.

Mannheim goes on to point out that it is necessary to comprehend thought in the concrete setting of the socio-historical situation in which people live. He (1936, p. 3) claims that: 'it is incorrect to say that the single individual thinks. Rather it is more correct to insist that he participates in thinking further what other people have thought before him.'

While it will later be argued that this is a rather strong statement, as Mannheim himself might acknowledge, it may nevertheless be argued that reflection is not a perfectly free response to a potential learning situation. Indeed, it is clearly more constrained than this. Since the potential learning situation is itself socially constructed and perception is also a social construct, it is perhaps not surprising that there is some constraint about the process of reflection. Unfortunately, those who have thus far written about reflection have not sought to demonstrate how the process of thought relates to the thinker, or the social situation in which the thinker is located.

However, as early as 1903 Simmel suggested that the dominant type of rationality of his time was related to the type of society in which people lived. He (cited from Thompson and Tunstall, 1971, p. 85) wrote:

the modern metropolis, however, is supplied almost entirely by production for the market, that is, for entirely unknown purchasers who never personally enter the producer's actual field of vision. Through this anonymity the interests of each party acquire an unmerciful matter-of-factness; and the intellectually calculating economic egoisms of both parties need not fear and deflection because of the imponderables of personal relationships. The money economy dominates the metropolis; it has displaced the last survivals of domestic production and the direct barter for goods; it minimizes from day to day the amount of work ordered by customers. The matter-of-fact attitude is obviously so intimately interrelated with the money economy, which is dominant in the metropolis, that nobody can say whether the intellectualistic mentality first promoted the money economy or whether the latter determined the former . . .

Modern mind has certainly become more calculating. The calculative exactness of practical life which the money economy has brought about corresponds to the ideal of natural science.

While this might also reflect Simmel's own regret that the more personal society was disappearing, it also suggests that the way in which people think is closely related to the social structures and social practices of the time in which they think.

This section seeks to highlight a number of the ways by which reflection may have social determinants. Three aspects of the reflective process are suggested here, each of which may be related to the social context: language, rationality and the type of conceptual thought. However, it must be recognised that there are a variety of other variables that require discussion and research within this context.

Thought and Language. It is perhaps also pertinent at this stage in the argument to recognise that thought is related to language and language itself is a social construct. However, before seeking to draw conclusions too hastily from this it is necessary to explore the relationship between thought and language a little more explicitly. Although there is not a great deal written in the literature of adult education about this relationship, there is a great deal of literature within psychology, socio-linguistics and anthropology. No attempt is made here to review it in total, although some of the main issues will be examined briefly. For instance, Jenkins (1969) suggested that there were five possible relationships between language and thought:

1. Thought is dependent upon language.
2. Thought is language.
3. Language is dependent upon thought.
4. A combination of all of the above.
5. None of the above.

He concluded that all of the first three were true in differing situations. Carroll (1969), in reply to this paper, wished to be a little more tentative and he suggested that in each of the first three the 'is' should be replaced by 'can be' in order to make this more correct. Even so, it is necessary to examine these three propositions a little further to see whether they are in fact true in any learning situation.

Thought can be dependent upon language. The significance of this position in the formation of the mind was argued earlier in this study, following the work of Mead. However, it would not be maintained here that the relationship between language and thought is simple or static throughout the life-cycle. Indeed, once there is a stock of knowledge which constitutes a basis for the memory, then the relationship between thought and language must necessarily become more complex than it was initially.

That people usually think in language terms means that there is a clear relationship between the two. Indeed, to summarise the position adopted by Jenkins (1969, p. 218): 'One is likely to conclude after studying the evidence that language *influences* thought processes in a variety of ways, but is unlikely to conclude that language determines thought processes . . .' (Jenkins' italics). Clearly, not all thought is dependent upon language since it is possible to think pictorially and even emotively without verbalisation. Articulation may be necessary in order to communicate some of the ideas, but even this would not be so for the artist who may try to communicate them through the medium of picture or sculpture, etc. At the same time, it is true that language does influence thought in certain situations because language is an expression of the cultural system in which the thinker is both experiencing and thinking. Indeed people have to learn the language of the culture before they can think in it, in other words they have to learn how the language is used and how it relates to the socio-cultural-temporal reality of their environment. Eco (1985) has recently pointed out that there is a sense in which the prevailing culture influences both the perception of colour and the manner in which colour is thought about and discussed. Language, therefore, may influence perception, experience and pre-reflective thought as much as it influences reflective thought. Hence, the social determinants of language, e.g. socio-economic class etc., influence the reflective processes and learning through reflection must therefore be constrained by the cultural and sub-cultural constraints of language.

Thought can be language. Clearly in its behaviourist manifestation, this position has been refuted earlier in this study. Nevertheless, it is recognised that in certain situations people think in language, simply because this is the most convenient way, or even the only way, to express thought. Hence, this proposition is acceptable here in its non-behaviouristic mode.

Language can be dependent upon thought. The anthropologist, Thomas Gladwin, describing the way that the Truk people navigate their small boats across hundreds of miles of sea to small islands, makes the significant point that:

> the Trukese navigator can point to his destination over the horizon, something the European generally cannot do, but he cannot put into words all the myriad perceptions which have led him to be sure at that moment where the island lies. This is not merely because the Trukese are unaccustomed to describing in words what they are doing. The simultaneous integration of several discrete thought-processes defies verbalization. The navigator can probably inventory all the factors to which he must be alert, but the process whereby they are weighted and combined is both complex and fluid. (Gladwin, 1973, p. 117)

Hence, it might be argued that in this case the thought processes are independent of language and any expression of the process is dependent upon the way that the Trukese navigator is thinking. Language is still a cultural manifestation of the complexity of the thought process and may be constrained by the vocabulary of the culture, but there is still a sense in which it is dependent upon the thought that is occurring in the mind which may actually be verbalised in itself.

Labov's (1973) analysis of language, intelligence and non-standard English among black Americans reaches similar conclusions; that is, that the thought process may be much more sophisticated than the language used to express it. Indeed, Labov makes the point that sometimes standard language, which appears to be learned language, actually confuses issues, while non-standard language appears to simplify much more complex ideas and conceptions.

Almost coincidentally, this discussion demonstrates another significant point about adult learning and intelligence; if intelligence is tested through the use of language then it cannot measure those abilities that cannot be expressed in language or those thoughts that are expressed in non-standard linguistic forms. Hence, it is hardly surprising that those people whose linguistic forms are not standard are usually labelled as less intelligent than those who employ standard language in formal educational processes.

Thus it may be concluded from this very brief discussion that it is possible to think without language and that thought is not always necessarily determined by language. Nevertheless, non-verbal thought may still be a cultural manifestation, so that it still reflects the social-cultural-temporal milieu in which it occurs. Hence, whatever the relationship between thought and language and its complexity that has been demonstrated here, thought does not appear to escape the constraints of the social situation. This leads to the further point that in order to develop a more sophisticated understanding of the learning process, it is important to begin to explore socio-linguistics and semiotics in greater detail.

Reflection, however, not only emphasises language but it also utilises certain taken-for-granted elements, such as personal philosophy and rationality, so that it is necessary here to demonstrate how these affect the thought processes. Two illustrations of this will be given and discussed in order to demonstrate the fact that there are other constraints upon relection and that these are also of a social nature: the first of these demonstrates the implicit assumptions in some interpretations of the position of women in society and the second questions the concept of rationality itself within the process of thought.

The thought process is often influenced by theories that the thinker has about society in general, so that any ideas that the person has about society will be constrained by the covert taken-for-granted philosophy that guides and constrains the thought processes. Mezirow refers to this in his typology of reflection when he recognises that at one level of reflection individuals are not always aware of the values, etc. that constrain their thought but at another they are able to recognise these. The position of women in society has been chosen as an illustration of this process because it has become a current area of concern, as the feminist movement has shown, although it would have been possible to have taken a large variety of illustrations from social living. Some people regard it as right and natural that, because the female of the species gives birth and feeds the offspring, they should remain at home and undertake domestic work whilst the man should go out and work to earn money for the family. Additionally, because the male has traditionally been regarded as the stronger of the sexes, it is the male's right to make the decisions about the family, etc. This patriarchal form of thought has been legitimated by religious texts, etc. and has become an accepted philosophy by some people when they reflect upon the world in which they live. It has become a taken-for-granted ideology that is not questioned in the thinking process. An example of this is where it has been argued in recent times that it is immoral for women to go out to work an take jobs from men, etc. Naturally, this form of reductionism is not a form of reflection that is critically aware, but it is one which is constrained by taken-for-granted ideology and legitimated by some manifestations of religion.

A much more complex example is that of rationality itself. Marcuse (1968) sought to show how Weber's idea of technical rationality was itself irrational and ends with the most irrational of all of his ideas — that of charisma. Perhaps Marcuse's position may be simplified in order to demonstrate the logic of his argument, in the following manner. The demands of capitalist society are such that a rational bureaucratic hierarchy has to be created in order to maximise efficiency. Hence, there has to be a form of control and the creation of a class of people who can only sell their labour power in order to create the most efficient system. Yet the form of production that operates in the separation of labour from the means of production is one that dehumanises some individuals and alienates them. Any form of labour that actually dehumanises people does not appear to be rational. But the capitalist entrepreneur who invests money in an enterprise would regard it as rational for the company in which the capital has been invested to maximise efficiency, even if this means that workers should be expected to work on an assembly line, in which they are separated from the product of their labour and eventually alienated in their work. Hence two apparently rational ideologies can be seen to be diametrically opposed to each other when they are operationalised and the form of rationality that dominates is in fact an ideology that assumes the status of rationality by virtue of its dominance. The dominant rationality/ideology then becomes a part of the taken-for-grantedness within society and individuals utilise it in order to give meaning to experiences.

It is not the intention here to explore these aspects any further, but it must be noted that both of these dominant but taken-for-granted ideologies occur because of the power relations within society. Consequently, it is important to recognise that reflection occurs within a social context in which the power elite of society has predetermined some of the dominant ideologies which have become a part of the taken-for-grantedness of society and internalised by its members. Indeed, it is also significant to note that these ideologies have become part of the educational institution, so that people learn in formal institutions that have incorporated these dominant ideologies into their own sub-cultures. This is the process which Gramsci regards as hegemonic. Entwistle (1979, p. 12) regards this as follows:

> In Gramsci's formulation, hegemonic direction is by moral and intellectual persuasion, rather than by control by the police, the military, or the coercive power of law: 'rule by intellectual and moral hegemony is the form of power which gives stability and founds power on wide ranging consent and acquiesence'. For this to be so, 'every relationship of "hegemony" is necessarily a pedagogical relationship' (*Quaderni*, vol II, p. 1331). Control of the subalten classes is much more subtly exercised than is often supposed: it operates persuasively rather than coercively through cultural institutions — churches, labour unions and other workers' associations, schools and in the press.

One final element that should be included here is conceptual development and its relationship with age. Following the work of Piaget with children, some psychologists have sought to investigate the extent to which conceptual development is related to age in adulthood. Allman (1984, pp. 74–5) summarises some of these findings. She notes that Arlin (1975) suggested that adults develop the ability to ask or discover important questions after the stage of formal operational thought, that Neugarten (1977) noted that middle-aged people developed an increasing amount of reflective thought and that Moshman (1979) also considered that after the stage of formal operational thought adults develop the ability to think about their own theories and their processes of theorising. Thereafter, Allman discusses the work of Riegel (1979) who suggest that adults develop a dialectic logic that enables them to tolerate contradictions in their thinking which leads to more original thought. Now it may be questioned whether these developmental stages are related to age or to experience, and even whether they are exclusive to adulthood. Certainly many questions asked by children are fundamental to humanity and most profound, although the language in which they are posed might not be as sophisticated as that of adults. This is certainly not the place to discuss this research in detail, although it is significant to note that if conceptual development is age related, then this is another social factor that relates to learning, although these findings do appear to be open to correlation with other variables, such as experience. But even then it might be possible to claim that if it can be correlated with any variables, then there are other social factors that have to be taken into consideration when seeking to understand reasoning, reflection and learning.

Clearly, then, the above discussion is about aspects of cognitive style, but it must be noted that cognitive style and learning style are not synonymous terms. The cognitive style relates to the thought processes, which are themselves related to the socio-cultural-temporal milieu of the thinkers, whereas learning style relates to the ways in which people endeavour to learn.

Thus it may be seen that in a variety of ways reflection is not a free process but that there are social pressures that constrain the manner by which people think and which, consequently, result in conformity in the outcomes of learning rather than the type of critical awareness for which some of the theorists discussed earlier have called. Mezirow, almost alone among the theorists of reflection, has recognised that one element in becoming critically aware is that of being aware of the processes that constrain the thinking process. Indeed, it would be recognised that the forms of reflection which are constrained by the social processes actually fall in the lower order of Mezirow's hierarchy, although the point at which he locates the commencement of criticality is perhaps open to question. However, being aware of constraints is not the same as being free of them and so it must be asked whether learning is so totally constrained that conformist outcomes are the only outcome to learning, even though the learner may be aware of the factors that have constrained the thought processes.

REFLECTION AS AN INNOVATIVE PROCESS

If thought were not innovative on occasions the possibility of social change would be limited and learning would be little more than assimilation and regurgitation. Thinkers such as Freire (1974) have regarded education as liberating, so that it may be assumed here that there is some potentiality for innovative thought but the processes whereby this happens need now be examined.

Mannheim (1936) was concerned about this problem and postulated that there was a single group of people in society who were most likely to be able to break free of the thought processes of their social group: these were the intelligentsia. He wrote (1936, p. 9):

> In every society there are social groups whose special task it is to provide an interpretation of the world for that society. We call these the 'intelligentsia'. The more static a society is, the more likely it is that this stratum will acquire a well defined status or position of a caste in that society. Thus the magicians, the Brahmin, the medieval clergy are all regarded as the intellectual strata, each in its society enjoyed a monopolistic control over the moulding of the society's world-view and over either the reconstruction or the reconciliation of the differences in the naively formed world-views of the other strata.

Mannheim goes on in this passage to explain how the intellectual stratum in society emerges, pointing out that in the middle ages, when society was rather static, this group did achieve its own status and had its own control over the world view of society, so that others were forced to accept its interpretation of the world. However, with the growth of modern society which, it could be argued, commenced with the growth in the division of labour that resulted from technological innovation, there was a breakdown of the traditional strata of society. The intellectual stratum was no longer drawn from a single sub-group within society, so that its members brought a variety of interpretations of society and a variety of thought processes to the situation. Hence, their social organisation was opened up and they sought to synthesise a variety of interpretations of reality. The result of this is:

> . . . the intellectual's illusion that there is only one way of thinking disappears. The intellectual is no longer, as formerly, a member of a caste or rank whose scholastic manner of thought represents for him thought as such. In this relatively simple process is to be sought the explanation for the fact that the fundamental questioning of thought in modern times does not begin until the collapse of the intellectual monopoly of the clergy. The almost unanimously accepted world-view which had been artificially maintained fell apart the moment the socially monopolistic position of its producers was destroyed. With the liberation of the intellectuals from the

rigorous organization of the church, other ways of interpreting the world were increasingly recognised. (Mannheim 1936, p. 11)

The significance of Mannheim's analysis is that once a variety of interpretations of reality, or of any phenomenon with it, are available it becomes possible to compare and contrast them, it becomes possible to pick and choose from them, to analyse and synthesise, so that the possibility of breaking away from established answers arises. The fact that the potentiality exists for the growth of new thoughts does not necessarily mean that this will automatically occur, since there are patterns of thought that are built into most people's thought systems as a result of early childhood socialisation which favour acceptance of the *status quo* and conformity to an external authority. These patterns were discussed above, and in Chapter 3 of this study, when the growth of the person was examined. Hence, it must be recognised that there is a propensity, in many people, to accept the ideas with which they are provided rather than to question them. Yet, the recognition that there are several solutions to a problem, many meanings to some experiences, etc. at least allows for the possibility of independent thought. Passmore (1967) recognises that teaching people to be critical is itself a problematic process and, writing about teaching children, he almost suggests that children will imitate a teacher who adopts a critical perspective, which is in effect suggesting that the propensity to conform should be utilised to create independent critical thought.

From the above discussion it may be seen that since the thinker uses the language of the sub-group, is likely to adopt the rationality and ideology of the sub-group and has a propensity to accept authority, it is hardly surprising that reflection often tends to reproduce the thought forms of that group and to be conformist. However, it must also be pointed out that when a pluralism of interpretations of an experience is possible then there exists at least the possibility of breaking away from the established pattern. It is this to which several writers on learning have referred when they have talked of double loop learning, innovative learning, learning for liberation, etc. This does not mean that the outcome of this form of critical reflection will always be innovation, since it is perfectly possible for the innovative thinkers to agree with established propositions and it is always probable that in authoritarian situations innovative thinkers may not voice their ideas and remain part of the silent majority. It does mean that in certain circumstances innovative thought is possible, although it is less frequent than some would like.

CONCLUSIONS

Reflection may be regarded as a significant part of certain learning processes, but reflection itself is to a great extent socially constrained. Thus learning will be socially constrained if thinkers find it difficult to get outside of these social processes. Hence, even reflective learning may well be conformist in nature, but within the framework of the model of learning produced in the second chapter, it may be seen that innovative learning can occur at any stage of the last tier of types of learning. In a sense, therefore, there are now twelve types of learning rather than the nine discussed in the model. However, the innovative forms of learning are outcomes of the same learning processes, rather than different ones, having similar routes through the learning process and so they are not separated in this analysis although the difference constitutes a major focus of Chapter 9.

The learning model does, however, contain a number of other stages and it is now necessary to examine some of these. However, this examination will be less extensive than that contained in this chapter, so that all the other elements in the model of learning are discussed in the following chapter.

6

Other Factors in the Learning Processes

It will be recalled from the model of the learning processes produced in Chapter 2 that there were other factors involved in learning than those which have thus far been discussed and each of these needs to be analysed. Hence, this chapter examines all of the remaining factors, including: practice/experimentation; memorisation, evaluation; the person changed and more experienced. These four factors constitute the four main sections of the chapter, and this follows the order suggested above. However, it is difficult to get an entirely logical sequence since the learning processes are so complex and overlapping. The reason why this sequence was chosen was simply because in each succeeding box in the model an increasing number of arrows flow in, indicating that that particular factor is present in an increasing number of different learning processes.

PRACTICE/EXPERIMENTATION

Practice and experimentation appear as a single box in the model of the learning processes and it might be objected that since reflection and memorisation have been separated, it would have been more logical to do the same for these two concepts. Clearly they are both different: experimentation refers to the possibility of doing something new, to creating something that has not existed before; while practice carries a connotation of repetition and even drudgery. The only element that they appear to have in common is that they are both practical.

Indeed, this is one of the reasons why they have been linked here, since the practical component of learning is recognised as being important. Even so, the interlinking does demonstrate one of the other problems in seeking to understand learning: the processes can be similar in structure but the outcome can be different; learning can be conformist or innovative. It is this paradox which is a significant factor in this discussion. Nevertheless, it is recognised here that they need some form of separate discussion and this occurs throughout this section.

Experimentation does not always result in innovation, the end-product can be in agreement with the already established practice and this complicates the discussion about learning. However, the term has been used here because it conveys the idea that the person has a degree of freedom to produce new knowledge and new procedures and it reflects Kelly's (1963) idea that human beings are, like scientists, always trying to experiment with life. Kelly gives the impression that people are totally free, which is not accepted here, but his idea that the person is free in certain circumstances to experiment is an important one to the theory of learning.

While experimentation and practice are different, they were interlinked in one box in the model in order to combine the common practical elements and at the same time to convey the complexity of the process, and it will be recalled from the diagram of the learning processes that a number of different arrows enter this box, one comes directly from the experience and another comes from reflection. Practice/experimentation occurs in a number of different forms of learning and so the discussion in this sub-section will be divided into those forms of learning that are non-reflective and those which are reflective, with the former being analysed first.

Practice/experimentation in non-reflective learning. Practice in non-reflective learning relates to skills learning, whether the skill be physical or social. Physical skills can be those of the manual worker or those of the sports person who trains in order to achieve a high degree of physical expertise. Social skills training occurs in many forms of education, including children's education, certain forms of affective education and also in therapy. Thus it may be seen that two apparently different phenomena, training and therapy, occur in this section.

Educationalists have frequently debated the extent to which these forms of training can be regarded as educational, or whether training is a process that is totally distinct from education (see Mannheim and Stewart, 1962, pp. 12–18 *inter alia*). This is not a debate that will be rehearsed in great detail here. The reasons for the distinction, however, appear twofold: education has been regarded by some as an end in itself (Dewey, 1916; Paterson, 1979, *inter alia*) and cognitive rather than psycho-motor. However, it is suggested here that some education does have an end beyond itself and, secondly, there is no reason why educational learning should not occur as a result of psychomotor experiences, so that the debate appears to be quite sterile. However, since knowledge has traditionally been regarded as having a higher status than skills, education has assumed higher status than training, as if they were different processes. However, it has been claimed (Jarvis, 1983a, pp. 86-6) that some forms of training can also be educational, but more significantly for the purposes of this discussion both involve learning, even if training is more likely to be seen as a form of 'learning by doing'.

However, 'learning by doing' is a phenomenon with which most people are familiar. Belbin and Belbin (1972, pp. 84-5) record how a manual worker who had low self-esteem considered that he was unable to learn from the initial experience and needed time to practise. This worker claimed that he 'learned by doing' and what he was actually claiming was that he required plenty of time to repeat techniques until he felt confident enough to undertake them. He was not really able to learn by being instructed how to perform a technique, although he might have needed the initial experience in the classroom in order to spur him to practise it. But he could only learn by doing it for himself, by practice. Now it is significant that Belbin and Belbin do not suggest that he lacks ability to acquire the skill. In fact they state quite specifically (1972, p. 84) that his main drawback was his lack of confidence. Once the technique had been mastered, the worker had the confidence to undertake a wide variety of tasks, so that the significance of the self-image to learning must be recognised as perhaps as significant as the concept of ability and the place of practice for such individuals given significant place. Additionally, it should be noticed that while the outcome of this learning, in skills terms, was conformity, a significant change had occurred in the person's self-concept that might have enabled him to tackle new learning situations with greater confidence and perhaps to have appeared more able.

The acquisition of physical skills is also something that sportsmen and sportswomen seek through frequent repetition of the same technique. While this is far from mindless, the end product is still physical, so that this is one which may be depicted in the diagram of the learning processes by the double arrow between practice/ experimentation and evaluation, rather than by the double arrow to reflection.

It would also be true that certain forms of therapy are learning exercises, where the learner practises the correct response to certain stimuli or experiences and is suitably rewarded when the outcome is acceptable to the therapist. Therapy of this nature is behaviourist which may be based upon the premiss that the human being is the result of experiences, without an independent mind to assess the process. Nevertheless, it is clear that behavioural techniques are used beneficially within therapy and that some patients do learn the necessary skills to take their place within the wider society. However, the extent to which therapy is educational, as opposed to a learning process, is debatable.

There is a sense that this form of practice suggests that learners acquire a correct way of doing something because they understand that the way being taught has to be emulated; consequently it may be regarded as non-reflective. In addition, there is at least one form of experimentation that might also be regarded as non-reflective. This occurs when a person is told how to perform a technique or a procedure and immediately, impulsively, attempts to practise it without any thought or analysis. Kagan (1971, etc.) has undertaken many students of impulsivity-reflectivity with children, in which he measured the reaction time to potential learning situations. Some children responded extremely rapidly, impulsively, while others were reflective. While Kagan has not attempted to isolate sociological variables to any great extent, concentrating rather upon psychological ones; he has suggested that impulsivity may be related to: what he calls 'constitutional predispositions', e.g. hypo-activity; involvement in the task; anxiety about the task. Hypo-active is minimally related to the development of analytic concepts. The greater the degree of involvement in the task the more likely it is that the learner will be reflective, but the greater the anxiety the less likely that the learner will be able to tolerate silence to think and so may appear to be an impulsive, non-reflective learner. Hence, those people with low self-images may not have the confidence to reflect upon a potential learning experience and to draw the fullest implications from it. Perhaps this form of response only occurs in certain social situations, such as an individual being questioned by somebody who has higher status, whereas in other social situations, like a formal classroom, where there are other learners, they can all remain silent and shelter behind each other, and maybe think about the situation, etc. Hence, the social situation which is a part of the experience has to be taken into consideration in comprehending the learning process. However, this does not mean to say that the impulsive person is always non-reflective;

Kagan (1971, p. 55) makes the following significant point:

> We do not wish to paint the reflective child as necessarily the better or the brighter child. It is likely that efficient learning and creative problem solving will occasionally be facilitated by a reflective approach, occasionally by an impulsive one.

Impulsivity is not, therefore, necessarily correlated with conformist practice, although there is a possibility that it may happen in this manner. However, impulsive experimentation may not result in satisfactory performance, so that there is a possibility that if there is no successful outcome to the performance that the impulsive person may be forced to reflect upon it and another learning cycle would commence, based upon the unsuccessful performance as a potential learning situation. It is interesting to note tht impulsivity was also a factor in intuitive learning, discussed by Bruner and referred to in the previous chapter.

Experimentation in reflective learning. Once again it may be seen that there are two types of situation within reflective learning where the practice/experimentation factor plays a part in learning — these are in reflective practice and experimental learning, but this time they will be discussed together.

Perhaps the most significant study of this form of learning in recent years has been Schon's (1983) work on *The Reflecive Practitioner*, in which he seeks to show that professionals in practice do not merely seek to apply the theory that they have learned to the practice situation, but that they use it as a potential learning situation from which they can learn and create new procedures and new knowledge, although this does not deny that they had a theoretical base to their practice in the first instance. Schon considers that the traditional idea that theory is applied to practice is false: this he refers to as the death of technical rationality. Jarvis and Gibson (1985) regard this as the interface of theory and practice, rather than the application of the former to the latter. Schon's main concern, however, is to demonstrate that the professionals reflect in the practice situation and on occasions produce new forms of practice and knowledge, appropriate for the situation in which they function.

However, this does not mean that every situation is so unique that no practice or procedure can be repeated, merely that when there are changes in the situation, changes in practice or theoretical knowledge might also be demanded. Schon demonstrates how a variety of practising professionals 'think on their feet' and produce unique responses to situations, some of which relate to new forms of practice and others to new forms of knowledge. Hence, it is necessary to note here that in his analysis the procedure or the knowledge may be traditional or it may also be innovative; he allows for both possibilities. Indeed, it will be seen from the types of learning that emerged from the analysis in the second chapter that this can relate to both reflective practice and to experimental learning. These may also be single loop or double loop, to use the language that Schon and Argyris employ elsewhere, but both of these forms of learning are possible within all three types of reflective learning.

This brief sub-section has begun to analyse some of the complexities of the practical dimension to learning, it has highlighted the fact that there are freedoms and constraints within learning and that these also relate to the extent to which learning produces change or conformity as an outcome. However, it is important to recognise that the manner by which learning is evaluated is another factor within this analysis and it is on this topic that the discussion must now focus.

EVALUATION

The word evaluation has connotations with curriculum evaluation in educational theory, and for that reason the choice of the term was problematic; the terms appraisal and assessment were initially considered. In some ways assessment was considered to be the best term, but it is so frequently related to the post-learning process of examining that it was decided not to employ it. Appraisal does not really convey quite the right meaning and so evaluation was finally selected. This term does convey the process that occurs within learning. Both in the cognitive and in the psycho-motor domains many learners consider the outcomes of their thought and action and decide whether they have achieved an acceptable end product. This is an evaluative process·and forms an intrinsic part of the learning sequence for many, but not all, learners. If the outcome is acceptable then it is memorised, but if not, then the outcome is rejected and the thinking or practising/experimenting stage continued. Hence, the arrows appear in the model in both directions.

The inclusion of this element within the model of the learning processes was itself open to debate because it could be argued that evaluation only occurs after the learning process is complete, or because there are some learning situations in which this process does not occur. While there is considerable strength in this position, it was also recognised that evaluation is an element within some learning processes and that it does relate to Schon's (1983) discussion. As it was recognised that in some learning processes there is no evaluation in the process *per se*, it was probably considered wiser to omit this box entirely from the model. This point illustrates just how difficult it is to construct a model of such a complex process, one that is relevant to everybody's learning.

Another, similar problem is that for some people the process of evaluation is one that they carry out for themselves. Whereas others seek another person to test them to see if they have learned correctly. This is an important difference and, at first sight, it would appear to be a difference between non-reflective and reflective learning. However, it is not as simple as this, since even in reflective learning situations — especially if the outcome is innovative — thinkers might seek to consult other people in order to try out their ideas. In these situations it might be asked whether the other persons are actually a part of the process or distinct from it. On balance, it would seem that they might be seen as a part of the process, but it has to be recognised that they do perform distinctly different roles in the process of learning. Indeed, it will be seen in this section that the whole process of evaluation operates differently in the different learning processes, but before this is discussed it is important to clarify a few further points.

A similar point to note at the outset of this discussion is that there are several different ways by which these processes can be evaluated. Each of these may be related to different learning sequences in the model developed in the second chapter, and each may also be related to different forms of knowledge, etc. that may be considered as outcomes of learning. Hence, in seeking to learn non-reflectively, it is possible to evaluate only the product of the learning/memorisation or also to evaluate the process in skills learning, whereas in the reflective learning there may be both a process and a product evaluated. It is for this reason that arrows flow into this box from memorisation, reflection and practice/experimentation, so that all forms of learning except pre-conscious learning can, but do not necessarily, incorporate this factor to some degree.

There is little evidence about how adults actually evaluate their learning, although some exists that shows that they have learned to do this. That evidence comes from adult learners who return to the education system. For example, many adult returners find it difficult to evaluate their work against any other set of criteria than those which they experienced within the authoritarian context of school education because they assume that there are objective, external standards of correctness, which appear to be the ones that many children internalise during their schooling, and that they can acquire the necessary knowledge by rote learning. Indeed, this approach causes problems to adults who return to learning later in life, especially when they are exposed to a variety of different theoretical perspectives about the same problem, because instead of being able to evaluate their learning with reference to an authority they have to choose between authorities and this leads to confusion for some adults. The confusion can be so great with some adults that they think that they need help and guidance to see them through this stage. Hence, some teachers in higher and adult education have attempted to teach learners the arts of learning and evaluating in order to overcome this problem (see Abercrombie, 1969, for an early example of this approach). Thus it may be seen that evaluation is itself dependent upon earlier learning experiences. If the learners' evaluation method relates to a different type of learning to the one in which they are engaged, or even to a different form of knowledge, then it is clear that the learners' own evaluation might be suspect, and this is one of the arguments against adopting self-assessment as an educational approach in an oversimple manner.

Another similar important element within this context is the nature of the self-image of the learner within the social milieu in which the learning is occurring. Those people with low self-concepts within the situation are more likely to assess their learning in conformist terms. In contrast, those with a positive self-image may be more prepared to adopt another set of criteria which are more independent, and perhaps more innovative, and judge their performance more realistically or even more leniently than they might.

Another factor that will affect the manner by which evaluation operates within the learning process is the way that the learning outcome is to be assessed. If learners know that their learning is going to be assessed by an external means, e.g. against correct memorisation or accurate performance of a skill, then there will be a tendency to utilise the method themselves, in as far as they are able. Consequently, it may be seen that the assessment process is internalised and becomes a part of the learning process.

A similar point to the above which has to be taken into consideration in this process is the nature of the environment within which learning occurs. If the situation is formal, there is more likelihood that the outcomes of thought and practice that lead to conformity will be evaluated as successful. By contrast, if the environment is more egalitarian, then there is a likelihood that another set of criteria might be utilised. But this might also depend upon the position of the person within the organisation in which the learning process is occurring. From sociological studies of change in organisations, there is evidence to suggest that some of those who are established generate a bureaucratic mentality and so they may judge the outcomes of their own learning by the procedures that are in operation within the formal organisation in which their learning occurs. (For example, see Merton's 1968 study of bureaucratic structure and personality.)

Since knowledge may be empirical, pragmatic, logical or belief, there are clearly a number of different ways in which it can be verified. Empirical knowledge can be verified by the sense experiences, so that the correct learning of empirical knowledge can be checked with reference to the 'fact' and this can be undertaken by the learner or by another person. Pragmatic knowledge can be evaluated by experimentation and logical knowledge by ascertaining the validity of the process by which the learning outcome was reached. This last form can be undertaken by the learner alone, or it is possible for the learner to have another person perform that role. Belief knowledge cannot be verified, but the 'rationality' by which the conclusions are reached can be evaluated by a person other than the learner.

Another way of undertaking this process is to examine whether the learning outcomes have reached an apparently acceptable objective set of standards or criteria and this allows for the external form of evaluation, referred to above, to occur. By contrast, since learning tends to be subjective as well, it is possible to have self-assessment, whereby the learners evaluate how far they have progressed from where they were when they began their learning exercise. Among the problems of self-assessment of learning outcomes is the fact that there could be considerable movement from where the learners were when the process of learning began, but if they were ignorant at that point, there is the possibility that they have still not reached an acceptable standard when they evaluate their own learning.

It will be noted that in the above paragraphs there are a number of sets of intertwining variables; those of subjectivity/objectivity, of whether the base line for evaluation is the point at which the learner started or whether it is the end product of the learning and also there are those which relate to the different forms of knowledge. Clearly it is difficult to untangle these in practice, although they are demarcated here for analytical purposes. It should also be borne in mind that knowledge is one of the products of learning.

The above discussion also makes the assumption that everybody who learns actually has a rational approach to evaluation. While this appears to be logical at first sight, there are at least two other broad approaches; the first makes the assumption that learners know intuitively when they have arrived at a correct solution to the process, while the second is that there is in some forms of learning no internal evaluation process at all. Both of these are quite normal approaches and can occur in non-reflective learning.

This brief section on evaluation has clearly not entered into the philosophical realms of the debate about the correctness, or otherwise, of the criteria for evaluation that are adopted. This lies beyond the scope of this study. Even so, it will have become apparent that many of the methods employed in this stage of learning relate very closely to the approaches used in moral philosophy in seeking to understand the nature of goodness, and those used in epistemological studies to determine the nature of knowledge. There are, however, some social implications of the above discussion that need to be mentioned before the discussion moves to a consideration of memorisation.

The first of these is to point out that the nature of the evaluation that occurs often relates to the type of learning that is taking place. For instance, it is much easier to understand the non-reflective learning processes if it is recognised that the evaluation that is occurring often presupposes that there are objective standards or empirical knowledge and that if there is an external assessment it is going to relate to the product of the learning. In addition, if the learning is to be assessed externally then the presupposition might exist that there is no need to evaluate it internally, or even that the learners are not able to undertake this because they are not the experts. In contrast, when the evaluation focuses upon subjective standards, logical or pragmatic outcomes, etc. there is a greater likelihood that the learning will have been of a reflective nature. However, it must be pointed out here that even in these instances the final outcome of the learning might not be innovative, but single loop learning — to use Argyris's terminology.

The second point to recognise from this brief discussion is that the nature of the evaluation within learning itself is social; it may have been learned by previous experiences both within and outside of the educational system, but also it may relate to the environment within which the learning is taking place. Where it has been learned by previous experience, it may result in a lack of congruence between the current learning process and the evaluation element within it. Where it occurs within a formal or an authoritarian environment, then the learners may evaluate their learning in terms of correctness or acceptability to the social system, rather than in relation to the learning process itself. However, there is one other point that must be raised here although further reference will be made to this later. There are learning situations in which the learners might decide that it is inappropriate to practise what they have learned as a result of reflection upon a previous potential learning experience considering the social milieu, so that the action is dissonant to their cognitive learning. Discontinuity between learning and action is another reason for rejecting the behaviourist approach to learning.

Having analysed some of the aspects within the evaluation which occurs within learning, it may still be seen why a great deal of learning tends to conformity rather than towards any form of innovation. However, this discussion will be referred to in greater detail in Chapter 9 of this book, but before this, it is necessary to look at the nature of memorisation since, having evaluated the learning thus far, it might be necessary to internalise it.

MEMORISATION

All the arrows in the models of the learning processes which relate to any form of learning, enter this box so that it is not surprising that the majority of books on the psychology of learning place considerable emphasis upon memory. While memory is a very significant element in the learning process, it is one upon which less emphasis is placed in this present study, not because there has been so much written about the subject already but because it is in the province of the psychologists and, increasingly, of other disciplines, such as biology, which are concerned with the ways in which the brain works.

Memorisation, rather than memory, was the term chosen here in order to try to make the distinction between the learning process whereby certain knowledge, skills and attitudes are committed to memory, and the function of the brain as such. In the earliest models of the learning processes in this present research this element was actually called internalisation in order to make the point clearer. This also distinguished between the process discussed in this sub-section and the non-reflective learning process that has also been termed memorisation in this book. However, the term internalisation was not used in subsequent models because it does not convey the idea of committing something to memory, so that memorisation was finally chosen.

It will be noted that the arrows come from the processes of experience, reflection and evaluation; all the learning processes have this stage within them, so that it may be wondered whether the process is the same for each of the separate stages and different types of learning. Obviously, further research is needed to answer this question with any degree of certainty, but there are at least two theories about the process of memorisation and both of them need to be examined briefly here. The first process appears to be a sequential one in which individuals first commit something to their short-term memory and thereafter it is internalised within their long-term memory. The second approach relates to the degree of meaning that an experience has, so that a meaningful experience is easily attached to memories of related experiences, whereas those experiences which are meaningless are much more difficult to commit to memory. Obviously a lot more research needs to be undertaken before firm conclusions can be drawn, but at the present time it would seem unwise to claim that the latter approach has superseded the former one, as Botkin *et al.* (1979, p. 22) have done. Indeed, it is perfectly possible to consider that the process of memorisation varies according to the type of experience that is to be memorised.

It is perhaps significant to note here that Habermas (1972, p. 9) claims that: 'only something already known can be remembered as a result and comprehended in its genesis. This movement is the experience of reflection.' Such a claim is perhaps rather imprecise and it might be noted that, according to Habermas, only something that is known by someone can be remembered, since this process of memorisation does not necessarily include reflection. The processes of learning that have been termed non-reflective learning in this study imply that the learner acquires knowledge without reflection. Even so, Habermas is right, as was shown in the last chapter, to place emphasis on the place of reflection in some forms of learning.

It will be recalled, however, that earlier in this study the ideas of meaningful and meaningless experiences were discussed and, consequently, this earlier analysis may be related to this present diverse understanding of the process of memorisation. Many adult educators (e.g. Brundage and Mackeracher, 1980, p. 103; Knowles, 1980, p. 44) have emphasised the fact that people learn better when they perceive the phenomenon to be learned to be relevant to their everyday life, and educators of children are also aware how important it is to make the subject being taught relevant to the life of the children. Hence, there appears to be a considerable amount of support for the idea that memorisation is more efficient if the content to be memorised is meaningful in some way. Meaningfulness is more likely to occur when the experience being memorised can be related to previous experiences that the learners have already had and have recorded within their memory. It follows from this that people are more likely to be able to memorise effectively those experiences which relate to previous experiences, or, in other words, that potential learning experiences that are far removed from the socio-cultural-temporal life of the learners may be harder to learn. This is not a surprising conclusion, but it is significant for understanding the learning process. People are more likely to memorise effectively those phenomena that relate to their previous experiences and they are less likely to memorise effectively those which are foreign to them. An example was given in the third chapter of an humanities specialist in a technological laboratory. Much more relevantly, however, the example could have been of working-class drop-outs from the school system seeking to return to education, but finding the formal middle-class adult education environment and method of presenting abstract knowledge foreign and difficult, not because of ability, but because both the environment and the knowledge are less meaningful to them than they might have been had they been organised and presented differently.

There are experiences, however, that are foreign to everyday experience that are memorised and recalled vividly; these are traumatic and some stressful experiences. Some of these experiences are obviously suppressed into the unconscious and the effects may become problematic and sometimes result in the need for psychotherapy. But at other times they may be used as a basis for learning and then therapy becomes unnecessary, or less necessary. It is, therefore, quite false for educators to claim that only the enjoyable experiences are effectively learned, although it might be quite immoral for educators to create situations of trauma and stress. Hence, it is correct to claim that within the limits of the educational situation enjoyable experiences are more conducive to learning. It is perhaps significant to note that either happy or stressful experiences have been mentioned here, indicating that the affect plays an important part in all learning, and not only in that which is sometimes referred to as experiential learning.

The opposite to meaningfulness is meaninglessness, and in Chapter 4 this was explored in some detail in relation to alienation and anomie. It is now necessary to analyse this from the perspective of memorisation. One of the fundamental features of meaningless experiences is the fact that there is no experience stored away in the reservoir of the memory to which the present experience can be related. Hence the memory must function differently in order for it to store such an experience. It is here where the ideas of short- and long-term memories might become much more significant. If an experience is new, then there is less relevant previous knowledge to bring to it in order to reflect upon it, so that what might occur in this instance is that the perceptions of that experience might be stored in the short-term memory and eventually some aspects of it transferred to the long-term memory. Thereafter, it takes its place within the store of memories that function in the same way as the memory works in relation to meaningful experiences.

Additionally, it might be that some types of learning contain a mixture of both approaches to memorisation, so that in some forms of rote learning, e.g. vocabulary learning in languages where it is possible to relate words with the same meaning from different languages, meaningful memorisation occurs, whereas in committing to memory historical dates, etc. the sequential approach to memorisation takes place. Indeed, it will also be recalled how many of the techniques employed to improve the memory try to change the memorisation pattern from sequential to meaningful memorisation.

Does all meaningful memorisation, however, have to be bound to the socio-cultural-temporal world of the learner? This is an important question and it appears that the answer to it must be negative. There are situations where the learners can solve apparently meaningless problems and in the process of thinking through the issues the whole problem becomes meaningful, so that in these instances new knowledge and attitudes etc. may be committed meaningfully to the mind. However, in many non-formal and informal learning experiences, the meaningfulness is related to the learners' life world and in these instances it would be possible to claim that memorisation is more effective when the experience is related to the socio-cultural-temporal life world of the learners. Hence, it is possibly easier to learn about the familiar than about the unfamiliar. This does not necessarily mean that the learning outcome will be conformist, since people appear more likely to think about and criticise from a standpoint of confidence those aspects which are at least familiar. The converse of this is also significant, if learners are taken from the familiar and expected to learn from less than meaningful experiences, there is a strong likelihood that the memorisation will be sequential and less effective. Indeed, it may also tend to be memorisation-type learning rather than critical reflective learning.

Like the other aspects of the learning process, it appears that memorisation may be a complex process in which the two types of memorisation process are related to the situations within which the learning occurs. It certainly appears that sequential memorisation is much more likely to occur when the experience is meaningless and the learning outcome is, therefore, much more likely to be conformist, whilst meaningful memorisation is more likely to occur when the potential learning situation is meaningful but the learning outcome may also be conformist although there is some possibility that the learning outcome may be innovative.

THE PERSON: CHANGED AND MORE EXPERIENCED

The end product of learning, it is maintained here, is the learner rather than the learner's behaviour. The learner may have acquired additional knowledge, a new ability to perform skills or even a different self-image. Herein is a major difference between this approach and that of the behaviourists. Behaviour change may be an outcome to learning but this also depends upon the social situation within which the learning occurs and also the situation within which the learning outcome is practised, since action is most frequently initiated by the individual. This is one of the topics that is discussed in this section. But first it is necessary to revert briefly to a study of the person who, as a result of the learning experience, is changed and more experienced. These are the two main themes of this section.

The person. Paterson (1979, p. 67) has argued that 'an educational activity is one which fosters the highest development of individuals as persons'. While Dewey (1916) would not disagree with Paterson, since he regarded the outcome of true education to be growth and development, he (1938, p. 25) was perhaps being more realistic when he claimed that 'some experiences are miseducative'. There is obviously a difference in emphasis here; Paterson is concerned to argue that liberal adult education has a developmental function for those who participate in it, but his concern is with liberal education and not with learning *per se*. The significance of this is not that learning does not occur during education, but that learning is a broader phenomenon than liberal education and so it might be asked whether learning experiences that do not develop the person are educational. This is a perfectly justifiable question, although it must be pointed out that the end product of the learning is not a sufficient conceptual criterion for distinguishing between education and learning. Dewey recognised this point when he claimed that not all experiences are educative, although it might have been conceptually clearer to have

127

argued that not all learning experiences are educative.

This would be a justifiable conclusion from the evidence of the analysis conducted in this book. Clearly many experiences result in learning that do develop the individual, but throughout the study there has been recognition that some potential learning experiences lead to the realisation that individuals cannot learn or that they result in alienation. An elderly person who, upon having an experience of the modern technological world, exlaims 'I don't know what the world is coming to these days' is, in fact, claiming that the potential learning experience has resulted in an inability to learn from a changed situation. This experience, however, might result in the self-image and confidence of that elderly person being changed in a negative manner. Having learned that the world is an alien place provides little or no incentive to go and learn more about it. In precisely the same manner, children at school who are expected to learn by memorisation phenomena which are meaningless find it difficult, if not impossible, and consequently might be labelled as 'not being very clever', might lose self-confidence, etc. and eventually bow out of the formal learning system. The labelling might be treated as if it were a reality and the children treated as if they were not clever, when the actual process that has occurred has been that they have been labelled in situations foreign to their experience, in which they have been unable or unwilling to show their actual ability. In both of these examples, there is learning, although it is not necessarily about the phenomenon which is the subject of the learning, it is about the learner. The experiences have not led to self-development. In Paterson's terms they are not educational and, in Dewey's they might be miseducative. Hence, it must be borne in mind that there are learning experiences that do not develop the learner's self-image. Perhaps the significant thing about both of the examples given is that certain social characteristics of the learners have to be provided in order to make the example relevant. This points to the fact that adult learning, and child learning, has to be understood within its social context.

Clearly, there are other forms of learning that change and develop the learner. These are the basis of many learning experiences, since it has been maintained throughout this discussion that the mind and the self are products of social experience. Hence, learning may, perhaps frequently, result in the individual growing and developing as a result of the learning experiences of living. While living is not synonymous with learning there are tremendous overlaps in the two concepts and with normal persons learning may be coterminous with conscious living. However, with mentally handicapped persons it might well be claimed that one of their problems is that they are unable to learn from the experiences of life. But with normal persons, there is an on-going process of learning from living which results in the reservoir of experience, which is the mind and the self, expanding with experience, which may in turn relate to age. Hence, Cattell's (1963) research into fluid and crystallised intelligence takes on significance. While Cattell showed that crystallised intelligence tended to increase until people reached the age of the early sixties, perhaps the subsequent research by Horn and Cattell (Horn, 1970) is even more significant for the purposes of the argument being presented here. They showed that after the age of sixty, increase in ability depended upon the experiences older people were having; indeed, those who were involved in intellectual pursuits continued to gain in crystallised intelligence. This research finds support from a recent report from the Open University, in the United Kingdom, that showed that the best degrees awarded in one year were awarded to those students who were between the ages of sixty and sixty-five years old. The converse of this is also significant: by the early sixties people may begin to disengage slightly from the world and have fewer experiences from which they might learn. Consequently, they may not continue to change and develop.

Not all development is of an intellectual form and so it is necessary to refer to a point made in the previous section of this chapter. It was suggested that traumatic and stressful experiences may be easily memorised because they are so meaningful. However, for some people such experiences are debilitating, while for others they are challenges to be overcome. Hence, for some people such experiences may become learning experiences from which they grow, while for others the experiences may be ones which induce other emotions from which they learn to restrict their activities and, perhaps, not develop and grow in the same way. The difference in the way experiences are treated clearly depends upon previous experiences which have moulded the person to some extent, but the fact that people respond differently to similar experiences may indicate the different ways in which the mind has developed.

Thus it may be claimed that the majority of learning experiences produce change in the person, even if that change is totally cognitive and unmeasurable. The change is the result of the learning. It is not the learning *per se*. That change need not be developmental, in the normal sense of the term; indeed it can be detrimental to the development of the person. More significantly, experiences in similar situations may produce different learning outcomes and affect the growth and development of a person differently, depending upon a variety of social characteristics and variables.

Learning and behaviour change. The behaviourist definition of learning specifies that behaviour change is necessary for learning to occur, and this was disputed from the outset of this present study. However, it was pointed out above that most learning results in some form of change, even if it is a cognitive one. But even if the learning demands behaviour change, the outcome is not automatic, since people's behaviour is itself socially constrained. Consequently, a person who learns specific knowledge that calls for behaviour change may be loathe to practise it if it appears to be inappropriate to the social situation in which the practice is called for. Krech *et al.* (1962, pp. 512–15) suggest that there are a number of factors that affect the way that an individual behaves in a group, including: the size of the group; its composition; the extent to which there is consensus within the group; the difference between the group's position and the individual's; the pressure the group exerts upon the individual; the wider social context. In addition to all of these factors, the person's own self-image and self-confidence will play an important part in the process.

A significant factor to note here also is that there can be no direct correlation between behaviour and a single act of learning since the new experience is only incorporated into the multitude of previous experiences that have constituted the person of the learner until that moment in time. Indeed, the learning experience might actually help to change people's reasons for acting in the way that they do, but not actually change their behaviour pattern at all.

Hence, it can be concluded that behaviour change is no measure of learning, since the individual learner may have learned a variety of things, such as the truth of a proposition and the appropriateness of adopting that position within a given social context. Additionally, this conclusion gives rise to the need for a theory of action within the context of society, rather in the terms that Giddens (1979) has undertaken. In addition, it must be recognised that as a result of a learning experience the person may have grown and developed but there need be no immediate outward sign of that change or that development.

CONCLUSIONS

This chapter has traced the other factors in the learning processes. It has been seen that learning is a very complex process and that the behavioural outcomes of learning do not necessarily correlate with the cognitive or self-image outcomes. Conformity may be the over-riding factor even though the cognitive learning has demanded that innovative action should follow from the process. Indeed, it has been shown throughout the whole of these last four chapters that there are social factors that affect the learning processes and that a number of quite specific conclusions can be drawn from this discussion.

First, a number of different learning processes have been demonstrated and something of their inter-relationship has been shown, since it must be borne in mind that a number of these processes can occur simultaneously. In addition, the relationship between different forms of knowledge and different approaches to learning has been highlighted. This is an important relationship and there will be some further discussion of it later in this book.

It has been demonstrated that the whole of people's socio-cultural-temporal milieu affects the way in which individuals learn, and that there are elements of culture that affect the process, such as language ability, etc. so that this may well be related to the way in which people learn. Berger (1966) regards this as a manifestation of the society within the person.

It was also shown that people learn more effectively if the context and content of what they learn is meaningful to them. This has a number of quite significant consequences, including the fact that people do not learn quite so effectively when they are learning out of their social context, where they have less self-confidence, and where the content that is to be learned is not very meaningful. This has considerable significance both for teaching methods and for the educational institution as a whole.

In addition, it has been noted that learning has a number of social constraints surrounding it, such as the social attributes of the learner, the social context within which the learning occurs and the relationship between them. Hence, it is suggested here that adult learning theory needs to develop within a broader context than adult development and psychological analysis.

Finally, it must be recognised that any person may experience a mixture of these types of learning during any brief time span throughout life; the extent to which one type, or even one category, of learning is associated with any particular social grouping in society is unknown and remains a topic for future research.

Having examined the various components of learning within this part of the book, it is now necessary to analyse the variety of types of learning that were shown to exist and specified in the second chapter. The next three chapters of this book will consist of an analysis of the various responses to a potential learning situation in their social context.

7

Non-learning Responses to a Potential Learning Situation

In Figure 2.2, there are three non-learning responses to a potential learning situation and these were called presumption, non-consideration and rejection. Presumption indicates that people have certain presuppositions about the social situation and provided that they are fulfilled they perform their role without question; non-consideration shows that in some situations people do not think about their experience; rejection demonstrates that there are certain situations in which individuals make a definite decision not to learn. None of these experiences results in the acquisition of any knowledge or skill, although there are some instances where the self-concept of the learners is affected by the experience. This change may be either negative or positive, negative because the actors have not been able to learn from the experience and recognise that this is the case, or positive because the actors recognise that an ability to cope with the experience has been manifest. Thus it may be seen that the self might be affected coincidentally by the non-learning response to a potential learning situation, and it will be shown in the next two chapters that whatever the type of learning response, the self must always be seen as an element in the experience.

It is now necessary to examine these types of non-learning in the situations in which they occur, since those situations may well have some effect upon the process. It will be recalled that four social situations were suggested: individual, informal, non-formal and formal, the latter three being group situations. It might be noted that, if education is the institutionalisation of learning, then in only the latter two types of group situation can learning in an educational situation occur.

In any situation the actors might be pro-active or reactive but it is suggested that with presumption the actors might be pro-active in creating a situation, while not necessarily viewing it as a potential learning situation. But obviously they can also react to such a situation. In contrast, actors are more likely to be reactive in situations when there is rejection.

The aim of this chapter, therefore, is initially to examine the relationship between the three different responses and the social situation, so that this constitutes the first part of the chapter and, thereafter, the social consequences of non-learning are examined.

NON-LEARNING IN THE SOCIAL SITUATION

The aim of the first part of this chapter, and similarly with the next two chapters, is to locate each of the respective types of learning into each of these four types of situation in order to illustrate the different ways in which learning occurs. This is a descriptive exercise to some extent, but it will serve to demonstrate the complexity of the learning processes and, perhaps, to show that even the model in Figure 2.2 is an over-simplification of the reality. Initially, then, the three non-learning responses are discussed.

Individual

It must be pointed out from the outset that the individual situation is still a social one because, as it will be recalled from the previous discussion, individuals are social beings who have internalised the culture(s) of the society in which they live, or have lived in the past. Peter Berger (1966, pp. 110–41) refers to this as 'society in man', where man is employed in a non-sexist manner, that is, 'the culture of society within . . . people'. Therefore, because people have internalised that culture in previous learning experiences and because they are a product of previous learning experiences, even when they act alone, they do so from the perspective of their social history. Hence, they are actually acting within a social context. Each of the three non-learning responses is now discussed within the context of the individual situation.

Presumption. When there is no disjunction between individuals' biographies and their experience, people act in an almost unthinking manner since the stimulus to act calls forth a previously learned response; put in a different manner, people know that in a given situation, which is meaningful to them, they are able to act in their usual

134

manner. Indeed, the situation is self-evident, so that they may not even consider whether they have been pro-active or reactive within it, but they could be either. People's life worlds are meaningful and familiar, they are self-evident, so that they presume that their normal response is self-evidently acceptable behaviour. This is a common everyday occurrence. Hence they gain no new knowledge or skill, but their self-image may be reinforced, almost coincidentally within the action, because they acquire additional confidence in negotiating another similar situation.

It is perhaps significant to note here that people presume that they are both free to conform or free to change their behaviour patterns, and that the structures of society do not appear oppressive to them. This perhaps highlights the fact that in these instances the structures of society enable people to feel confident in a meaningfully structured situation and to act without thought because of their previous experiences. It is important to note this since so often structures are treated as if they are always negative and restrictive, but they are also fundamental to a great deal of human behaviour. Indeed, it should be noted that there could be no social living unless this were among the most common responses to a potential learning situation.

Non-consideration. For a variety of reasons some people respond to a social situation without giving it a great deal of further thought; this may be because they have no time to think about it or because there may simply be too great a gap between the experience and their biographies, so that they do not bother to consider it. They might also feel threatened by the experience that they could have, if they allowed themselves to have it, so that their fear prevents them from entering such a situation. Clearly this is very close to one of the responses in the rejection situation, but this is when people have the experience but refuse to think about it. This point illustrates that these responses are not discrete nor easily classifiable.

There may, but need not be, disjuncture between people's biography and their present experience. Indeed, in some situations the actors might be aware that there is a disjuncture and might even be motivated to reflect upon the experience but for a variety of reasons, such as being too busy, they may never turn their minds to consider that experience. Since they have been unable to consider these experiences the actors' self-concept remains unchanged.

Rejection. Since the modern world is changing very rapidly in many ways, it must be recognised that everybody enters a variety of social situations in which there is a disjuncture between their biography and that experience. This disjuncture is often the trigger that sparks off the learning process, as Aslanian and Brickell (1980) show. But in some situations the actors might feel that the gap between their biography and their experience is too great to be bridged or, alternatively, they might feel that their self-image is threatened by their experience. In both cases their reaction might be to reject the possibilities of learning from the situation. The actors might, for instance, turn off the television rather than consider the implications of a certain programme, or not read a page of a book, etc. A variety of reasons for acts like this exist, such as fear. But even more significantly, these might be the reactions of a bigot or a prejudiced person. All of these cases are much more deliberate acts than the one mentioned in the previous section, since they initially involve some thought being given to the experience.

In some of these cases the self-images of the actors might be harmed in such a way as to inhibit them from learning from similar situations in the future. Indeed, this is the beginning of the spiral of reaction that might lead to anomie, which was discussed in Chapter 4. In addition, this might be a significant feature in the so-called disengagement process in the elderly, a process that seems to occur more frequently with the elderly in Western individualistic societies than in other types of society, since elderly people appear to be more isolated and might be less involved than they were when they were younger (Cowgill and Holmes, 1978, pp. 24–5). In such situations the individual may feel that the structures of society are very oppressive and that the only freedom that an individual has is a negative one.

However, certain forms of rejection, such as bigotry and prejudice, might result in the actors' self-image being reinforced, because they see themselves as being strong enough to resist the 'temptations' of the potential learning situation. To a lesser extent, the religious person who seeks to shun certain experiences which might be viewed as tempting also falls into this category and so it can be seen how close certain forms of response to experiences are. There are clearly some that would be viewed positively and others negatively, by different individuals, depending upon their position and biography in relation to the situation. There are many studies of prejudice, etc. so that it is unnecessary to delve into them any more deeply here (but see Allport, 1954; Fisher, 1982, *inter alia*). Prejudiced people may be pro-active in initiating situations because of the low threshold that often accompanies it, but less likely to be pro-active in initiating situations that they see as potential learning ones, unless they think that the experience will reinforce their own world view. All of these examples might also be viewed as examples of negative freedom, where actors can resist the social pressures that operate upon them which sometimes seem oppressive to them.

Informal

It will be recalled that the first group-type of interaction discussed was informal; that is, an apparently non-structured type of relationship that most people experience frequently during their lifespan. However, the fact that it is informal does mean that it is by definition bounded by social parameters that are common to all the actors in the social situation and taken for granted by them, so that any learning or non-learning that occurs must be bound by those parameters, irrespective of whether the interaction be pro-active or reactive. Additionally, it is precisely because the interaction is informal that there may be many situations where there are no learned outcomes, because the actors are involved in the familiar and acting in a meaningful manner. Even so, each of the three possible non-learning outcomes will be discussed briefly below in order to demonstrate the validity of the position suggested here.

Presumption. Since actors enter into informal situations with their parameters already structured, there is a taken-for-granted form of behaviour between actors. Indeed, the strength of this taken-for-grantedness can be demonstrated by considering the situation where the social situation of an actor has drastically changed in relationship to a second actor. The second actor often finds it extremely difficult to enter an interaction where the patterns of behaviour have to be learned afresh. An example of this is the problem an individual faces on entering into an interaction for the first time with an acquaintance who has been recently bereaved. It is these patterns of relationship learned previously that provide the basis for habitualised behaviour and give it the appearance of freedom. This type of situation can once again be seen as a possible reinforcement to a self-image, whether the actor was pro-active or reactive at the outset of the experience.

Non-consideration. Very little can be added to the previous discussion on this topic, in as much as it is important to understand the motivation for not considering a potential learning situation and this remains a topic for future research, but it may be similar to some of the ideas already suggested.

Rejection. In this situation a gulf may well exist between the actors' biographies and their experiences, but the need to learn that this gulf creates is not necessarily responded to in a positive manner. There may be a variety of very good reasons why this response should have occurred in an informal relationship. For example, if following certain actions were to produce strains in the pattern of relationship, even if the actors might learn something from the action, then one or more of them might decide not to pursue the issues. Hence, the exercise of tact and social skills might be seen as a rejection of learning in certain situations, but the significant thing about these situations is that they are meaningful to the actor, whereas the previous discussion on rejection of the potential learning situation was one of meaninglessness. Thus it must be recognised that not every rejection is necessarily damaging or self-inhibiting. Indeed, in these situations it might be possible to demonstrate that the exercise of the social skill in rejecting learning sometimes results in an enhanced self-image. A problem might arise, however, when an individual has been socialised to respond to a specific situation in one direction, e.g. by not asking questions about certain personal matters, and regards silence as tactful, whereas another person in the interaction interprets the failure not to ask those certain questions in a tactful manner as disinterest. This example demonstrates very clearly the extent to which interaction and social learning are governed by social parameters. But it also shows the importance of experiences being meaningful to actors at the outset if meaningful action, whether learning or non-learning, is to occur. In addition, it shows the extent to which individual freedom, or agency, might itself be seen as a product of social structure.

Non-formal

Following Coombs and Ahmed (1974), it will be recalled that non-formal interaction was regarded as a more structured form of interaction than the informal type but not one that occurs within a bureaucratic organisation. The teacher-practitioner (Jarvis and Gibson, 1985), or mentor, was used as an example of a teacher who performed away from the formal structure of the classroom. Hence, there are certain forms of non-formal interaction that might be considered as educational, since there are social interactions provided by educational institutions which are on a different basis to that of classroom teaching and learning. However, there are other non-formal interactions where learning might, or might not, occur, such as mentoring, learning on the shopfloor with some expert advice and learning in the community situation. Since there is a degree of formality within the interactions that are now being discussed, and because many of these forms of social interaction are potential learning situations, it is necessary to recognise that non-learning becomes a more problematic concept than it was in the previous type of situation. For the sake of this discussion the teacher-practitioner/student-practitioner interaction, and the community educator, in a teaching and learning situation are both used to demonstrate this aspect of some of the elements that are relevant to these types of situations.

Presumption. Once the patterns of relationship between the actors has been established it might be fairly easy for student-practitioners to assume that they know the routine for a specific practice and to perform it without reference to the teacher-practitioner. This presumption might be a sign that learning has already occurred and that the student-practitioner has the confidence to perform the procedure in the presence of the teacher-practitioner. Successful performance might result in reinforced self-image. Presumption, or taken-for-granted behaviour, must always be a sign that some learning has occurred. However, one of the problems with such behaviour is that an habitualised pattern of behaviour is enacted when the social situation for which that response was appropriate has changed slightly. It is at this point that a teacher-practitioner can intervene with a student-practitioner in order to help them to recognise how the situation has altered, but when they become independent professionals presumption in such circumstances becomes a hindrance to good practice.

Non-consideration. When a gulf between biography and experience is recognised but the student-practitioner does not wish to respond to the potential learning situation, it may be one of the teacher-practitioner's functions to generate a learning process. However, it is easy within professional practice to have too many commitments, so that practitioners are prevented from considering the lessons that could have been learned from a potential learning situation. It is sometimes the job of the teacher-practitioner, the supervisor, etc. to ensure that the practitioners, student-practitioners, etc. do at least consider the situation. Even so, there are many potential learning situations within a non-formal relationship where, for a variety of reasons, the actors fail to consider the situation within which they both interact and practise. For instance, in the third world where non-formal education is widely practised, it is not hard to envisage situations where the 'teacher' comes to a village with a message, technique, etc. which is so far removed from the cultural pattern of the group that individuals within it do not wish to consider it. In precisely the same way, working-class clients of middle-class professional practitioners may not consider the advice that they are given if it is far removed from their biographical experience in such a situation.

Rejection. It is not difficult to conceptualise situations in which actors within a non-formal context have interactions which result in rejection of a potential learning experience. Indeed, some of the examples discussed in the above section might be conceptualised as rejection as easily as non-consideration, apart from the fact that in this form of non-learning the actors actually consider the potential learning experience before they decide not to learn from it. Similarly in professional preparation a skills demonstration could have been conducted by a teacher-practitioner for student-practitioners, but because they were already proficient in that skill they decide not to observe the procedure carefully and they might actually miss something from which they might have learned. This shows one reason why demonstration as a teaching method should be employed with some degree of care.

It should be noted here that the degree of meaningfulness is a factor in the decision to reject the opportunity to learn. In the first example the situation and the biography were too far apart and in the latter they were too repetitive so that there appeared to be no disjuncture between them. Perceived disjuncture is a necessary precursor for learning, unless there is an authoritarian situation in which the learners have no choice but to respond or the learning is pre-conscious.

It will have been noticed that within the non-formal context the relationship has been treated slightly differently and this is because it does involve the potentiality of hierarchy and so a power and/or status dimension begins to appear. If people are expected to learn from a specific situation and, for a variety of reasons, they treat the situation as a non-learning experience, the outcome may be that the structures, or persons with authority, exert pressure to try to create a learning experience. It is also quite easy, in the light of the previous arguments presented in this book, to recognise that if the teacher-practitioners' social backgrounds are different from those of the student-practitioners', then there is a possibility that the interaction itself fails to establish the type of rapport that enables learning to occur. For instance, it would be difficult for a student-practitioner whose ideology of professional practice was different to that of the teacher-practitioner to learn as effectively in that situation as would a student-practitioner whose role ideology was similar. But role ideology may itself reflect socialisation, etc. and even the social class, ethnicity, sex, etc. of the practitioner. But failure to respond to the teacher-practitioner's authority may result in the learners being regarded as unintelligent, trouble-makers, etc. This form of labelling may bear no relationship to the actual ability of the persons concerned, only with their non-learning responses to socially constructed situations within which they were expected to learn. This argument might be pursued one stage further and it might be asked whether unintelligence is created by society? Why people do not learn in such situations is a significant question and one that requires further research.

Formal

Much of the foregoing discussion might be applied to this situation, since a great deal of teaching and learning occurs within the context of the formal organisation, with its rules and regulations. However, it is not considered appropriate here to repeat this and so it is now necessary to examine non-learning within the formal organisation. Clearly there are two types of formal organisation that could be considered here, the first being the adult classroom where the learner is placed within a formal relationship to the class teacher and, secondly, where the learner is a member of the organisation such as the workplace. This distinction becomes very important in considering professional continuing education, where the workplace may well be the place of learning. Indeed, there are now situations in which the teachers may be released from both formal instructional duties or from practice to act as 'roving' teachers, or mentors, within the organisation. This has certainly occurred within nurse education in the United Kingdom and also with some recent educational work in factories. However, for the purposes of this discussion, the main theme will be the learner as a role player within the organisation.

Presumption. Many role players within formal organisations go through the bureaucratic processes without learning from their experiences, simply because they see themselves as functionaries within the organisation and presume that the organisation's procedures are acceptable and unchanging. Merton (1968, pp. 175–260) highlights two types of person within the bureaucracy who conform to the procedures of the organisation, the conformist and the ritualist (who merely goes through the motions). In both of these instances, the actors merely conform to the procedures and do not learn from them; indeed, Merton also suggests that the structures of the formal organisation act upon the person creating a bureaucratic-type of personality. Hence, these people merely perform within the organisation and may not learn a great deal from their experiences because their biographies and their present experiences fit together harmoniously.

Non-consideration. Once again, there may be many reasons why a potential learning experience is not considered. The previous discussion is appropriate here but will not be reiterated. However, an example of the formal teaching and learning situation may be used to illustrate another aspect of this response. People listening to a formal lecture might become aware that the speaker is saying something interesting and is actually creating a disjuncture with their biographical experience. Hence, they may start to think about the point being made, still half listening to the lecturer. Before they have finished thinking through the implications of the point, the speaker makes a second relevant point, and later a third, and the listeners are no longer in a position to think through the implications of all the points that are being made by the speaker. By contrast to this, the lecturer may be providing the listeners with experiences that are so far removed from their biographies that they do not bother to concentrate upon what is being said. Bourdieu (1973) would point out that some of these potential learners do not have the cultural capital to be able to learn from such experiences. Hence, the working-class child, or adult, in a sophisticated middle-class environment might not be able to appreciate the carefully but tortuously argued aspects of a lecture on an abstract topic, or even the intricacies of a display in a museum. Hence, the method of presentation ensures a form of cultural reproduction and also ensures that those who do not have the cultural capital are not able to consider what is being presented. Thus, some reasons why the lecture is an inefficient teaching tool become more apparent.

Similarly, if the culture of a formal organisation is totally foreign to individuals, they might not endeavour to understand it and prefer to remain estranged within it. This might also be true of certain groups of people who settle in different countries but do not seek to assimilate anything of the culture of their new country. Schutz's (1970, p. 87) insightful analysis of the stranger in the community is significant here, since: 'The stranger . . . becomes essentially the man who has to place in question nearly everything that seems to be unquestionable to the members of the approached group.' Clearly the stranger is in a potential learning situation but if the gulf between the situation and the stranger's biography is too great, and if there is nobody to help the stranger to bridge that gap, then he may not consider the possibility of learning from the situation and remain alien within that society, or he may reject that group and this, while it falls under the next sub-heading, can lead to potentially damaging situations for both parties. Even so, within a bureaucratic society or organisation people might pre-consciously acquire some of the cultural characteristics, but this type of learning will be discussed in the next chapter.

Rejection. Merton (1968, pp. 207–9) highlights one type of rejection response to a formal situation; this he calls retreatist. The retreatists are persons who do not share the values of the organisation and who therefore remove themselves from the social situation rather than learn from it. They may do this physically, like the tramps who remove themselves from the organisational society, or mentally, like the school children who close their minds to what is happening in the classroom, or who, like some migrants, for very understandable reasons, deliberately seek to retain their own cultural life-style in a new society, etc. In some of these situations, such as the classroom, there is the potentiality of an anomic outcome, as was pointed out earlier, while in others there is an ideological reason for the rejection. Certain evangelical Christians, for instance, would claim that they have to reject 'the world' and so they endeavour not to learn from it.

Conclusion. This section of the chapter has examined some of the possible non-learning responses to social situations that were posed in the model discussed earlier. It may be seen that the examples utilised here are not exhaustive and it would be possible to find other illustrations to make the points being made. The significance of the non-learning responses are probably self-evident, but the second part of this chapter seeks to expand on some of the points that have occurred in this section.

NON-LEARNING AND THE SOCIAL STRUCTURES

It will be seen from the above discussion that non-learning is closely connected with both the cultural environment and the social structures, so that it is now necessary to extend this discussion a little. This will be undertaken by considering each of the three forms of non-learning response individually.

Presumption. It was noted in the first instance that there are situations when people, by virtue of their presumptions, feel quite free within the social structures. Indeed, it might be argued that in these circumstances, the structures enable the actors to perform their roles. They might consider that they are agents, able to act freely and rationally within the structures that surround them. That they feel free may not be doubted, but this feeling of freedom may merely reflect that in these circumstances the actors have internalised the behavioural patterns that are appropriate to the situation and have conformed to them.

Where there is a voluntary conformity neither the strength of the social structures, nor power, manifest themselves. It is perhaps significant that at the outset of this discussion between the relationship between non-learning and the social structures, that where there is conformity the aspect of power does not appear to be operative, but then there is no need for it to do so. This apparent lack of demonstrable power is what Gramsci called hegemony. Williams (1976, p. 205) described hegemony as:

> . . . a whole body of practices and expectations, our assignments of energy, our ordinary understanding of the nature of man and his world. It is a set of meanings and values which as they are experienced as practices appear as reciprocally confirming. It thus constitutes a sense of reality for most people in society, a sense of absolute because experienced reality beyond which it is very difficult for most members of society to move, in most areas of their lives.

Thus hidden within the presumptive non-learning response, it is possible to see why power need not manifest itself openly in specific social situations. This is especially true when people accept media definitions of reality, etc. since, as it may be recalled, these are someone else's selection and interpretation of reality. Provided that the social structures etc. do facilitate the 'good life' for most people, such interpretations may be generally acceptable, but this does not mean that they should not be understood by a critically aware people. This response to a potential learning is discussed more fully in Chapter 9.

Non-consideration. The above discussion is also appropriate in this instance to some extent, since those people who are too busy to stop and reflect might always consider that given the time it would have been possible to have thought about the situation and to have learned from it. This might be true, but the fact remains that there are situations where people appear to choose to conform and not to stop and consider what might have been learned from a specific situation. In a similar manner, those who choose not to consider a situation because they might be threatened by the outcome also demonstrate the significance of the fact that if people choose to conform, for whatever reason, there is no need to exercise power to enforce them to do so.

That there are people who do not learn, cannot learn, because they are cultural strangers means that there are barriers that prevent individuals approaching the group and learning. Sometimes these may be deliberate whereas on other occasions they may not even be recognised. For instance, in the case of the lecture cited above, those taken-for-granted elements within the presentation were precisely the reasons why the listeners might not have sought to learn from it, whereas in the instance of the migrant they may be more deliberate.

However, whilst the choice not to consider the potentiality of a learning situation is made, it is clear that the social structures might not appear oppressive and the actors think that they are free to act but do not do so because they are too busy, etc.

Rejection. In contrast to the above discussion, those who do consider the situation and then reject the opportunity to learn from it may experience the structures of society in a different light. For them, the structures may appear firm, immoveable and even oppressive. Hence, the social forces seem too strong and insurmountable, so that they actually reject the opportunity to learn. By doing this, they have no effect upon those structures because they choose to retreat and the overall effect is upon their own self-image because they appear unable to cope with the new situation. Once they have begun to opt out, there may be a spiralling effect downwards, because they no longer feel confident to cope with the social structures within which they are expected to live.

In this type of situation, the structures of society do seem to be oppressive but it is still unnecessary for power to be manifest because the person is apparently choosing to retreat. Hence, it might well be asked whether this is an act of freedom. To some extent the answer to this must be in the affirmative, but whether that apparent freedom is merely a reflection of previous learned knowledge, skills and attitudes is much more debatable. Without pursuing the philosophical question very far, it is possible to claim that the freedom to opt out of a potential learning situation exists in as much as it does not demand the exercise of power to force someone to act against their will. This, then, is an exercise of negative freedom.

However, there were some illustrations cited above where commitment to, or merely socialisation within, another ideological or cultural pattern was suggested as a reason for non-learning. Such rejection might actually result in reinforcing the position already held since the actors do not see the necessity of that which they reject.

CONCLUSIONS

This chapter has sought to explore issues of non-learning in response to experience in the social situation. In some ways it might appear to be a negative chapter and yet it demonstrates clearly some of the inter-relationships between individuals and their socio-cultural environment, and it also highlights the significance of meaningfulness to the social experience of the actor. These are very important questions because they impinge upon the debate about individual freedom and the freedom to be an agent within the structures of society. It is clear that further reference will have to be made to this discussion in future chapters. Indeed, the next two chapters follow a similar pattern to this one, but they discuss the other types of response to a potential learning situation.

8

Non-reflective Learning Responses to a Potential Learning Situation

Three non-reflective learning responses were itemised in the second chapter of this study; pre-conscious, skills/practice and memorisation. In many ways these are the most common forms of learning that occur in everyday life, and also they are the ones that are most frequently defined socially as learning. Additionally, they are the ones that most people seem to think that initial education instils into its participants, so that 'good' teaching is regarded as being able to get students to reproduce the knowledge/skills, etc. with which they have been prepared. Indeed, analyses such as Bourdieu's and Passeron's (1977) point to the fact that education is viewed as a means of cultural reproduction which, in turn, demands that the forms of learning be dominantly non-reflective. Indeed, they argue that certain forms of teaching are symbolic violence, since they seek to impose upon learners arbitrarily a cultural form which may be foreign to them. Hence, it must be recognised that where imposition occurs there is a power relationship in existence and that this is implict in many forms of education. Indeed, this was the point made earlier, following the suggestion by Yonge (1985), that pedagogy and andragogy reflect different ways by which the learner is accompanied through the learning experience, so that children are less likely to feel on equal status with their adult teachers and so they learn (memorise) what is required of them. However, adults might be expected to learn a skill or memorise a procedure of a regulation, in the same way that children are expected to learn their mathematical tables at school, and so this might be viewed as a form of pedagogy which results in conformity. This is not to deny that reflective learning might also produce conformity, but it is to suggest that non-reflective learning cannot result in innovation. By contrast, adults in other learning situations may feel on a more equal status to their teachers and might, therefore, engage in a more reflective form of learning.

The opening paragraph has tended to focus upon the teaching and learning interaction, rather than learning *per se* and this is because it is a situation within which these forms of learning occur most frequently. However, the ensuing discussion seeks to show that they occur in all types of social situations and, indeed, they occur when the individual is alone as well as in the group. Prior to this, it is necessary to explore briefly the relationship between these forms of learning and some of the other aspects mentioned earlier in this book, such as the meaningfulness of the social situation, the self-concept, etc.

It is shown below that there are some situations when this type of learning occurs when the self is hardly affected at all. For instance, it would be possible to consider a situation where an adult learns a procedure that lasts for only a very short time, e.g. working on an assembly line, and that the learning of this very brief procedure is simple and by rote, so that the self-concept of the learner may not have been changed since it was hardly challenged by the act. This is not to deny the possibility that the self may be changed by working on an assembly line. But it is also possible to envisage some situations where learners master a skill that they never thought possible and, while it is still non-reflective learning, the success that they experience gives them confidence to proceed to greater things. Hence, the self may be affected through this form of learning, and the person may grow and develop as a result of successful learning of this type, but this need not necessarily occur. The point is that the outcome of the learning in relation to the self depends upon the biography of the person until the moment of the learning experience and also upon the social situation of the learner.

It is perhaps significant to note also that the content to be learned may or may not be meaningful to the learner. Now this is an important point, since some of the things that children might be expected to learn in school might be foreign to their experience and consequently quite meaningless to them. As a result, they may experience great difficulty in memorising the knowledge or skill to be learned. It is, consequently, a part of the skill of the school teacher to make such meaningless information into meaningful lessons. By contrast, adults may very easily absorb knowledge which relates quite specifically to something within their experience and may find memorisation of such phenomena easy. The significance of this observation is that it calls into question such memory tests as those which require the memorisation of random numbers, since this is only testing one form of memorisation, that of remembering meaningless events or phenomena. (See Cross, 1981, pp. 163ff. for a discussion about remembering meaningless phenomena in relation to ageing.) However, it might be recalled that in Chapter 4, some of the problems of learning within the meaningless situation were discussed and it was suggested that continual experience of meaninglessness might result in anomie or alienation, phenomena that can occur with children in the school situation as easily as it can with workers on the assembly line.

From the above discussion it might also be seen that many of these forms of learning are more reactive than they are pro-active. Indeed, it is dificult to regard pre-conscious learning as anything other than reactive learning, although the same might not always be the case with skills learning or memorisation. The reactivity of pre-conscious learning is clear in the way that Reischmann (1986) refers to this form of learning as 'learning *en passant*'. Skills learning or memorisation might also be reactive, especially where the situation is, or has become, meaningless to the learner. Indeed, this form of reactivity may also be a reaction to a form of authority. However, there are many instances where skills learning and memorisation are pro-active.

Clearly the debate about the nature of education and training becomes relevant at this point, since it might be claimed that the latter is about non-reflective learning. However, this would be an over-simplification of the reality since it could also be claimed that indoctrination, brainwashing, saturation advertising and a multitude of other techniques also involve non-reflective learning. But it will be necessary to return to some of these points in the ensuing pages.

Before discussing these three forms of learning within the social context, it is perhaps important to note that people do experience the world through all of their senses and not only through the aural and visual, so that all sense experiences constitute data in learning, and some of the learning might involve an unconscious reaction to some of the sense data. Indeed, Brundage and Mackeracher (1980, p. 31) make the point that: 'Adults learn best when novel information is presented through a variety of sensory modes and experiences, with sufficient repetitions and variations of themes to allow distinctions in patterns to emerge.' That adults learn best when information is presented through a variety of sensory modes is significant, especially for pre-conscious learning. But the claim might be just as valid for children's learning as well.

Having made these general introductory points, it is now necessary to place these three forms of learning within the social context, so that this forms the first part of this chapter; thereafter, the relationship between these forms of learning and the social structure is discussed.

NON-REFLECTIVE LEARNING IN THE SOCIAL CONTEXT

It will be recalled that there are four types of social situation and, consequently, this section follows a similar format to the opening section of the last chapter, taking each of the different social situations in turn and discussing the three types of learning within each.

Individual

It was pointed out in the previous chapter that even in the individual situation people are still social constructs, so that learners never escape their social biography. Hence, even when they are totally alone they are influenced by their previous experiences, so that the need to learn that they might experience remains a social construct. Each of these three types of learning is now discussed within the context of the individual learning situation.

Pre-conscious. It has been pointed out on a number of occasions thus far in this book that people learn through all their senses. Hence, people 'soak up' the atmosphere of a situation without necessarily being aware of what they are doing. Even so, their perception of the event is stored and might be recalled at a subsequent time. The memories that are stored need not always be of a cognitive nature, for they might be aesthetic experiences, art forms, etc. so that on subsequent occasions people trying to express the positive or negative feelings that they hold about certain phenomena may find difficulty in articulating their feelings in words since they transform experience into knowledge or attitudes without ever explaining in words why they feel the way that they do. The extent to which this can be defined as learning is clearly open to debate, but it is maintained here that pre-conscious experiences are learning experiences.

There are other ways by which people may learn pre-consciously, since they are all recipients of a variety of social pressures/forces that are emitted from a multitude of cultural sources. While some of those forces may stem from sources of which the learners are conscious, others may stem from sources on the periphery of the consciousness and be received and store in an almost unconscious manner. In this manner they are merely acquiring impressions about which they may reflect at a later time (note the dotted line in Figure 2.2. from memorisation back to experience), but reflection might never occur although the sense impressions might affect subsequent action.

Saturation advertising might well operate in this manner, so that people are frequently exposed to certain brand images, etc. and when at a later time they desire to purchase the product it is almost taken for granted by them that they buy that particular brand as a result of the image they have internalised. That this type of learning occurs automatically as a result of social living cannot be denied, but the deliberate utilisation of it for the purposes of advertising and the sale of merchandise raises profound moral questions. While discussion of such issues is very necessary, it falls beyond the scope of this study. Even so, this topic was discussed in relation to the media (Jarvis, 1985a), when it was argued that all learners ought to be taught to think critically in an information technology society.

It is clear from the types of examples discussed here that the learners usually react to a situation and that it might be meaningful, but need not be so, for them. People might be aware that they are receiving a wide variety of sense impressions, but they are certainly not aware of all that they receive. This process is a natural one in social living and one that cannot be avoided. However, it also becomes clear that it is possible for other people to utilise their knowledge of this process to try to get people to acquire 'knowledge' in a pre-conscious manner. Certainly the knowledge, etc. that is stored, because it is not reflected upon, will tend to reflect that with which they have been presented.

Skills/practice. This form of learning might be either pro-active or reactive. For instance, a person might seek to become a better swimmer and spend long hours in the swimming pool trying to improve physical fitness. Others might be concerned that they do not know the correct social skills for a certain occasion, so that they closely observe other people who are much more poised than they and seek to imitate their behaviour. Imitation is a well-known form of learning, important for children and adults in the acquisition of necessary skills, etc. to live socially, even the skills of language itself (Hilgard, Atkinson and Atkinson, 1979, p. 265). Naturally, further reference will be made to imitation in the next sub-section when informal situations are discussed. It is perhaps as significant to note that some people are unable to get close enough to others to learn to imitate them, and so they appear to be strangers. Cultural and socio-economic class factors might inhibit them from getting close enough to their models to imitate their performance but, by contrast, some people deliberately seek to model their performance upon significant others, often without them being aware of what is happening.

151

Memorisation. Like the previous discussion, this form of learning might occur as a result of either pro-active or reactive behaviour. Learners might seek to memorise a variety of phenomena alone, because they wish to or because they have been instructed to. The latter might occur within the context of children learning vocabulary at home and merely seeking to memorise or adults seeking to learn procedures about their work situation. In neither case need they actually understand fully what they are doing, or even the rationale behind what they are doing (although they may!), but they might be doing it because they have been instructed to do so. By contrast to this, other people may endeavour to memorise the words of a poem because they wish to do so. In this instance they are pro-active and undertaking what they are doing voluntarily. This is a significant factor about self-directed learning, it involves nearly all of the forms of learning, and it might be either pro-active or reactive in the first instance.

Perhaps memorisation occurs most frequently in society simply because people recall the events from their primary experiences of everyday life, which do not appear to demand further critical reflection. Similarly they are exposed to the secondary experiences of the media and they may remember the interpretation of a social event reported on the television, or the interpretation that the newspaper provides. In these latter instances the interpretation becomes the fact of the learner's experience, rather than the fact *per se* and this is stored and recalled to mind at some later stage; but the secondary experiences are treated as if they were primary ones. There is clearly an inherent danger in this process, as was suggested in the previous section of this chapter.

In both of these forms of learning the self-image of the learners might or might not be affected. If the skills/practice or the memorisation resulted in a sense of success, then the learners' self-image would have been enhanced and a sense of development occurred. By contrast, if the learning had occurred as a result of instruction and the learners had not necessarily been interested in the topic, then it might have had little or no effect upon the self-image. Hence, in Figure 2.2 it is possible to trace the learning path in both directions from the point of memorisation.

It is clear from the above discussion that these types of learning reproduce the knowledge, skill, etc. to which the learners have been exposed and it has been implied that even though some of the actual learning occurs alone, it might well occur as a result of the learners being instructed to learn specific information or skills, etc. This is clearly not always the case, since much early socialisation occurs through imitation and children can be seen practising a skill that they have observed, so that in these instances the learning is pro-active and voluntary. Having examined these forms of learning in individual situations, it is necessary to do so within group-type situations.

Informal

Informal social interaction occurs most frequently in society and it will have become evident from the previous section that it is difficult to demarcate the two clearly, simply because what is often noted and learned in an informal situation is practised in an individual one. However, it is necessary to examine non-reflective learning in the context of the informal and so each of the three learning types are discussed below.

Pre-conscious. Once again it must be stressed that since pro-activity is necessarily conscious, pre-conscious learning tends to be reactive. In social interaction with friends, peers or family, it is commonplace to find that people have acquired habits, expressions, etc. from those who are close to them. This occurs without conscious effort, merely because interaction has resulted in the habit, or whatever the learning in question might be, being acquired. Reaction in this way is frequently to situations in which the meaning is taken for granted by those who learn; but in certain instances the interpretation of the situation given by the learners is incorrect, which might have humorous outcomes since their ensuing action relates to their own interpretation of the situation rather than that which is generally accepted as the situation in question. It must be recognised that in most informal situations the meaning is taken for granted, since this is one of the factors that allows informality to occur, so that the possibility of pre-conscious learning occurring is fairly strong.

Skills/practice. The informal situation is often one in which people like to practise new skills, since they feel that they are less likely to meet with ridicule, etc. if the skills that they are acquiring are not perfect. At the same time, it is the type of social situation in which people note the skills of others and determine to imitate them. This is especially true when learners look to trendsetters and seek to imitate their behaviour, be it in the workplace, in fashion or in any other form of social life. Hence, both childhood and adult socialisation is facilitated by informality. In these social situations people can get close enough to others to observe their skills, etc. and to imitate and practise them. Obviously these situations are both meaningful and proactive for the learners. It is much more difficult to think of meaningless situations where people react and learn a skill in informal situations.

Memorisation. In everyday discourse with friends, neighbours, etc. people acquire a great deal of information which they proceed to store in their minds. They may not actually define this as a learning situation, but they learn and remember the contents of many of their informal conversations. These impressions of social reality are learned within the social context and may well affect future behaviour. But because of the informal nature of the interaction much of the information that individuals gain may be memorised uncritically, since the informants are trusted as reliable sources of information. Just as trendsetters may determine a certain fashion, a similar process occurs with opinion leaders, who are respected by learners as reliable sources of information and whose views are memorised and repeated by their followers. Thus the process of socialisation occurs, not totally but frequently, through the informal primary groups and thereafter through other informal situations.

Once again it will have become clear that in these informal situations the knowledge, skill or sense impressions of a social event, etc. that are acquired tend to reflect the social-cultural-temporal milieu in which the learning occurs and in this instance it might do so without the exercise of power or control. Once again, however, recognition must be given to the hegemonic processes that operate within society. At the same time, it is possible to utilise those people who are known to be trendsetters or opinion leaders in order to disseminate practices or information, and in this sense a more overt form of control might be exercised. However, the desire to conform to someone else (Mead's significant other), or to conform to an overall pattern of behaviour (Mead's generalised other), of a social group is sufficient for imitative learning to occur. This discussion approaches the non-formal situation and is referred to again in the next section. Clearly overlap between situations must occur since reality is not so obviously subdivided as is any model seeking to depict it. However, it is beyond the scope of this study to enquire why the majority of human beings do seek to conform in this way, but it does appear to be a major reason for certain forms of learning to occur.

It must also be recognised that the informal groups are often very powerful reference groups, so that when individuals have to make a choice between these and formal groups, often the former prevails; at other times, naturally, it is the latter that is the more powerful. It is important to recognise in social learning that this conflict of reference groups sometimes occurs, which reflects Figure 3.2, in which a variety of sub-cultures are depicted. However, it must be pointed out that there is no indication in the model of the learning processes (Figure 2.2) of this type of conflict. It is perhaps at this point that the meaningfulness of the situation is significant, since individuals may well resolve their conflicts by opting for the familiar, which also indicates why there is a strong tendency to reproduce certain cultural patterns.

Non-formal

It will be recalled that non-formal situations are those which occur in a relatively formalised manner outside of the confines of the bureaucratic framework of the large organisation. However, these are formalised enough to include a hierarchical relationship between the actors. The example used in the last chapter was that of the teacher-practitioner with a student-practitioner. Additionally, the concept of mentor might have been employed. In the previous section it was also suggested that opinion leaders or trendsetters may also operate in the non-formal situation. However, non-formal education is a term also employed in the third world. LaBelle (1982, pp. 162–3), it will be recalled defined this as 'any organised, systematic, educational activity carried on outside the framework of the formal system to provide selected types of learning to particular sub-groups of the population, adults as well as children'. Hence it is employed in this book to relate to formalised but non-bureaucratic environments in which learning might occur.

However, the formalised nature of this provision does mean that learners do not always consider themselves to be on an equal status with the person(s) who facilitate their learning, so that the power/authority dimension must be taken into consideration in any analysis of learning in this context. If power is considered to be too strong a concept, then the idea of status differential might be a useful one. Indeed, the opinion leaders or trendsetters might actually be the mentors or the teacher-practitioners discussed here. It is now necessary to discuss these three types of learning within this type of social situation.

Pre-conscious. One of the factors that Jarvis and Gibson (1985) concentrated on in their discussion of the teacher-practitioner's role was that of ensuring that the relationship between the teacher-practitioner and the learner-practitioner was warm, friendly and trusting, so that conditions were conducive for the learner-practitioner to gain the most effective learning from the situation. The reason for this was simply because the conditions established were such that the pre-conscious learning experiences of the learner-practitioner might give the learner confidence to explore facets of the work environment in a much more critical and reflective manner. Naturally the opposite can occur if the situation is authoritarian and formal. It has been maintained throughout this study that several types of learning may occur simultaneously and this is one of the occasions when it is most likely to occur. Another pre-conscious form of learning that might occur in this type of teaching and learning interaction is role-modelling. Many students do not think that they model their role on the performance of their teachers, but role-modelling certainly occurs and, on occasions, it is pre-conscious. Thus it may be seen that usually this is a reactive form of learning, but it also usually occurs in meaningful situations.

Skills/practice. Learners may well seek to copy the performance of an expert in their work situation, especially if that expert is assigned to help them acquire a specific skill. Without a great deal of thought, the learners may acquire the sequence of a skills performance and practise it until it is efficient. The expert may actually demonstrate to the learners 'the way in which it is done' and, thereafter, the learners practise it until the performance approximates to that of the expert. Demonstration is a common teaching method with teacher-practitioners and experts, since they sometimes regard it as their task to do no more than to transmit to the learners the way that they themselves perform a procedure. This form of skills/practise may be either reactive or pro-active on the part of the learners. It is pro-active if the learners actively seek out the expert and then endeavour to perform the technique in the way that it is taught, reactive when they are instructed by managers or the teacher-practitioners themselves to follow the demonstration. Naturally, this occurs in a meaningful situation with adults, although it is possible to conceive of situations where the skill that the learners are expected to master is meaningless to them. This might occur when children are seeking to master a complicated piece of music on the piano when they do not really understand the music or its structure. Such meaningless performances do not appear to be conducive to furthering a desire to learn this particular skill or technique.

Memorisation. The argument in this section is very similar to the previous one, since the process of memorisation is similar in nature to that of skills learning, only in this instance the learners acquire knowledge rather than skills. Clearly the learning of procedures or certain forms of information without reference to situations or to the theory underlying the procedure, etc. is of this type. Opinion leaders certainly provide information in a non-formal setting that is memorised; such information may be about the work performance but it may also be about a variety of non-work situations. Considerable research suggests that opinion leaders are better read and more informed than are the majority of their colleagues. Hence, they are referred to for advice, guidance, information, etc. However, it is more likely that memorisation is expected of learners in the formal rather than the non-formal situation. Even so, when it occurs it might be in either a meaningful or meaningless situation, but usually when the latter happens it does so in a reactive rather than pro-active situation.

Once again it is clear that these types of learning are reproductive rather than innovative in any way. The learners are the recipients of the cultural form and reproduce it at a later time. Clearly both demonstration and instruction are methods utilised by mentors or teacher-practitioners in the process of helping the learning to take place, but there appears to exist an expectation that the learners will not produce anything other than that which they have been taught. This is not a particularly surprising conclusion, since mentors and teacher-practitioners are not always given the opportunity to consider the educational implications of their role, and often they may not be professionally prepared for it. This point will also occur in the final sub-section of this part of the chapter.

Formal

The final section of this part of the chapter analyses these three forms of learning in the context of the formal situation or organisation. The most common teaching and learning environment of this type is the school, college or university, although many teachers from these educational institutions would deny that this was the dominant form of learning expected from the students. However, there are other formal situations that are also significant here, and these are any formal organisation where work or any other activities are conducted, so that all the references here will not only be to the school.

Pre-conscious. This type of learning has been described throughout this chapter as 'soaking up the atmosphere', since this appears to be a very common form of pre-conscious learning. This is also the type of learning that occurs as a result of the hidden curriculum in most educational institutions; it is the atmosphere of bureaucratic control that is often learned and which occasionally functions to inhibit people from wishing to return to education once they have left the compulsory sector. Indeed, it is the type of learning that pupils and students acquire when they are in the very authoritarian teaching and learning situation, which might inhibit any other form of learning than memorisation of the 'correct' answers, etc. Hence, many adult educators, recognising this problem, have emphasised the need to create the type of atmosphere which, when entered, leaves a positive feeling in the minds of the learners. Lovell (1980, p. 35) notes that this is a form of classical conditioning.

This is the same type of situation that occurs in the workplace, where workers might learn that their views are not very important to management, so that they cease to express ideas that might actually be useful to the future of the company. This type of authoritarian approach is contained in the philosophy that 'the management must manage' and workers soon realise, at first pre-consciously, and then usually very consciously, that acquiesence is what is expected of them.

This form of pre-conscious learning occurs when new workers, new recruits to an occupation or profession and new students to a school or college are socialised into the ethos of the organisation concerned. The new arrivals acquire the 'culture' of the organisation and rapidly learn that they are part of it. Almost without conscious thought they find themselves identifying with it and becoming part of it. Ultimately, it produces a conscious awareness of a new identity, an occupational identity. It produces a conformist mode, so that the recruits 'learn the way that it is done' in the organisation concerned.

Naturally a great deal of this form of learning must be of a reactive nature since the organisation is there before the learners experience it, and its structures frequently appear to be irremovable barriers, so that all that the learners do is to acquire the ethos of the inert environment. Since much of this learning is pre-conscious, it usually means that there is no specific meaning placed on those elements which are learned, since most meaningful learning is conscious learning. Nevertheless, where the situation is taken-for-granted meaningful, it is quite possible to learn in a pre-conscious fashion.

Skills/practice. There are always social skills to be learned to play a part in the organisation and it provides plenty of opportunity to practise those skills. New recruits learn to follow the same social conventions as do others in the organisation, and socialisation is a function of this learning process.

However, there are many other forms of skills learning within the formal organisation. For instance, in industrial training the instructor might demonstrate how a procedure is carried out, and the learners are expected to master that skill or procedure through constant repetition and practice. In these instances, the learners might be either proactive or reactive. For example, a learner may wish to acquire a certain skill and seek out the expert who can provide assistance. By contrast, a manager might consider that the skills necessary to perform an operation effectively were lacking in a certain operative and consequently place that person with an expert so that the expert's skills might be viewed by the worker. Indeed, this is the classical model of apprenticeship — where the young apprentice is given the opportunity to see the master at work and then is expected to react to the skills seen and to practise them until they are acceptable to the expert.

Situations in which this form of learning can occur are meaningful to a varying extent. It is certainly possible to envisage situations where the situation is very meaningful and the learners either pro-act or react to them. However, it is also possible to think of situations where the worker is expected to acquire certain skills, but which might appear meaningless at the time of learning, such as placing a manual worker in a formal learning situation to learn some of the theory underlying the skills performance of the job. Clearly, in situations of this type there is at least an element of coercion experienced by the worker.

Memorisation. Many of the arguments presented in the above section are also relevant to this one. Information must be digested and represented in certain examinations, even though it may not necessarily be understood. Mathematical tables and vocabularies are often learned by rote. Significantly, it can be argued that these examples are ones in which this is the best way of acquiring them, since mathematical tables do not change and few people are likely to have such a profound effect upon a language, etc. Indeed, it might be possible to argue that certain empirical facts are best learned in this way, irrespective of the age, sex, class, etc. of the learner. However, there are other forms of knowledge and other ways of experiencing the world, and perhaps it would be more questionable if these were learned in the same way. Indeed, it is actually debatable whether empirical facts should be learned this way either, especially if the facts are meaningless to the learner. Of what value is learning a mathematical table if it is meaningless to the student? The same question might be asked about learning a vocabulary, or a procedure in an organisation. However, when the learners are under authority, this might be expected of them. Yet it might be necessary to learn about certain drug dosages, if the learner is a student doctor or a nurse, etc. In these meaningful situations, learners might be pro-active or reactive, discovering in practice that they do not know certain facts that they should know.

The outcome of such memorisation within the formal situation is that the learners acquire the necessary skill or knowledge, or both, in order to conform to the smooth running of the organisation and the retention of the *status quo*. They learn to fit into the smooth operation of the bureaucracy and not to disrupt its operation. Indeed, Figure 1.2 (the model of the individual receiving the social forces from objectified culture) is a fairly good reflection of the individual within an 'ideal' bureaucratic organisation. In this situation the person is expected to embody the culture of the organisation. The self is expected to become a mirror of the wider world in which the person lives and knowledge a mere rehearsal of what already exists. This is the picture of Merton's (1968, p. 194) conformist, following all the means and accepting all the goals that are prescribed within the social organisation.

Clearly this happens sometimes, maybe often, but it does not always occur. If the learners do not have the cultural capital, then they will neither consider nor reject the learning opportunity and if they have been educated to treat information differently they will approach their learning differently. This latter aspect will be discussed in the next chapter. However, much of what has been presented in this chapter relates closely to a functionalist model of learning and it also relates to behaviourism. It contains a conception of the person, one that many have found unacceptable. It was Wrong (1976), whose classical paper 'The Over-Socialised Conception of Man in Modern Sociology', who highlighted a great number of the theoretical weaknesses of this position. However, it has been argued throughout this book that this is not the only approach to understanding the person, or actually to understanding learning, so that the next chapter focuses upon this. Prior to this, however, it is necessary to locate this discussion within a wider context.

NON-REFLECTIVE LEARNING AND THE SOCIAL STRUCTURE

The first section of this chapter has sought to locate the three types of non-reflective learning within a social context; it has sought to show how these types of learning can occur; whether or not the actors are fully conscious of the situation; whether or not they are in meaningful situations and irrespective of whether they have been pro-active or reactive. The major conclusion that can be drawn is that these forms of learning do reproduce the culture and social structures that exist already and that they can in no way be seen to be innovative. Indeed, one thing that has been apparent in many of the situations described has been the fact that the learners are often under authority and this might not encourage any form of learning other than the non-reflective. This is true whether the learners are children or adults, and it is in accord with the case argued by Yonge (1985), when he concentrated upon the manner in which the learners are accompanied through the learning process. It need not be a matter of accompaniment, it is merely a matter of how the learners perceive their social situation. For them, the social structures are immoveable; indeed, they may not have even considered the possibility that there can be, or need be, any change. Hence, in this instance, learning is merely reproduction.

If the above is so, then it does call into question Knowles's formulation of andragogy. Adults under authority may be mature human beings but this does not mean that they are always, or have always to be, self-directing. Indeed, they can be pro-active and still seek to do no other than reproduce what they have been taught. Occasionally, adults may not have a reservoir of experience which they can use in learning, so that they may not have the self-confidence to do other than reproduce what they have been taught. It would be possible to examine all of Knowles's points in a similar fashion, although it is not considered necessary to do so here. The significance of this analysis, however, is to show that there are certain types of social situation that produce the type of teaching and learning which Knowles would regard as pedagogic, even though the learners could as easily be adults as children. Knowles's analysis depends upon the fact that there is an egalitarian relationship between teacher and taught, which is fundamentally an ideological position rather than an educational one. The ideology, however, is covert. He assumes that there is no power/authority/status in the teaching and learning relationship which might be unrealistic. Hence it would be unwise to consider the andragogical approach, as defined by Knowles, to be the only approach to the education of adults. Clearly Knowles (1980, p. 43) has acknowledged that there are occasions when the andragogical method is applicable to children, but he has continued to treat andragogy as if it is predominantly an adult method of teaching and learning, rather than one that can occur under a variety of appropriate social conditions, whoever the learners.

Some current research (see Marsick, 1987, forthcoming) shows that some bureaucratic and hierarchical industrial and commercial organisations are beginning to adapt their in-service continuing education in a less authoritarian manner, but this has by no means been universally adopted and many companies are still treating their continuing education in the traditonal manner which, it must also be emphasised, is also ideological! However, even when there have been attempts by these organisations to adapt their approach, they have not always been successful, for a variety of reasons such as management not really wanting to release the reins of power, or the workers not really trusting the situation, etc.

Reproduction of the situation is quite crucial to understanding these types of learning and it must be emphasised that there are situations when this is what both learner and teacher seek. For instance, if there is empirical knowledge to be learned, then there might be a place for just learning it and not necessarily seeking to understand it. This is especially true of skills learning as well as empirical knowledge. However, this form of learning may be self-directed or other directed, pro-active or reactive and meaningful. Hence, it is not necessarily always an inappropriate approach to learning, although it might be appropriate less frequently than some people in authority would wish. It is important to emphasise this because a considerable amount of the ensuing discussion is going to focus upon the element of power/authority/status and by no means all non-reflective learning occurs in such situations. Indeed, it must be emphasised that pre-conscious learning is reproductive by its very nature, without the need to make reference to the dimension of authority at all. At the same time this does not rule out the issue of hegemony, that the information that the learners learn, whether pro-actively or reactively, is controlled by the in-built biases in the culture in favour of the current social system. Hegemony was discussed quite fully in the last chapter, so that it is unnecessary to pursue it here. Suffice to note that if non-reflective learning does occur within such social situations, then there is no need to exercise power overtly since the learners are going to acquire and internalise these biases. This can obviously lead to false class consciousness in the manner highlighted by Freire, so that people have to undergo a process of conscientisation in order for them to recognise that their learning has resulted in their constructing their life world through the experiences and from the perspectives of others in perhaps more privileged positions than they themselves occupy in the social hierarchy. Having made this point, the remainder of this chapter will focus upon the dimension of power as it relates to the other two types of non-reflective learning.

The dimension of authority/power/status lies close to the heart of some of the previous discussion in this chapter, so that it is necessary to expand this dimension here. Most authoritarian situations demand conformity from the participants and Milgram (1965) discovered that one of the main factors behind obedience is a denial of personal responsibility and a transfer of that authority to an authority figure. People participated in experiments in which they thought that they were administering electric shocks to a person in an electric chair in order to make the person learn, because they were told to do so, even though the shock might have been sufficient to kill the person. (The subject in the chair was an actor but none of the research subjects knew that he was playing a role as the recipient of the electric shocks that they were administering!) The first person to refuse to participate in the experiment was a person of equal status to Milgram, i.e. a university professor. People under authority tend to conform to the authoritarian figure, so that learning is reproductive rather than critical.

Learning in an authoritarian type of situation must necessarily produce conformity, so that the educators are either people in power or representatives of those who exercise power. This may be a conscious or an unconscious aspect of the teachers' awareness of their own role. It is this point that Marxist analysts of initial education make most clearly. Bowles and Gintis (1976, p. 103) summarise their position thus:

> We shall argue that beneath the facade of meritocracy lies the reality of an educational system geared towards the reproduction of economic relations only partially explicable in terms of technical requirements and efficiency standards. Thus we shall first suggest educational tracking based upon competitive grading and objective test scores is only tangentially related to social efficiency. Thus we shall confront the technological meritocratic ideology head on by showing that the association between the length of education and economic success cannot be accounted for in terms of the cognitive achievements of students. Thus the yardstick of the educational meritocracy — test scores — contribute surprisingly little

to individual economic success. The educational meritocracy is largely symbolic.

The educational institution, like other social ones, functions to reproduce the social conditions of power, so that during the process people learn their place in society. They learn to reproduce the type of knowledge, etc. that the social elite approve, which is Freire's 'banking concept of education', and there is little reward for any form of innovation. Indeed, no power elite could tolerate an educational system that calls into question the types of society, etc. in which they exercise power. Hence, it is hardly surprising that there is emphasis in some initial education, and also in learning in the workplace, upon non-reflective learning that produces conformity. Consequently, teachers may exercise authority because of their position within the hierarchy rather than because of their expertise, which is a totally different form of authority.

This authority might be exercised by the use of teaching methods which are largely didactic and which test for excellence by correct memorisation. Instruction, demonstration, lecturing, etc. are all types of teaching methods through which teachers can exercise the type of power that expects reproduction of the requisite knowledge or skill, irrespective of whether it is fully understood. Thus it might be asked whether such techniques as indoctrination and brainwashing fit into this schema. Clearly there have been numerous debates about the extent to which educational institutions, such as schools, actually indoctrinate their pupils (see Hollins, 1964; Snook, 1972, *inter alia*). Indeed, many of the same arguments could be raised from many types of secondary experience, such as that of the media. It is not without reason that many of the most successful capitalist entrepreneurs seek to control newspapers and commercial television; nor that governments generally, even in the more democratic countries, also seek to exercise authority over the media. It is perhaps beyond the scope of this study to pursue this track any further here. Learning techniques, such as imitation and role-modelling, are also approaches to learning that tend to be reproductive and non-reflective. But the point that must be made is that non-reflective learning might actually be encouraged in certain authoritarian situations and forms of education, whether the learners be children or adults. In the latter case, the adults might actually be those who are at the lower end of the social hierarchy, since those higher up the social ladder might be expected to think more critically and even encouraged to innovate.

The above discussion may also reflect some of the debate that has been conducted in educational circles about education and training; the former has been regarded as learning knowledge and perhaps learning it in a critical manner, whereas the latter involves learning skills, procedures or formulae in an uncritical manner. The debate about education and training is a large one, lying slightly beyond the scope of this study, although it is perhaps illuminating to try to discover precisely what type of learning is required in the more formal structures: it might be argued that they are often similar in so-called educational and training situations. Such a conclusion would make much of the debate about the apparent differences seem sterile. Indeed, in many ways this might be the case. However, if education were about reflective learning and training about non-reflective, then the debate may be much more significant.

However, not all people are conformists, some might have the confidence to disagree openly with those in authority, but this might well relate to the self-confidence of the people concerned. Those whose self-image has become such that they accept authority and obey it automatically may not think to question the ideas, knowledge, skill, etc. that those in authority expect them to learn. Others, however, may have the self-confidence to do so, and this will no doubt depend upon the type of socialisation process that they have undergone; it might also relate to the fact that in other facets of life the persons who have the confidence to question and who do not automatically learn in a non-reflective manner hold positions of responsibility, so that they are used to thinking about things before making decisions. Socio-economic class is not the only variable in this: learners might bring different ideologies and belief systems to learning situations which clash with the information with which they are presented and this clash might lay the foundations for reflective thought. However, this leads the discussion into the final three forms of learning and this constitutes the focus of the next chapter.

CONCLUSIONS

This chapter has considered three forms of non-reflective learning. It has demonstrated that they are fundamentally reproductive in their mechanism, reproducing the knowledge, skill and attitude and also the social and cultural system.

It was also noted that this form of learning is on occasions important, since it might be necessary to learn empirical knowledge, and it might be as necessary during the process of language-learning to undertake the rote learning of vocabularies, etc. Indeed, but is also important for learners to find their place within the larger organisation, so that it is sometimes necessary to learn new information in a non-reflective manner initially. While this might be pro-active because the learners wanted to succeed in their task, there are other situations when non-reflective learning occurs as a reaction to power/authority/status within the social context. In these situations the learners might not feel free to question, so that rote learning is taken as the norm.

Finally, it has to be recalled that there are other forms of learning and that in some situations people might decide not to learn or in others to question and debate the issue. It is this third type of learning that constitutes the focus of the next chapter.

9

Reflective Learning Responses to a Potential Learning Situation

In Chapter 5 it was suggested that even in the processes of reflective learning a strong possibility exists that the outcome might be of a conformist nature since learners bring to every new situation their own biographies, which are social constructs. Hence, even the way in which individuals define a situation and the manner in which they think about it thereafter relates to aspects of their previous experience. As social beings, individuals are constrained by the very processes that have made them what they are. Consequently, the outcome of many, but not all, reflective learning experiences might be predictable. This is not a simple behaviourist type of solution, rather it recognises the reality that people live within a patterned society and that the nature of their own learning must necessarily reflect something of their previous experiences, even their mental experiences and cognitive processes. This is in accord with Argyris's (1982, p. 88) single loop learning, which he claims functions within the constraints of the theory-in-use. However, this does not deny the possibility that innovative responses to a potential learning situation can occur, although it recognises that these might be less frequent than some educators might hope, because the plurality of interpretations of various phenomena suggests the possibility of new interpretations occurring and consequently new knowledge emerging. Hence, it is recognised from the outset of this chapter that there are at least two types of possible outcome to any reflective learning process: conformity and innovation. The use of these terms is similar to Botkin *et al.* (1979), who employ maintenance and innovation and to whom reference has already been made in Chapter 2. Throughout this chapter, conformity refers to those reflective learning processes that result in an outcome that does not greatly disturb the *status quo* within the social group or even the life world of the individual, whereas innovation is any learning process, the outcome of which is orientated towards changing some aspect of the situation or the life world of the individual. This does not mean that the conformist process is exactly the same as the processes discussed in the previous chapter, namely skills/practice and memorisation, but it does mean that new solutions are still reached from within a traditional framework, so that the fundamental structures of the life world or even of society are not disturbed. In this way it is similar to Argyris's single loop learning, while innovation is actually a new way of looking at things and is similar to Argyris's double loop learning. It is also recognised that at least two other possibilities exist: cognitive innovation but behavioural conformity and cognitive conformity but behavioural innovation; the former is probably more common than the latter.

Cognitive innovation is clearly the same process as Mezirow's (1977, p. 159) perspective transformation: 'a development process of movement through the adult years towards meaning perspectives that are progressively more inclusive, discriminating and integrative of experience.' Clearly he is correct about this being a process of development but he might more accurately have regarded it as a lifelong process. He (1981, p. 7) actually described the process as one having the following ten stages (1) a disorientating dilemma; (2) self-examination; (3) a critical assessment of personally internalised role assumptions and a sense of alienation from traditional social expectations;(4) relating one's discontent to similar experiences of others or to public issues — recognising that one's problem is shared and not exclusively a private matter; (5) exploring options for new ways of acting; (6) building competence and self-confidence in new roles; (7) planning a course of action; (8) acquiring knowledge and skills for implementing one's plans; (9) provisional efforts to try new roles and to assess feedback; and (10) a reintegration into society on the basis of conditions dictated by the new perspective. Mezirow recognises that the paths of change can be sudden or gradual and this is clearly in accord with some of the points made about reflection in Chapter 5 of this book. However, a number of the above points are not in total accord with this study, since it is clear that learning, even cognitive innovation, can occur in individual situations and so his fourth point is not accepted here, nor is his final one, since he is suggesting that individuals are free to dictate the conditions of their actions, whereas people's actions will be partially dependent upon their social situation.

Even so, it might well be asked whether there is any relationship between these types of outcome and the levels of reflectivity that he (1981) suggests. He certainly considers his three higher stages of reflectivity, those he classifies as critical reflectivity, as quite crucial to perspective transformation. Cognitive innovation might only occur through the exercise of critical reflectivity, but it is by no means the necessary outcome of such a process since people can be critically reflective and yet produce cognitive conformity.

There are once again three main routes through the reflective learning process; these are contemplation, reflective practice and experimental learning. It is important to note that the term 'reflective learning' is not used here to refer to a learning style, but to three distinct types of learning. These three types were briefly discussed in Chapter 2, but before they are examined within their social context it is necessary to explore their relation to the dimensions of pro-activity-reactivity and to meaningfulness-meaninglessness.

It certainly appears that reflective learning can occur both pro-actively and reactively; the former can happen when people seek to be creative in any way and the latter when they react to a problem. Reactive reflective thought can also occur when people respond to authority or to a suggestion to think about something, etc. but also to the experiences which have raised questions in the mind. The point about the disjuncture between biography and current experience is that an outside authority can both create it and recognise it, so that it is then possible for them to help learners engage in reflective thought, especially when the external authority is perceived to be benevolent. Frequently the situations in which these forms of learning occur are meaningful at the outset, although they are ones in which necessarily there is disjuncture between biography and experience. On occasions, it is possible for them to be meaningless at the outset, and then for the meaningless itself to constitute the problem that has to be solved by providing meaning to the situation. However, it must also be borne in mind here that meaningless situations may create a non-learning response, as was noted in Chapter 7, so that the question of motivation is also an important one in understanding why some people respond differently to situations which they define in similar ways. Examples of these will occur in the ensuing discussion.

It will also be noticed in the discussion of the different forms of learning in Chapter 2 that it was assumed that these three types of learning result in personal change, usually growth and development, since not only has the potentiality of acquiring new knowledge and skill been experienced, but also the very process of engaging in thought and reaffirming the position held or learning a new one is a fundamental mechanism of human growth. It is at this point that learning and living converge. All life means growth, claimed Dewey (1916, pp. 19–53), and it is maintained here that most conscious learning results in growth and that when people are able to consider their own situations they are able to influence the direction of that growth. Indeed, of all the types of learning that contribute to growth and development, these three are the most significant, even though the process is not automatic. Once again the structure of this chapter is similar to that of the previous two, in which each form of learning is discussed in relation to the four different types of social situation in the first part of the chapter, and in the second part the relation between these forms of learning and the social structure is discussed, showing that different people at different levels in the social hierarchy might experience these structures, and therefore learning, differently.

REFLECTIVE LEARNING IN THE SOCIAL SITUATION

The four types of social situation once again form the sub-sections within which these three types of learning are discussed. Consequently, the individual constitutes the first part and, thereafter, the informal, non-formal and formal group situations are discussed.

Individual

Individuals may think alone either when they are alone or when they are in a group. In either situation the action is individualistic, it may be pro-active or reactive, even though the process is affected by the social experiences that led to the individuals being what they are. People can rarely escape from their previous experiences, so that they operate in all the learning processes discussed here. Once again the three types of learning are examined in order from the lowest to the highest in the hierarchy produced in the second chapter.

Contemplation. This is the process of learning through pure thought, without any reference to behaviour. The term employed here has certain religious overtones and, indeed, meditation can be included in this form of learning. Hence, it is obvious that belief knowledge, that is knowledge that cannot be verified, can be acquired through this type of learning. Knowledge of this type is certainly one major element in the universe of meaning of most people. However, it is by no means the only form of learning that can occur through this means, since rational knowledge, i.e. that knowledge that can be verified through logic without reference to empirical reality, can also be acquired through contemplation. The philosopher who thinks through certain problems engages in this form of learning. It is also the method of the pure mathematician, who thinks through the problem and seeks to verify the outcome by no other means than the internal logic of the mathematical argument. This is a form of learning that can be self-directed, but it can also be other-directed, since learners can respond to Socratic-type approaches in teaching, but also to questions posed in the normal interaction of everyday life.

Contemplation can occur when a thinker discovers a problem and seeks to solve it through the processes of thought, either as a reaction to a situation, or pro-actively. However, the problem would be regarded by the thinker as a meaningful problem. Since the thought processes might follow the inner logic of the discipline and the processes themselves are bound by the previous experiences of the thinker, it might be unlikely but not impossible, for major paradigm shifts to occur, so that there is a general expectation that the outcome is likely to be a form of maintenance learning. At the same time it must be pointed out that since the structures of social reality do not bind the thinker, especially when there are alternative explanations available, there is the potential for considerable creativity in many areas. Hence, drama and fiction, flights of fantasy, thoughts about the meaning of existence etc. are all possible and do occur in this mode. In other words, people evolve their own personal philosophies by this means. But also the policy-makers, who are not always exposed to the rigours of practice, evolve their policies by this approach, and herein lies some of the potential problems of isolated policy-making.

It might be asked here if this form of pure thought is actually learning and it is maintained here that since these thoughts are initially stimulated by experience in the life-world, and since the end product may be new ideas and new knowledge, it is a form of learning. The point is that the new ideas, philosophies, knowledge, etc. are the end product of the thought process even though there need be neither a behavioural nor a measurable end product. By contrast, it might be claimed that this is surely of the highest forms of learning, since pure knowledge, uncontaminated by the world, is the highest form of knowledge obtainable. This is certainly a position that was adopted by certain religious and Greek thinkers and it has been prevalent in some contemporary thinking, as Young (1971, p. 38) so clearly demonstrated, when he suggested that high status academic curricula contain knowledge that is 'abstract, highly literate, individualistic and unrelated to non-school knowledge'. However, it is maintained here that those forms of knowledge that relate to practice are actually more complete since they combine theory and practice, so that their acquisition constitutes a higher form of learning than does pure contemplation, since people live in the world and without a combination of theory and practice the full human potential is not attained. Mind without body is as incomplete as body without mind.

Reflective practice. The term for this form of learning immediately relates to Schon's (1983) seminal study on professional practice, as Chapter 6 showed. In this Schon points out that the majority of professional practitioners do not merely learn theory in the professional school and go out and put it into practice; this is what he refers to as technical rationality. He claims that this apparently logical approach to the preparation of professionals is wrong because it does not relate to how professionals actually practice. He shows that professional people actually bring their knowledge to the situation that they experience and that they think on their feet, creating both new knowledge and perhaps, even more significantly, new skills in that situation, ones which are unique to the situation. Schon refers to this as 'reflection-in-action' and it is through this process that new skills, techniques, etc. are evolved. Clearly this is a much more meaningful form of skill performance than that discussed in the previous chapter, since it relates skill to knowledge, so that there is no divide between theory and practice. Schon points out that this form of reflection both on practice and in practice prevents over-learning or mindless performance skills. It is obvious from this discussion that the process that Schon refers to here is also relevant to the next section of this chapter. However, the point about this is that the skills performed might be innovative, but they need not necessarily be so because the normal practice might be considered still to be the most acceptable. Such a conclusion would not be surprising since the norm might have been discovered by many practitioners in similar situations. However, there is a danger in assuming that the norm is always applicable and always the best solution, since similarity does not equate to congruence, and people and situations are different and unique.

There is a sense in which this approach to learning tends to be reactive, since it occurs when practitioners are confronted with a situation and then reflect upon it. Some practitioners, however, might merely perceive the situation as being similar to previously encountered ones and immediately act as if it were the same. This is perhaps the point at which to note that Kagan's (1971) research on learning styles and impulsiveness is significant, since the impulsive learner might respond in a taken-for-granted manner to a situation which is similar to but not the same as other situations. (This work is also cited by Knox, 1977, p. 448.) However, it must also be noted that impulsiveness and intuitive thinking are similar to each other but that they are not the same process. Additionally, it might also be true to claim that people with a high degree of self-confidence might be more prone to reflect prior to action than the less confident.

This same type of approach has been used in skills training in what has become known as the discovery method. Smith (in Howe, 1977, p. 199) writes:

> the discovery method is a style of teaching which structures a situation so that the trainee learns by actively finding out the principles and relationships himself. Thus, for example, instead of a trainee being shown a piece of equipment and given a lecture on how it works, the trainee would be given the actual piece of equipment with the parts clearly labelled. Provided the safety considerations are taken into account, the trainee learns the functions of each part and how the equipment works by operating it himself.

Thus it may be seen how certain teaching methods are being used in relation to a clear understanding of how adults learn. This is a topic on which the final chapter of this book focuses.

Experimental learning. The difference between this final form of learning and the one in the previous section is that the final outcome in this instance is new knowledge rather than new skills. However, it is knowledge that has been tried out in practice, so that it can be either empirical or pragmatic. Empirical knowledge is generally regarded as that which is experienced through the senses, while pragmatic knowledge is that which is accepted because it is known to work in reality. Hence, this form of learning results in knowledge that has been verified. It is beyond the scope of this study to enter the philosophical debates about the nature of knowledge, but Scheffler (1965) has discussed this very clearly.

It was pointed out in the previous section that one of the logical outcomes of the reflective practitioner is that new knowledge is produced by the process of thinking about practice, so that the individual thinking about a professional performance, or indeed thinking about the knowledge upon which the action is based, might actually produce new knowledge. However, it must again be recognised that in many situations the thinker is bound by previously learned thought processes, so that both the meaning attributed to the event and the learned outcome of the process might be forms of cognitive conformity rather than innovation.

The term experimental suggests that the learning has been pro-active rather than reactive. In these cases the learners might be problem-solving and trying out solutions in practice. The experience upon which the thinker reflects might have been provided by some agency other than the actor, such as the media, through reading a book, just through observation of social reality, etc. and in these instances the learning processes are certainly reactive.

However, the situation within which the act occurs is usually a meaningful one to the actor, although it is clearly not one which can be taken for granted, a disjuncture between biography and the experience triggers off the thought processes which result in this form of learning, even though this disjuncture might not have been realised in the first instance by the learners themselves. It is suggested that most of these forms of learning result in some form of personal development for the learner, as suggested above.

There are many different ways in which these forms of learning occur and the above examples have been selected in order to illustrate some of the complexities of this process. It is now necessary to undertake the same task for learning within group situations.

Informal

In the informal setting the meaning is usually taken for granted but the learning might be both pro-active in as much as the learners might deliberately seek to discover something by asking a companion a question or reactive because an associate has posed a question or during the interaction certain events occur that could not be taken for granted, so that the actors are forced to think about it.

Contemplation. The very terminology employed here suggests that this form of learning is undertaken alone. However, this does not preclude the possibility that the learners might be with other people but might shut them out from their thought processes. In these instances, the learning might actually be reacting to an experience, to something that has occurred that caused participants to think about it. But such an experience might be meaningful and then it might subsequently lead to the experience constituting a contemplative learning process when the actors are alone. Hence, there is a dotted line that joins memorisation to experience in Figure 2.2, which depicts this possibility.

In certain adult education settings, educators might utilise this type of learning in the first stage of snowballing, where the participants are asked to respond to a problem individually, so that each actor thinks about it. Thereafter, the participants are invited to join together in twos and then in fours and to continue to think about the problem. Other adult techniques, like buzz groups, also use similar informal groups to think about and discuss problems and ideas, etc.

At the same time it has to be recognised that in informal interaction it is quite possible for people to think on their feet and reach new solutions and ideas very rapidly. The self-confidence that comes from being in an informal situation might prove an effective stimulus for such a process.

Reflective practice. In the informal situation people often need to negotiate precisely how they are going to play their roles in the interaction, so that there is a form of experimentation and evaluation in the role play. If the people with whom the learners are interacting seem to approve of the performance, then the skill is memorised, but if the other participants show disapproval then the role performance is changed. Now it should be noticed that in informal situations like this, conformity to the social norms and mores is still quite rigorously enforced, so that many of the outcomes to the learning are still conformist norms. However, this must be understood only from the situation of the group concerned, since if the learners have chosen to share informal relations with a deviant group the learning outcomes are likely to conform to the practices of the deviant group. If the learning outcomes are innovative, then the learners appear to have three choices: to try to change the practices of the group, to do nothing and retain behavioural conformity with cognitive innovative ideas, or to leave the group and seek membership of a group whose practices are more akin to the new skills, procedures etc. that the learners have embraced. Perhaps the first choice is the hardest to operationalise, and if the learners remain in the group then conformity to the group norms is likely to be the outcome, even though the learners are aware of the dissonance between their ideas and the practices of the membership group. In the longer term the learners may be forced to resolve this problem by further learning.

Experimental learning. In any genuine informal dialogue there is always the potentiality of exchanging ideas with people and reflecting upon the exchange, so that new ideas and new knowledge can emerge. In such a dialogue some of these ideas can be tried out and tested, so that the new knowledge can be seen to relate closely to practice.

In informal situations a great deal of learning can occur, often because it is informal and it is not therefore recognised how much happens. However, it has to be recognised that informality occurs most frequently in situations where people come from the same social background and have similar biographies, so that the learning outcomes might well be fairly conformist. Indeed, too many innovative learning outcomes would put the stability of the informal group at risk. At the same time, the informality of the group might also be conducive to innovation because the actors might have sufficient self-confidence to be deviant with friends and acquaintances. Hence, it would be unwise to draw over-simple conclusions about the complex processes of learning, which are related to the process of everyday living.

Non-formal

This social situation is a more formalised group situation, but it is one which remains outside of the bureaucratic organisation. It is the type of situation where learning occurs in the workplace as a result of collaboration or because an expert-student type of relationship has been established. In addition, it is also the type of situation where the educator goes to work with people in the community or in the village in the third world, in which a formalised but non-bureaucratic, and often non-hierarchical, relationship is created. The three types of reflective learning will now be discussed in this type of social context.

Contemplation. This form of learning occurs if the mentor, expert, teacher, etc. encourages the learners to think for themselves. It can come as a result of an open-ended question which cannot be easily answered, since this type of question can create a disjuncture between the learners' biographies and their experience. Indeed, this is often a rationale for Socratic teaching, since the question creates disjuncture and the learners endeavour to resolve the dissonance within their life worlds. If the mentors leave the students with unanswered questions, the learners can then think about their experiences and seek to discover a response for themselves. As long as the relationship is one of trust, etc. rather then an authoritarian one, the learners might be encouraged to discover innovative answers for themselves instead of seeking the type of conformist answer with which they think their mentors will agree. In some ways this approach is similar to that discussed in the previous section.

Reflective skills. In precisely the same way as in the previous section, the mentor, teacher-practitioner, etc. can help learner-practitioners to think about their own professional performance by asking questions about the skill, techniques etc. that they employed. Open-ended Socratic type questions, without answers being provided by the mentor, allow the practitioners to consider their performance for themselves. If the expert also encourages experimentation in practice, then learners might try out new ideas about their skills or techniques and discover those which are the more suitable for them. Indeed, this approach was discussed in the context of the informal group, and it is also relevant here (see Smith, 1977).

Experimental learning. The end-product of this form of learning is knowledge, as opposed to the skills and techniques of the former section, but many of the learning situations are the same. Mentors or teacher-practitioners can stimulate the learners to think about problems that appertain directly to the workplace. Additionally, and perhaps more significantly, learners can be encouraged to think about the workplace when they are away from it, even in the formal educational setting, and generate new knowledge about it as a result of thinking about innovative practice. Hence, pragmatic or empirical knowledge can be derived from thinking about practice. This form of knowledge generation is precisely the opposite from the traditional idea of applying theory to practice. Here, theory is also derived from practice: new theoretical insights are learned as a result of practice.

The possibility of innovative outcomes of the learning must always exist within this context, but the extent to which they occur is less well known since there have been few rigorous attempts to find out how the non-formal teaching and learning situation in the workplace leads to such outcomes. However, this is not the case with non-formal education in the third world, where participatory learning is quite central to many development projects. There are many examples of this reported in the pages of *Convergence* and other journals that concentrate upon development (see Rahman, 1984, *inter alia*).

It was in this type of non-formal situation that Freire evolved his method, which was clearly very effective or else he would never have been imprisoned by the right-wing military regime in Brazil after the 1964 *coup*! The significance of Freire's (1972b) approach is that he sought to make the situation meaningful to the learners by using words and situations that were familiar to them. Since he was seeking to liberate their thought processes, he was obviously not expecting his learners to learn what had been prepared for them in a slavish manner. Indeed, conscientisation is the actual process of becoming aware that the learners are able to step outside of the forces that lead to conformity with the dominant culture and see that they are able to be innovative for themselves. Hence, it is obvious that certain deliberate attempts to enable people to learn and become independent of the teachers' perspectives have been successful in the third world. In a similar manner, educators like Horton (Adams 1975; Clark, 1978) have managed to achieve this in the United States. However, with both of these educators, and others like them, there has been a deliberate attempt to help the learners realise the meaningfulness of learning new ideas and also to free themselves from the conformist outcomes of learning. This has involved them in a deliberate attempt to make the learning situation totally meaningful throughout by involving the learners in the complete process of preparing the learning process. It is perhaps also significant that Horton, like Freire, suffered considerable opposition from the political establishment because of his approach.

Clearly, the majority of situations in which these types of learning arise are meaningful to the learners, although they are not so meaningful as to be taken for granted. Perhaps the meaningfulness of the situation from which the learning and teaching occurred is actually the major reason for the success that Freire has had in Latin America.

Most of the illustrations given here are of reactive learning, where the teacher-practitioner has taken the initiative in the learning situation. However, there are situations where the learners can be pro-active, i.e. when they pose questions to their mentors about the way that they have performed their tasks or about the knowledge upon which their occupations are based. The questions might arise because the learners are not sufficiently confident about their own knowledge, etc. or because they discover a problem during the performance and they initiate a dialogue with their mentor, or with a colleague, in order to learn more about the area that concerns them. However, this form of pro-activity is inhibited when either professional practice or organisational ethos is based upon individual performance and when asking questions is viewed as an indication of ignorance rather than an intelligent response to a situation.

It is now necessary to explore this type of learning within the context of the formal organisation, which is the final sub-section of this part of the chapter.

Formal

Contemporary society may be viewed as organisational, so that most people are forced to function at some time in their lives within a formal organisation; this may have been during schooling but it is also likely to occur in the workplace. Hence illustrations in the earlier chapters have not all been drawn from the formal classroom setting, although it must be remembered that in contemporary society the school is not the only location of an educational setting (see Eurich, 1985). However, people may be learners whether they are in the bureaucratic organisation primarily to learn or whether they are there to work, or even to receive a state service or benefit. However, one of the problems with bureaucratic organisations is that they are prone to inertia and in consequence, their formal procedures appear less likely to change than do those in less formal institutions; whether in fact the appearance reflects the reality is another matter. A significant recent study of bureaucracy notes that bureaucracy is often a carrier of the modern consciousness, but at the same time its own organisation gives the impression of autonomy. Berger *et al.* (1974, p. 59.) write that:

> As a client of bureaucracy he (the individual) is always *passively involved*. In encountering bureaucracy, the individual does not basically do things, rather things are done to him. Therefore the individual's encounter with bureaucracy engenders a greater sense of impotency than is typically the case in his work situation. (Authors' italics)

Berger *et al.* may have been selective in their choice of work situation, since there are those in which the workers experience alienation precisely because they are reactive rather than pro-active to the demands of the job. Nevertheless, it may not be surprising that many people who function within such an organisation seek to solve problems and learn without disturbing the structures that have themselves become taken-for-granted, that is, in Argyris's terminology, they learn through single loop learning. This issue will recur throughout this section, the purpose of which is to explore the three types of reflective learning in relation to the formal organisation, starting with contemplation.

Contemplation. The religious terminology of this type of learning perhaps suggests one of the ways in which this form of learning occurs within the formal group, since in many a church service where there is a formal ritual structure, or liturgy, the congregation are expected to contemplate the mysteries of the universe and of the divine while the service proceeds. Ironically there are many such religious services where there is little or no time for such contemplation to occur! In a similar manner it might be possible to argue that the same type of learning is being encouraged during a formal lecture, or even more likely during a lecture discussion, where the speaker is making suggestions for the audience to think about. Hence, an individual or a group can stop and think about the ideas put forward, knowing that within the context contemplation is the only response that the learners can have to the ideas being suggested. This might, indeed, be the motive of the lecturer. Hence, it must be recognised that the lecture can be used to stimulate thought without seeking to enforce the learners to accept the ideas contained within it. In contrast to this, a formal lecture might be so meaningless to a group of learners that they cease to concentrate upon what is occurring in the classroom and spend time thinking about that, or about another, experience. In this case they may be learning, but not learning what the teacher might wish them to gain.

Another possible way of thinking about this is to envisage a supervisor, or a manager, examining the way that the organisation is functioning and seeking to make it more effective — whatever that should mean. Hence, managers may be observing organisational performance and contemplating how it can be improved.

Thus it may be seen that the contemplative method is primarily a reactive method when employed within the formal organisation. However, it can be used pro-actively when, for example, the managers of a formal organisation are faced with a situation which they define as a problem and then elect to spend time thinking about it and discussing it, etc. Such contemplation may have a practical outcome in terms of policy, but unless the policy is tested in experimentation and practice it still remains belief knowledge. The extent to which policy statements are based upon contemplation and belief knowledge is perhaps more extensive than often supposed. But the fact that such decisions determine certain structures for other people may be indicative of the fact that those who are lower in the hierarchy might feel themselves more constrained by the structures of the organisation than do others higher up its ranks. Quality circles is a method employed within formal organisations which can utilise this type of pro-active learning to think through problems. However, it might be that the quality circle *per se* is best classified as a non-formal or even an informal group.

Others who voice innovative learning outcomes within a bureaucratic organisation might only be prepared to do so if their own reference group is other than that organisation. Hence, professionals, whose reference group is the profession rather than their employing organisation, might actually feel freer to voice learning outcomes to specific problems than do others whose reference group is the employing organisation. Similarly, those who have a broad range of knowledge and who see alternatives to the problems being analysed might actually see other ways of responding to the problem than do those whose previous experiences have been more circumscribed.

Reflective skills. A similar argument to that presented above might be produced about techniques and procedures within a formal organisation. While the learning might be either pro-active or reactive in meaningful situations, it might be the position that the learner holds within the organisation relates to the operationalisation of innovative practical outcomes of learning. By contrast, if people are reacting to authority they may produce new skills, etc. provided that they feel free to express and demonstrate their new reflective skills within the organisation, and to some extent that depends upon the way in which they perceive authority.

However, many procedures and techniques are prescribed by organisational management, so that potential learning situations may not be perceived in this way because the practitioners do not see them as such. Hence, the formal organisation may actually inhibit learning.

Experimental learning. At the risk of being repetitive, few people might have the confidence to experiment within an organisation. It is for this reason that there often needs to be participation in the whole process, as was discussed in the non-formal section above. One of the problems that formal organisations have encountered in seeking to create environments in which there might be innovatory learning has been to create an atmosphere of trust.

Teaching methods, such as the group project, have been devised in schools in an attempt to get groups of young people involved in experimental learning. Obviously there are great advantages to this, but there are also dangers inherent in the situation. Leaders might emerge in the group and impose their views and ideas upon the remainder of the group members, so that only those in the group hierarchy engage in experimental learning.

Perhaps there have been sufficient illustrations in this section to demonstrate some of the major issues in reflective learning and to show that there are both situational as well as biographical problems that have to be overcome if the learning outcome is to be innovative rather than conformist. Having pointed to some of these issues it is now necessary to draw some conclusions about reflective learning and the social structure.

REFLECTIVE LEARNING AND THE SOCIAL STRUCTURE

Having examined the three types of reflective learning within their different social contexts, the aim of this section is to relate that discussion to the wider issues of the social structure in general. Once this has been completed, this chapter will conclude with a brief overview of the last three chapters.

Contemplative learning might be a relatively free form of learning since no behavioural outcome is necessarily demonstrated, so that the social pressures only operate upon and within the thought processes themselves. Hence some of the learning outcomes might be of an innovative nature as the possibilities of fiction, drama and flights of fantasy suggest. Yet there is still a strong possibility of conformist outcomes and this indicates that there is a strong bias in this direction to learning processes. But there is a degree of freedom created by alternative explanations, as Mannheim (1936, p. 10) suggested:

> . . . in contrast to the situation during the Middle Ages . . . a free intelligentsia has arisen. Its chief characteristic is that it is increasingly recruited from constantly varying social strata and life-situations, and that its mode of thought is no longer subject to regulation by a caste-like organization. Due to the absence of a social organization of their own, the intellectuals have allowed those ways of thinking and experiencing to get a hearing which openly competed with one another in the larger world of the other strata.

However, one of the features of modernity is that there are competing explanations of many phenomena freely available for anybody to contemplate, if they so desire. Hence there may be less need for an intelligentsia, as such, although there is always need for a critically aware group of people in any democracy, even though management or government might not immediately appreciate them! Nevertheless, it may be a myth that many people actually do think freely all of the time. That all people could do it some of the time is a reality. Reflective learning can liberate anybody from the constraints of their environment, and even from those of their socialisation process; this has been demonstrated by Freire in the process of conscientisation. The significant thing about this conclusion is that all people may have the opportunity to think and learn in such a manner, but they may not respond to it. It may be necessary that people are taught this skill (Jarvis, 1985a), so that they may interpret their secondary experiences from the media etc. in a much more aware manner. Those who have the cultural capital, i.e. those who are aware of the competing explanations, may be those who respond most frequently, and since they are usually in the middle or higher echelons of the social hierarchy it might mean that they are less frequently inclined to seek to change the existing social structures. Indeed, this reflects the fact that those most likely to embrace the classical liberal ideology are those who are in the higher socio-economic classes in society.

Precisely the same type of argument holds good when there are behavioural outcomes to the learning. Learners might be cognitively innovative as a result of their reflective learning process, but they might consider that the social milieu in which they act is not conducive either to their expressing their new-found knowledge or to their exhibiting their newly acquired skills. Consequently, they might behave in a conformist manner, even though they possess innovative knowledge. The higher up the social hierarchy are the learners, the more likely it is that they might feel free to demonstrate their new knowledge or skills etc. Hence, the manager in an industrial organisation might feel freer to do things differently than would the employees, unless of course that manager had first gained the trust of the employees and then they might also feel free to do the same. Additionally, it is recognised that the only other group of people who are likely to exhibit innovative ideas within an organisation are those who have nothing to lose from their not gaining popularity with those in the higher echelons, i.e. the professionals and those at the bottom of the social hierarchy, the former group because their reference group tends to be their profession and the latter precisely because they have nothing to lose by innovating because they are at the bottom.

In precisely the same way, learners in the formal setting of a classroom might seek to give the teacher the answer that they believe the teacher wants, until such time as they trust the teacher sufficiently to provide an innovative response. This is more likely to occur with adults than with children since they either do not feel that the teacher is at a different level in the social hierarchy or because they are more likely to trust their own judgement. Age is a social barrier to children learning in the same way and so it is hardly surprising that some adult educators have thought that adults learn differently from children, as was instanced in Knowles's (1970) early formulation of andragogy.

Within formal schooling in Western society, the examination system might well inhibit reflective learning and even where it claims to encourage it, innovative thinking may still be inhibited because learners feel that they have to reproduce certain specified knowledge and follow certain pre-specified paths in their thinking, rather than producing totally new ideas. Hence this innovative form of learning might not occur very frequently, since there are social pressures exerted upon teacher and taught to learn only that which relates, for example, to the examination syllabus. Only when there is no examination at the end of the educational course, e.g. in primary school and in liberal adult education, might innovative reflective learning be encouraged to emerge with any regularity. Since very young children are less inhibited by social hierarchy, etc. they may actually feel as free to experiment with their learning as adult learners in a liberal adult education class, even freer since adults have to overcome the problems of their previous experiences. It is significant that some recent innovations in formal examining have attempted to encourage a more innovative approach to learning, although the extent to which they have achieved their desired ends is still open to further evaluation.

It is precisely in the non-formal situation, where the teacher has little or no bureaucratic authority, and especially where the teacher expects novel or different solutions, that innovative learning outcomes might occur. Hence, Freire's theory of praxis. People who have learned new knowledge or new skills should seek to use them to act back on the world, change it and make it a better place in which they might live. However, the concept of better is relative — what might be better for the masses might be worse for the elite, and since the elite exercise power they might try to prevent change. The masses would then experience the social structures, not perhaps as immovable but certainly as powerful social forces. Consequently, Freire, and other educationalists who think like him, recognise that in a less than perfect world learning that is reflective and innovative might also be revolutionary. A similar conclusion might be drawn for truly professional practitioners, who always endeavour to keep abreast with changes in the knowledge and skills base of their profession, but who are employed within a bureaucratic organisation: they might always be seeking to change the procedure and the structures of the organisation in order to facilitate their changing professional knowledge and skills. Bureaucrats, however, may be more prone to prefer standardised responses and dislike procedural change.

Clearly at certain times in history certain societies are better able to cope with such freedom than they are at other times. For instance, it could be claimed that when the social structures, which Mary Douglas refers to as group and grid boundaries (Douglas, 1970), are weak then the social climate is much more conducive to this innovatory approach to learning than it is when the boundaries are strong, since at these times change is more easily accepted by members of society. Hence, it might be true to claim that during the expressive revolution of the 1960s and early 1970s in Western Europe and the United States, there was a greater concern for innovative thinking than there is in the mid-1980s when the group and grid boundaries have been re-established and are strong. Now it might be claimed that it may be more socially acceptable for people who engage in reflective learning to understand the situation but to arrive at conformist solutions.

Thus it may be seen from the above discussion that agents may arise more easily at some times in history than in others. It is also easier for those from the upper echelons of society to learn reflectively and put their innovative ideas into practice. But when agents arise from the lower strata of society they are likely to be resisted by the elite. Coincidentally, those who appear to be successful in getting their new knowledge, etc. accepted within society are frequently co-opted into the elite, so that they cease to be a threat to them.

Why then do some people reflectively learn different things from similar experiences? Clearly this relates to Argyris's idea of espoused theory and theory-in-use, since people bring their own theories and values to every situation and as a result their learning is in some way related to these values. Hence, a non-formal community educator would bring a different set of values to a potential learning experience than might a senior politician and a group of workers might bring different values to a potential learning experience than might the organisation's manager. Consequently, the meaning that they give to any experience might differ considerably and the learning outcome might also be greatly different. While these differences are related here to social and class positions, other variables, such as sex and ethnicity, might be substituted in the discussion with similar results. Indeed, age might also be considered a variable in as much as it is related to different perceptions of reality. However, biography is more significant as a concept because it combines these variables and points to the fact that people construct their own social reality in accord with their own social biography.

It is perhaps significant in the light of the above discussion that independent professional practitioners, who have been prepared to reflect upon practice, might be an ideal group of people to be innovative, since these professionals appear less inhibited by the constraints of their profession or by the pressures of the organisation. Nevertheless, there may be other pressures that prevent their being innovative, such as their own socialisation process and the habitualised actions that follow, the expectations of their clients, and also the bureaucratic procedures that even small organisations are forced to employ within contemporary society.

Thus far in this section the argument has been exploring why people are not always liberated through reflective learning, as if it were good that this form of learning should always happen. However, it has to be recalled that one of the important conclusions from Chapter 7 was that non-learning maintains the stability of the social group. Hence, the opposite might be true: if there were too much innovative learning then the stability of the social group would be put at risk. Indeed, this is clearly the revolutionary potential that is recognised in Freire's approach to non-formal education. Consequently it is possible for education to regain an ideal about freeing the mind, etc., but it might not be socially acceptable if it were to be too successful in achieving such an aim. Clearly this is a conclusion with which Argyris (1982, pp. 159–60) would agree, for he writes:

> First is the misunderstanding that the goal of Model II implies that Model I is somehow bad or ineffective and should be suppressed. On the contrary, Model I is the most appropriate theory in use for routine, programmed activities or emergency situations (such as rescuing survivors) that require prompt, unilateral action. We must not forget that the strategy of all organizations is to decompose double-loop problems into single-loop ones. The major part of everyday life in an organization is related to single-loop learning. Double-loop learning is crucial, however, because it allows us to examine and correct the way we are dealing with any issue and our underlying assumptions about it. Therefore, Model II

may be the appropriate theory-in-use for the nonroutine, non-programmed, difficult issues that cannot be solved unless we reexamine our underlying individual and organizational values and assumptions.

The point about Argyris's distinction is that some people seek to problem solve in their learning and they do so within the accepted framework of the society or social group, and they thus produce conformist-type responses. By contrast other people seek to solve the problem by problematising the situation within which the original problem occurred, so that the outcome of their learning might result in changing the social structures in some way, which is an innovative, even revolutionary approach.

Argyris, then, certainly does not seek for the type of social instability that can come from everybody seeking to be innovative all the time. However, the extent to which such social innovation is regarded as necessary will always depend upon the ideologies and beliefs that any observer, learner, educator, etc. brings to the social situation. In different social situations it is clear that people regard different ideologies and outcomes as more or less appropriate. The extent to which 'society as a whole' adopts a common policy about education and learning must depend to some extent upon the manner in which social attitudes are controlled by the elite through the media and other means.

CONCLUSIONS

It is evident from the discussion in the past three chapters that there may be quite clear relationships between the types of learning that emerge and the social context within which the learning occurs. Hence, it was suggested that where authority is exercised over the learner, however benevolent, there is a greater tendency to produce non-reflective learning, unless that benevolent authority actually encourages innovative reflective learning. Where there is a more egalitarian environment learners might feel freer to reflect upon their experiences, but even then their previous social experiences might only lead to conformist-type responses. Hence, while Knowles (1980, p. 44) is obviously correct when he claims that learners' previous experience is an increasingly rich resource for learning, he is not totally correct, since those previous experiences might actually result in learning being entrapped within them and hindered from innovative reflective learning in new situations. Innovative reflective learning might occur where it is encouraged and when learners do not feel inhibited by the social environment. However, it might also occur in situations that are not conducive to it, but it may not become evident to observers because the learners might choose to act in a conformist manner.

In addition to this, it has also been recognised that there is a relationship between the social structures and the types of learning. It was suggested, for instance, that when the structures of society are weak then there is a greater chance of innovative reflective learning occurring, but when they are strong this is less likely to occur. This is a significant conclusion, since it suggests that social policy about education could change greatly, reflecting the varying strengths of the social boundaries at different times in history.

It was also recognised that non-learning does not disturb the stability of society at all. Indeed, this form of response is crucial to the stability of society and power does not have to be displayed overtly in order to ensure that the structures are not disturbed. By contrast to this, covert power may be manifest in forms of authority, or even more overtly in such situations as indoctrination and brainwashing, in order to encourage non-reflective learning so that the structures of society should not be disturbed. Hence, governments frequently seek control of the media and the school curricula, especially in times when social stability is perceived by those in authority to be at risk. Finally, it was recognised that conditions have to be conducive to reflective learning; in some situations reflective learning might result in conformist outcomes, so that the social structures remain unaffected but there are instances where innovative learning results in those structures being questioned. In these situations there is always a potential for social disruption, as the work of Freire has demonstrated, even though it does not have to be of such a revolutionary nature. Freire worked in third world societies that were unstable because of the vast inequalities of power and material resources, so that especially after a military *coup*, innovative and disruptive ideas could not easily be incorporated into the system. Indeed, the elite of any social system that is monolithic and totalitarian would be forced to suppress any opportunities for such forms of learning, in specific relevant areas of knowledge, if the learning outcomes were perceived to be threatening to the social stability. But in the much more complex social systems of the first world, especially if the society is stable and the elite confident, new ideas might much more easily be incorporated into the social fabric. Nevertheless, it should be recognised that such innovative reflective learning is always potentially a force for change; in other words, reflective learning is always potentially subversive.

If the society were a large organisation and government were management, it would be possible to produce a similar argument to the above, since learning outcomes could have the same effects upon the organisational structures as upon the social structures. Hence, the tremendous need for workers to feel that they can trust them if managers try to get the workers to think innovatively in the workplace, or at least to share their innovative ideas with management.

It has also been recognised throughout these chapters that where there is no teacher, then the perceived need to learn relates to the disjuncture between biography and experience, but that when there are teachers in a teaching and learning situation then the new information that they may present, or experience that they may provide, should create a feeling of disjuncture between biography and experience if they are to facilitate learning, but at the same time they should not create too great a gulf, or else it might create a non-learning response. Nearly every response to a potential learning situation has longer-term effects: where reflective learning occurs there will be growth and development, but where non-learning occurs there might be a tendency to habitualise current practice and thereby inhibit the potentiality for future growth. There are, consequently, a number of inferences that might be drawn for teaching and these constitute the basis of the final chapter.

10

Implications for Educators of Adults

The original aim of the first workshop from which this research emerged was to relate learning theory and teaching techniques; the workshop concluded with a general discussion about the implications for teaching of understanding learning. Hence, it is perhaps not surprising that this book should conclude by reverting to the original idea, not just because it was the start of this process but because one of the most important things that has emerged from this study is the conclusion that learning and teaching must be more closely related if the teaching process is to be more meaningful to the learner.

Throughout this book it has been clear that there are a number of totally different processes whereby knowledge, skill or attitude is acquired through the transformation of experience and each of these is seen as a learning process. However, the question has to be posed at the outset of this chapter as to whether this simplistic use of language, in having only one word for learning, hides the reality of the complexities of the learning processes. This problem is compounded by the fact that other words, like conditioning, are used to refer to types of learning but they are not socially defined, nor generally regarded as referring to learning. In teaching, it has long been recognised that there are a variety of different teaching processes, or methods and techniques, which are totally different in their execution, even if not in their intention. Perhaps this reflects the fact that teaching has been the subject of research in a more natural setting whilst learning has been studied by psychologists within the laboratory. In a similar manner, it might help to relate teaching and learning if the different learning processes were actually recognised to be different processes. It might be claimed that this is merely making the process more difficult for the sake of theoretical precision. Yet it might be more accurate to recognise that there are different processes and that they happen in reality, but because of the way that language is employed they often remain unrecognised. Coincidentally, these different processes partially relate to the different teaching methods. In this book, for instance, a number of different learning processes have been discussed, and for each it has been necessary to add a prefix to the term 'learning' in order to explain precisely to what type of learning reference was being made.

The different types of learning referred to in this book may not exhaust the types that there are, so that the terms employed here are used only in order to demonstrate something of the complexity of the learning process, rather than as a final formulation of a typology of learning. Indeed, it would be quite possible to relate different types of learning to the self-concept in a more complete manner than has been undertaken here and then it would be quite possible to construct a totally different typology of learning.

Once it is recognised that there are different types of learning, it raises questions about the varieties of lists of conditions of, or principles for, adult learning that scholars have produced. For instance, Miller (1964) listed six principles, Darkenwald and Merriam (1982) produced eight and Brundage and Mackeracher (1980) produced a list of thirty-six. Now each of these approaches is clearly helpful to teachers of adults but, since they tend to assume both that learning is a unitary phenomenon and that it occurs within an organised teaching and learning situation, they may not offer so much help in understanding learning itself. It might be true to claim that there is only one basic condition for adult learning, that a disjuncture exists between the present experience and the adults' biographies (present or future and idealised) and their experience. This disjuncture may be self-induced by the experience of daily living, or other-induced, e.g. by a teacher. It must be recognised here that self-induced and other-induced are not the same as pro-active and reactive. Other conditions, such as how the teaching material is produced, depend upon the type of experience that the teacher provides for the learner, but these conditions or principles are basically ones of teaching rather than of learning.

In order to relate teaching to learning a number of significant points have arisen during this discussion, so that the purpose of this chapter is merely to draw together the strands of the previous discussion. It is not the intention to provide some basic tips for teachers of adults, so much as it is to explore in a theoretical manner some of the implications of the foregoing discussion for teaching adults. It has been almost self-evident through many of the chapters of this book that there are specific implications for educators of adults and it is these that are now discussed. For the sake of convenience and clarity the chapter follows the basic structure of the original model of the learning processes (Figure 2.2), so that there are sub-sections on each of the following main themes; the person, experience, reflection, practice/experimentation. Finally, the chapter has a concluding discussion.

THE PERSON

Throughout this study no intrinsic value has been placed upon learning; it has been recognised that the outcome of learning could be beneficial to the learner, but that it can also be inhibiting. Dewey's (1938, p. 25) claim that some education can be miseducative has been used here to refer to learning rather than education, but this is not to deny that education can also be miseducative. However, education is about planned learning (see Jarvis, 1983a, pp. 1–9), and as such, education must be normative, the value being implicit in what is planned, which will tend to reflect the value contained within the planners' own ideologies. This has been recognised earlier in this study, since it was pointed out that adult educators tended to bring a humanistic perspective to their practice and this could be seen in their emphasis upon the self of the learners. However, it was recognised that the person is more than just a self; the learner is body, mind and self. Even so, this does not negate the ideological perspective of those adult educators, only demands that the rationale for such a perspective be broadened. Hence, in this section there are four sub-sections: the body, person-in-society, growth and development and meaning.

The body. little emphasis was placed upon the body in this discussion because it was claimed that while socio-biology might be an important field of study in the future there is not sufficient evidence of its claims at present to build them into a theory of the person. Nevertheless, the significance of the body has to be taken into consideration, both in constructing a theory of the person and also in endeavouring to expound a theory of teaching adults. It is recognised that the learning potential of any human being is to some extent controlled by its physical accuities and even the physical position it is in at the time of learning.

Person-in-society. The position adopted in this book has been to recognise that both mind and self are social constructs, so that it is false to treat the person as if each one is totally individualistic without consideration being given to the social processes that underly the individual. While no denial is made here about individualism, it is claimed that persons are always persons-in-society, so that in seeking to understand both mind and self, the social element has taken a predominant place in the discussion. Each person, therefore, brings to a teaching and learning situation a social past and this has to be recognised by the teacher. Learners cannot just throw off their social past when they enter a formal learning situation, because there is a sense in which they are, in part, that past. Their minds, their thought processes, their language etc. all reflect that past, so that their definition of the teaching and learning situation, and their understanding of the knowledge, skills and attitudes to be learned, are affected by that past. Therefore, learners have to be recognised as people who are not totally responsible for what they are, even though all people do develop their individuality as they mature, and with it a considerable degree of autonomy, depending upon their previous experiences and their social situation.

If such a social background inhibits people from coming to the formal teaching and learning situation, perhaps it becomes necessary to recognise non-formal techniques and to experiment with outreach rather than to bemoan the fact that certain groups of adults do not darken the doors of formal educational organisations. Research into non-participation is one thing, but educational outreach is another response. Consequently, community education programmes become important (see Fletcher and Thompson, 1980, *inter alia*), learning in the workplace also becomes significant (see Chisnall, 1983, *inter alia*) and in the third world there is a variety of non-formal programmes (see Duke, 1985, *inter alia*). In all of these approaches it has been recognised that learning might be more efficacious and meaningful if it is conducted outside of the formal organisation, and it is the task of the educator to make this move rather than await a move from the potential learner. Indeed, it will be argued later in this chapter that it is not only a move of physical location that is important in this respect.

Growth and development. The model of the learning processes in Chapter 2 suggested that learning changes the person and this point has been made on several occasions throughout this book. However, all learning does not automatically result in growth, and some learning experiences result in the curtailment of the potential to grow, so that it has been recognised that people are to a great extent what they have learned. Consequently, the humanistic emphasis of adult education has been a significant one in human development terms, but it is important that all teachers should recognise the fact that people are what they have learned, and this may also relate to their apparent level of intelligence and ability, so that teachers always create environments and provide experiences that facilitate such growth in all people. Moreover, educators would be unwise to regard people as unable, or even stupid, merely because they cannot perform to the educator's standards within the formal educational situation, since in other situations it may be that it is the educators who cannot function as adequately as the apparently stupid learners.

People are more than their selves, but the emphasis upon the self has been beneficial in adult education. Nevertheless, it is necessary to recognise that there are certain limitations to the idea that self-development is the highest end product of learning, as some adult educators have claimed. It will be recalled that the person is more than self, and also that the person does not exist in isolation but only as person-in-society. Hence, it might well be argued that the highest end product of learning is the enhancement of the person-in-society. This calls into question some of the high claims made by Paterson (1979) *inter alia* about liberal adult education. Because of this, it is possible to argue that Dewey's (1916, p. 50) claim that 'education has no end beyond itself' is flawed because it assumes that the development of the person is the highest achievement of education. Such liberal approaches to the person need to be reconceptualised in terms of both individual and social good, recognising the reality of the development of the person. This does not deny the importance of the person, it only seeks to locate the person within society. However, such an argument does not mean that the person is solely the product of society and that education should be utilised for instrumental purposes only. It is important to discover a *via media* between the two, and to achieve educational forms or programmes that are beneficial for both the person and the society.

Meaning. It will be recalled that Luckmann (1967, pp. 41-9) claimed that the birth of the self occurs in the construction of 'objective' and moral universes of meaning which enable people to make sense of their own life world. Luckmann's position was modified slightly in order to highlight the fact that the person consists of mind and body, as well as self. However, the significant element in Luckmann's analysis is the emphasis that he placed upon meaning. This analysis is important because, like Mead's work, it demonstrates that the meaning attributed to the life world actually emerges from that relationship between the person and the society, and that the body of meaning, which is the mind, emerges from the questioning process whereby people seek to understand the world in which they live. In order to construct this universe of meaning it is necessary to undergo a process of questioning.

The fact that there is disjuncture between what is already known and the immediate environment that is being experienced gives rise to this process. It is this that results in the development of the mind and the self. Hence, the significance of the disjuncture and the resulting process of questioning cannot be over-emphasised in the process of teaching and learning. A need to learn is felt if there is disjuncture between biography and experience and this may result in the questioning process beginning that will need to be satisfied before it eventually comes to a halt. Recognising the point which the learners have reached, in some form of diagnosis early in the teaching and learning situation, there is an initial requirement of relevant teaching, and then teachers can help create this disjuncture through a variety of teaching methods, which can be didactic, Socratic or facilitative.

For instance, didactic teaching can be an instrument that generates questions just as efficiently as another form of potential learning experience, so that it would be wrong to rule out the lecture as an adult method of teaching and learning, but it is important that it should be used in order to generate questions and also to provide alternative solutions rather than only to inform and to expect memorisation learning to occur as a result of the presentation.

It is perhaps important to note that if the meaning system of some people is perceived to be threatened by their current experience there is a tendency not to consider the potential learning that might be gained from reflection upon the experience. Hence, prejudice and bigotry prevent learning and educators have to be aware that people holding such attitudes do not necessarily respond to the disjuncture in a positive manner and learn from their experience. More research is necessary to explore why people cannot or will not learn, even when they are in a social situation which is conducive to it.

This section has concentrated upon the nature of the person in relation to the process of teaching and learning and a number of the points made here will be referred to again later in this chapter, since some of them are quite fundamental to an understanding of adult learning in the context of teaching. Having examined the person, it is now necessary to relate this discussion to the person's experience.

EXPERIENCE

It was shown in the fourth chapter that experience is a subjective apprehension and comprehension of a social situation, but it has also been acknowledged throughout this book that adult educators have recognised the value of experience in their teaching (see Knowles, 1980; Usher, 1985, 1986, *inter alia*). Like Knowles, they have employed the term in a similar manner to the way that biography has been used here. It is important to recognise that this is only a terminological difference. As in the previous part of the chapter, there are four sub-sections to this one: biography, the relationship between biography and experience, the provision of experiences, and utilisation of experiences.

Biography. Knowles (1980, p. 44) uses the term experience in two different ways; in the assumptions of pedagogy it is employed as a particular incident in the teaching and learning process, whereas in the assumptions of andragogy he employs it as the accumulation of previous experiences, in the same way as biography is employed here. It is important to note that Knowles is perfectly correct to use the term in these two different ways. However, when he assumes that all past experiences are a rich reservoir for present learning he is perhaps being a little over-optimistic. The learners bring their own biographies to every learning situation and certain previous experiences may prove helpful to the learning process while others hinder it. For instance, the people who switch off the television, or even the mind, rather than hear things that they do not want to hear are being inhibited from learning something new by previous experiences. Sometimes educators of adults have to spend a considerable amount of time trying to break through such blockages in order for adults to learn effectively. Here the work of the educator is similar to that of the therapist, who has to help patients to overcome the problems that beset them. It is perhaps at this point of similarity that some of Roger's (1969) most telling points about teaching and learning can be seen.

At the same time it must be recognised that adults bring a wealth of experience to their learning, so that the teacher who omits to consider this is in danger of both alienating the learner from the teaching and learning situation and also of losing a most valuable learning resource. This means that certain methods, such as the uninterrupted lecture, might not always be the most beneficial way of helping adults learn. Adult educators have for long recognised this, but as other teachers from schools, higher education and industry and commerce, etc. begin to play a role in adult teaching so it is important to recall some of these basic principles. Even so, it is recognised that hearing adults recount previous experiences is not necessarily always a good use of time. However, it is important for educators to diagnose the position, experience and knowledge of students prior to teaching and so techniques that reach out to that biographical experience and seek to understand it become important. It was suggested above that adult educators have to go out of the formal organisation to reach people in certain situations and it is now being suggested that educators have to bridge the cultural divide in order to understand the previous experiences of learners, and learn their learners' language and life world. Goulet's (Freire, 1974, p. viii) analysis of Freire's method is perhaps pertinent here; he analyses it thus:

> participant observation of educators 'tuning in' to the vernacular universe of the people:
> their arduous search for generative words at two levels: syllabic richness and a high charge of experimental involvement;
> a first codification of these words into visual images which stimulate people 'submerged' in the culture of silence to 'emerge' as conscious makers of their own 'culture'
> the decodification by a 'culture circle' under the self-effacing stimulus of a co-ordinator who is no 'teacher' in the conventional sense, but who has become an educator-educatee in dialogue with the educatee-educators too often treated by formal educators as passive recipients of knowledge;
> a creative new codification, this one explicitly critical and aimed at action, wherein those who were formerly illiterate now begin to reject their role as mere 'objects' in nature and social history and undertake to become 'subjects' of their own destiny

Here Freire's approach is well summarised and, while it is recognised that he was working in the third world, this is a typical adult education method of reaching across the cultural boundaries and seeking to understand the ways in which the educator can help the educatee by understanding where the educatee stands. While Freire wrote about the third world, the persons with whom he worked were also persons formed by and affected by their social-cultural-temporal milieu in the same way as are other learners, and so the principle of teaching method is the same, whoever the persons are. But in the process the educators become learners too. They learn about a different social-cultural universe and maybe, as a result, view their own universe in a different manner. However, it is only from knowing about the biography of the learners that the educator can use that wealth of biographical knowledge to enrich learning, and also ensure that the learning experiences that are created are most meaningful to the learners. There is one problem, at least, with the educators trying to cross the bridge of the cultural divide between themselves and the learners; the latter have their own expectations of how the former should play their role and if the educators do not negotiate that role performance with the learners they might actually lose their respect, which in turn would inhibit the learners learning effectively.

Biography and experience. It may be seen from the above that the relation between biography and experience is most important to the processes of teaching and learning. Indeed, it has been claimed consistently throughout this book that meaningfulness in the potential learning situation is crucial to the learning process. However, it has also been claimed that the significance of this relation needs to be fully recognised. Learning begins when there is some disjuncture between biography and experience. Learning is not innate, in the way that instinct is, but the potential to learn exists in all persons, and it is also important for human beings to be in some kind of harmony with their environment. When there is disharmony or discontinuity — both subsumed under the idea of disjuncture — then people have to seek to adjust (learn), so that harmony can be re-established. Often the disjuncture is epitomised by the question, 'why?' Every parent is aware of the questioning process of the child, every adult is aware of the questioning process of their own adolescence — even though it was not articulated as loudly as it was in early childhod. Disjuncture lies at the heart of learning and the closer it is to the person's system of meaning the greater the imperative to respond to it. Hence, the significance of the ideas of meaningfulness and relevance. If situations are not meaningful or relevant then they may not prove to be learning situations.

It is interesting to note that another way of looking at the idea of disharmony between biography and experience is to view it in terms of a potential conflict between the two. Change, however, often results from conflict, so that learning may be viewed as a form of change, or adjustment, in order to respond to a potential conflict.

Adults will respond to disjuncture, often in a pro-active and self-directed manner, if it is relevant and meaningful. Hence, it might be that one of the most significant aspects of teaching adults is first to raise meaningful and relevant questions in their minds, so that they can seek to respond to the disjuncture that has been created. Now this does not give the educator the right to be destructive in the way that these questions are raised. It means that educators help adults in a very humane manner to probe their own experiences a little deeper and with a more critical awareness. Indeed, teaching through questions is a most fundamental way of creating a potential learning situation. Educators have to be aware of the dangers of creating too many questions, since attitudes function to protect the self and if the self is too threatened then learning may be inhibited rather than facilitated. Clearly the environment can also threaten a person, so that educators have to be aware of the effect of an authoritarian situation, even memories of authoritarian situations in educational buildings, etc. in the process of creating a questioning attitude.

Provision of experience. All learning begins with experience, and all people experience the world in a variety of ways at the same time, through different sense organs, etc. Perhaps the studies of the hidden curriculum in school education have highlighted this to some extent (see Jenkins and Shipman, 1976, pp. 17–18, *inter alia*). Since the experiences can be had through such a variety of modes, any teaching method can be used to provide an experience, whether it is didactic, Socratic or facilitative (see Jarvis, 1983b, pp. 120–57), and it does not have to be 'experiential' in the affective educational sense of the word. It is the environment within which the experience is provided that helps determine the type of learning that ensues. For instance, a lecture provided in an authoritarian situation might lead to memorisation, whilst a lecture provided in an egalitarian setting might result in contemplation or in experimental learning. By contrast, an affective approach, like role play, provided in a threatening situation might not result in any learning, whereas if it is provided in an informal atmosphere it might lead to reflective skills learning, etc. Hence, it is not the experience so much as the environment within which it occurs which plays a significant part in the creation of the learning that follows, since it is the meaning that the learning places upon the situation that affects the learning process thereafter.

Utilisation of experience. Usher (1985) highlights some of the advantages, while recognising some of the problems and disadvantages in using adults' own experiences as a base for teaching. He also highlights some of the weaknesses in Kolb's learning cycle. Indeed, Usher clearly summarises much of what would be considered good practice in adult education, although he is writing about learning within the formal situation. However, a great deal of adult education also occurs in relation to the workplace; either the learners are being prepared for their vocation or in continuing education adults are relieved of their work duty for a limited time in order to be updated. The interplay of the workplace and the classroom has often created learning difficulties which have resulted in a division being drawn between theory and practice. The traditional approach has been that theory is learned in the classroom and then it is applied in the workplace. The application of theory to practice approach has been correctly attacked by Schon (1983) as being untrue to practice, but it has also been unhelpful to teaching. Schon has called his attack 'the death of technical rationality', and indeed, this false division is one that has been recognised by adult educators as many of their teaching methods have demonstrated, evolving as they do from workplace situations. However, it is essential for educators of adults to recognise that it would only be the most mindless of individuals who would have attempted to apply theory learned in the classroom unthinkingly to a practical situation. Much professional practice lies at the interface of theory and practice, where the worker brings knowledge and skills, etc. (biography) to the situation and is frequently forced to think and learn in an unique situation. In such instances, new knowledge, skills or attitudes may be created, even though it is often unrecognised as such. However, it is this type of response to unique situations where new knowledge has been generated that adult educators can utilise when learners return to the classroom. Teachers can, through the use of Socratic or facilitative methods, help adults to crystallise that new knowledge and to articulate it so that they recognise the breadth and depth of new knowledge or skill or attitude that they may have generated. This can be undertaken through discussion-type techniques which are designed to help learners to share their unique understanding. This, naturally, means that the educator might also benefit from joining in such discussions as a learner, so that the new knowledge from practice might be incorporated into future teaching and learning situations within the profession, etc.

While the method of teaching adults is clearly important, it is also necessary to note the significance of teaching style, a point Kidd (1973) also observed. Although he did not explore research into this, it is important to note that authoritarian teaching might always produce a non-reflective form of learning. Rogers (1977, p. 101) highlights some of the characteristics in a teacher that might produce the most effective learning.

Educational research has quite unsurprisingly confirmed at least in outline, that this open, relaxed style of teaching is both more effective and preferred by students. It is possible to identify perhaps five or six characteristics which seem particularly important: a warm personality able to show approval and acceptance of students; the social skill to weld a group together; an 'indirect' manner of teaching which allows and generates the use of students' ideas; conscientious efficiency in organizing subject matter and administration; skill in identifying and resolving student difficulties and the sort of enthusiasm which shows itself in animated demeanour; plenty of eye contact and varied voice inflection.

In the above it is important to note that some of the characteristics are personality based but others are skills based. Among both aspects, however, there appears no place for authoritarianism.

This section has endeavoured to draw together some of the points about experience and learning that might be utilised within the teaching and learning situation. it should be noted that there is no condemnation contained here for so-called traditional teaching methods, only a recognition that whatever method is used it should both be appropriate to the situation and to the environment within which it is employed.

REFLECTION

It has been very clear throughout this study that the type of situation in which the teaching and learning occurs may well affect, even determine, the type of learning that follows. Hence, in certain types of situation memorisation occurs. However, it is not really the intention to discuss memorisation here, although it has to be recognised that memorisation within meaningful situations is likely to be more effective than in meaningless ones. The purpose here is to explore briefly the relationship between reflection and teaching. Clearly it is important that teachers encourage learners to reflect upon experiences and, consequently, to recognise that the end product of the reflection may differ from the teacher's own ideas. Teachers of adults should both encourage and expect that there will be differences between their ideas and the outcomes of reflective learning. But, it might be asked, is the teacher never correct? Of course the teacher may be correct, but this depends upon the type of knowledge involved in the teaching and learning situation. If the situation is one which involves empirical fact, then the teacher's experience is usually greater than that of the learners; if the situation is one which involves skilful practice, then the teacher may have a more efficient approach than the learner — but the learners may evolve more efficient techniques for themselves than the teacher's technique; if the situation involves pragmatic knowledge, then the teacher's understanding may be more complete than the learners'. However, merely because the teacher is the expert of the authority does not mean that the teacher should demand uncritical compliance. And, if belief knowledge is involved, then there may be no difference in authority, etc. so that learners should be encouraged to explore ideas for themselves. Hence, there are many situations in which adult learners may be greatly helped by teachers but not agree with them at the end of the teaching and learning process.

In order to explore some of these ideas this section also has five parts; questioning; teaching techniques; innovative thinking; teaching critical thinking; conscientisation.

Questioning. Earlier in this chapter it was pointed out that creating a questioning situation by generating disjuncture between biography and experience leads first to the learners questioning and then seeking to recreate the equilibrium between biography and experience. However, the teacher can also employ the Socratic approach of posing the questions. Such questioning might follow an experience that the teacher had facilitated, or any other experience of the learners. Posing questions is merely a technique for creating disjuncture. But it has to be recognised that if the disjuncture created by the questioning is too great it might not result in reflection but in the closure of the mind, so that the questions must not threaten the learners too much. Hence, the significance of the art of questioning for the educator of adults. Whilst the art of questioning is an important one for the teacher of adults, it is one that is not always incorporated into curricula for the preparation of teachers of adults.

Teaching techniques. However, teachers might wish to encourage reflection through other methods, and there are a number of ways in which this can happen. Techniques such as snowballing (where individuals are first encouraged to think about a problem and then individuals are paired and encouraged to discuss and then put in larger groups of two pairs and the discussion continues), buzz groups, individual thought in times of silence, individual and group projects, etc, all encourage independent thought. Some teachers use group discussion methods in the hope that this will happen. However, it has to be recalled that groups take on lives of their own and group dynamics demonstrate quite clearly that individuals are as affected by group pressures as they are by other social pressures. Hence, some learners in the groups might be encouraged to adopt the attitudes of other members of the group, etc. which is merely a process of memorisation or, at best, conformist reflective thinking (see Asch, 1951; Crutchfield, 1955, *inter alia*).

Innovative thinking. Both Botkin *et al.* (1979) and Argyris (1982) have been concerned about the innovative approach to thought. Argyris recognised that even in his single loop learning, the thought processes were still constrained by the immediate environment, so that the solutions to problems were usually conformist. Double loop learning, where it is not the immediate problem that is examined, but the problematisation of the situation within which the problem occurs, is much harder to achieve. Such techniques as brainstorming have been tried in order to seek to overcome the immediate cultural and group problems. However, the success of such approaches is open to some questioning since the individuals are still operating within a group situation. However, it may be that individuals operating within completely safe environments might be able to produce such learning. Argyris (1982, pp. 165–74) suggests that there are two principles that need to be recognised by learning; that individuals are responsible for actions that create feelings of threat and failure and responsible for their actions but they are not responsible for the theory-in-use that leads to their actions. If they can recognise these points, then they can begin to think innovatively. However, Argyris points to the difficulties and it is significant that he finds similarities between the role of the non-directive counsellor and the teacher of adults, since it is when students feel confusion and frustration that they are beginning to struggle with their meaning system and perhaps break through the barriers which have inhibited innovative thought.

Teaching critical thinking. This is a topic that has concerned adult educators and, in a sense, this is the other side of the coin to the previous paragraph. Because many adults consider learning to be memorisation, they have a great deal of trouble in acquiring the facility of critical thought. Yet once teaching techniques are employed that encourage adults to exchange ideas and to evaluate knowledge in group discussion, the ability to recognise the vulnerability of many viewpoints gradually emerges. From this adult educators can help students to recognise that knowledge is culturally constructed and, therefore, it is open to critical appraisal. In the same way, if adult educators present students with diverse interpretations of the same event, they can recognise the need to evaluate positions. Such techniques as the debate, using visiting speakers who hold different viewpoints, the interview, etc. are all methods that enable learners to see the variety of interpretations of single events that might lead to students gaining an awareness of the relativity and contextuality of a great deal of knowledge and becoming more critically aware as a result.

This has increasingly become recognised as an important element in teaching adults because the information society is constantly providing secondary experience for people, e.g. media interpretations of world events, but frequently the interpretation is presented as if it were the fact and also the recipients of the interpretation treat it as if it were fact.

Conscientisation. This is the process whereby people become aware that the meaning system that they have imposed upon their life world is not the only system and that there are alternative systems of meaning. Having become aware that their original system is not necessarily the only one, or the best one for them, they might rethink their position and then try to act upon the world in order to transform it. This is not necssarily a process of teaching critical thought in quite the way discussed in the paragraph above, it is the recognition that in the education of adults, people's meaning systems might well be subject to self-evaluation and that adult educators should be aware of the responsibility and delicacy of their task. Freire (1972b) clearly regards the acting back upon the world to transform it as the logical outcome of reflective learning and conscientisation, since failure to act is to create a disjuncture between the new meaning system and action. There are many instances where adult educators have to be aware that they are dealing with subjects that do impinge upon the meaning system of the learners, especially in dealing with such topics as racism, sexism, politics, etc. However, if adult educators seek to impose new meaning systems upon the learners with whom they are working, then they are guilty of indoctrination. At the same time, there are occasions, such as in vocational preparation, when certain attitudes are not regarded as acceptable to that form of professional practice, e.g. racism among community nurses, and so there are situations in which learners might have to be confronted with the implications of their own meaning systems. But it is clearly better for teachers of adults if they can help learners to a state of conscientisation without direct confrontation, utilising teaching methods as diverse as debate and role play, etc.

This section has sought to raise some of the issues that surround reflectivity in the teaching and learning environment. However, it is very important that teachers of adults assure adults that it is expected that they will not agree with all that they are presented during the course of teaching and learning sessions, so that they will feel free to be critical and to think innovative ideas and learn new knowledge. What adult educators should not try to do is 'to teach them all that they know' because if they create situations in which adults do think for themselves, then they might be able to claim that 'they have taught them more than they knew'. Certainly things that the teachers did not know!

PRACTICE/EXPERIMENTATION

Little needs to be discussed here, since it has been pointed out throughout this study that adults feel free to experiment if they feel that they are in an egalitarian situation. Only in experimentation will learners gain an understanding of the skills that they utilise and perhaps develop greater proficiency in their reflective skills learning. If they do not feel this, then they may feel inhibited and practice rather than experimentation occurs, so that the context within which the learning occurs affects the type of learning that ensues.

CONCLUSIONS

This chapter has sought to apply some of the ideas about learning to the teaching and learning situation. It is possible to search much of the documented research to illustrate more fully the points that have been raised here, but it was considered wiser to continue with the internal logic of the discussion of the previous chapters and to illustrate the outcome of the position adopted here. Hence, this chapter seeks only to raise some questions and ideas about a theory of teaching adults rather than merely provide evidence about how adults should be taught.

The book itself began with a theory of learning; it has suggested that there are a variety of different types of learning and that adults utilise them all — sometimes some of them occur simultaneously but all of them are utilised by people during their daily living. Indeed, there is nothing unique about the learning processes and since they occur every day they are often taken for granted. Yet they are the same processes that occur in formal teaching and learning and because they are suddenly placed within a formal context they take on a more formalised significance. Hence, the behaviouristic approach to learning, because it was researched under 'scientific' conditions, assumed higher status in teaching theory than perhaps it deserved. But more than this, it actually artificialised the normal, natural processes of learning and, therefore, failed to examine the richness or the completeness of the human learning processes. This book reports on a research project that occurred in a much more naturalistic environment, its conclusions are tentative and its endeavour has been to try to locate learning within the normal context of everyday life as well as in the more formal context of the teaching and learning situation. The book is, therefore, about the way people learn in society.

Ultimately, the person *per se* is a learner throughout life for the person can be no other. People are a result of learning and continue to be what they are because of learning. Whilst learning and living are not the same phenomenon, they are co-terminus and those who help others learn (whether or not they are called teachers) bear some of the responsibility for helping people grow and develop through the complexities of social life, but that is a human responsibility since people are and must be interdependent because they live in societies.

Bibliography

Abercrombie, M.L.J. (1969) *The Anatomy of Judgment*, Harmondsworth, Penguin Books

Adams, F. (with Myles Horton) (1975) *Unearthing Seeds of Fire*, Winston-Salem North Carolina, John Blair Publisher

Alexander, I.W. (1957) *Bergson: Philosopher of Reflection*, London, Bowes and Bowes

Allman, J.F. and Jaffe, D.T. (1977–78) (eds.) *Readings in Adult Psychology: Contemporary Perspectives*, New York, Harper

Allman, P (1984) 'Self Help Learning and its Relevance for Learning and Development in Later Life' in Midwinter (ed.) 1984

Allport, G.W. (1954) *The Nature of Prejudice*, Cambridge, Massachusetts, Addison-Wesley

Argyris, C. (1982) *Reasoning, Learning and Action*, San Francisco, Jossey Bass

Argyris, C. and Schon, D. (1974) *Theory in Practice: Increasing Professional Effectiveness*, San Francisco, Jossey Bass

—— (1978) *Organizational Learning: A Theory of Action Perspective*, San Francisco, Jossey Bass

Arlin, P. (1975) 'Cognitive Development in Adulthood: A Fifth Stage?', *Developmental Psychology*, vol. 11

Asch, S.E. (1955) 'Opinions and Social Pressure', *Scientific American*, vol. 193

Aslanian, C. and Brickell, H. (1980) *Americans in Transition*, New York, College Board

Baltés, P.B. and Schaie, K.W. (eds.) *Lifespan Developmental Psychology*, New York, Academic Press

Barash, D. (1980) *Sociobiology: The Whisperings Within*, London, Souvenir Press

Beard, R. (1976) *Teaching and Learning in Higher Education* (third edition), Harmondsworth, Penguin Books

Belbin, E. and Belbin, R.M. (1972) *Problems in Adult Retraining*; London, Heinemann

Berger, P.L. (1966) *Invitation to Sociology*, Harmondsworth, Penguin

Berger, P.L., Berger, B. and Kellner, H. (1974) *The Homeless Mind*, Harmondsworth, Penguin

Berger, P.L. and Luckmann, T. (1967) *The Social Construction of Reality*, London, Allen Lane

Bergson, H. (1920) *Mind-Energy*, translated by H.W. Carr, London, Macmillan

Bernstein, B. (1971) *Class, Codes and Control*, London, Routledge and Kegan Paul

Beynon, H. (1975) *Working for Ford*, Wakefield, E.P. Publishing

Blonsky, M. (ed.) (1985) *On Signs*, Baltimore, Johns Hopkins University Press

Bloom, B.S. (ed.) (1956) *Taxonomy of Educational Objectives*, London, Longman

Borger, R. and Seaborne, A. (1966) *The Psychology of Learning*, Harmondsworth, Penguin

Bosquet, N. (1972) 'The Prison Factory', *New Left Review*, No. 73

Botkin, J., Elmandjra, M. and Malitza, M. (1979) *No Limits to Learning: Bridging the Human Gap*, London, Pergamon Press

Bottomore, T. and Rubel, M. (eds.) (1963) *Karl Marx: Selected Writings in Sociology and Social Philosophy*, Harmondsworth, Pelican

Boud, D., Keogh, R. and Walker, D. (eds.) (1985) *Reflection: Turning Experience into Learning*, London, Kogan Page

Bourdieu, P. (1973) 'Cultural Reproduction and Social Reproduction', in Brown, R. (ed.) 1973

Bourdieu, P. and Passeron, J.-C. (1977) *Reproduction — in Education, Society and Culture*, London, Sage

Bowles, S. and Gintis, H. (1976) *Schooling in Capitalist America*, London, Routledge and Kegan Paul

Brookfield, S.D. (1986) *Understanding and Facilitating Adult Learning*, San Francisco, Jossey Bass Publishers

Brown, R. (ed.) (1973) *Knowledge, Education and Cultural Change*, London, Tavistock

Brundage, D.H. and Mackeracher, D. (1980) *Adult Learning Principles and their Application to Program Planning*, Ontario, Ministry of Education

Bruner, J. (1977) *The Process of Education*, Harvard University Press

Carroll, J.B. (1969) 'Reflections on Language and Thought' in Voss (ed.) 1969

Carver, V. and Liddilard, P. (eds.) (1978) *An Ageing Population*, London, Hodder and Stoughton in association with the Open University Press

Cashdan, A. and Whitehead, J. (eds.) (1971) *Personality, Growth and Learning*, London, Longmans, published for the Open University

Cattell, J.R. (1963) 'Theory of Fluid and Crystallised Intelligence: A Critical Experiment' in *Journal of Educational Psychology*, vol. 54, no. 1

Child, D. (1981 — 3rd edn) *Psychology and the Teacher*, London, Holt, Rinehart and Winstone

Chisnall, H. (ed.) (1983) *Learning From Work and Community Experience*, Windsor, National Foundation for Educational Research and Nelson Publishing Co.

Clark, M. (1978) 'Meeting the Needs of the Adult Learner: Using Non-Formal Education for Social Action', in *Convergence*, vol. XI, nos 3–4

Coombs, P. and Ahmed, M. (1974) *Attacking Rural Poverty: How Nonformal Education can Help*, Baltimore, Johns Hopkins University Press

Cowgill, D.D. and Holmes, L.D. (1978) 'Ageing and Modernization' in Carver, V. and Liddilard, P. (eds.) 1978

Cross, K.P. (1981) *Adults as Learners*, San Francisco, Jossey Bass

Crutchfield, R.S. (1955) 'Conformity and Character' in *American Psychologist*, vol. 10

Dahlgren, L.-O. (1984) 'Outcomes of Learning, in Marton *et al.* (eds.) 1984

Dale, R. *et al.* (eds.) (1976) *Schooling and Capitalism: A Sociological Reader*, London, Routledge and Kegan Paul in association with the Open University Press

Darkenwald, G.G. and Merriam, S.B. (1982) *Adult Education: Foundations of Practice*, New York, Harper and Row

Dewey, J. (1916) *Democracy and Education*, New York, The Free Press

Dewey, J. (1933) *How We Think*, New York, Heath
—— (1938) *Experience and Education*, New York, Collier Books
Douglas, M. (1970) *Natural Symbols*, London, The Cresset Press
Duke, C. (ed.,) (1985) *Combatting Poverty Through Adult Education: National Development Strategies*, London, Croom Helm
Durkheim, E. (1952) *Suicide: A Study in Sociology*, New York, Free Press
Eco, U. (1985) 'How Culture Conditions the Colours We See' in Blonsky (ed.) 1985
Elias, J. (1979) 'Andragogy Revisited' in *Adult Education*, in vol. 29, pp. 252-6
Entwistle, H. (1979) *Antonio Gramsci: Conservative Schooling for Radical Politics*, London, Routledge and Kegan Paul
Entwistle, N. (1981) *Styles of Learning and Teaching*, Chichester, John Wiley and Sons
Eurich, N. (1985) *Corporate Classrooms: The Learning Business*, New Jersey, The Carnegie Foundation for the Advancement of Teaching
Fisher, R.J. (1982) *Social Psychology: an Applied Approach*, New York, St Martin's Press
Fletcher, C. and Thompson, N. (eds.) (1980) *Issues in Community Education*, Lewes, The Falmer Press
Freire, P. (1972a) *Pedagogy of the Oppressed*, Harmondsworth, Penguin
—— (1972b) *Cultural Action for Freedom*, Harmondsworth, Penguin
—— (1974) *Education: The Practice of Freedom*, London, Writers and Readers
—— (1978) *Pedagogy in Process: The Letters to Guinea Bissau*, London, Writers and Readers
Fromm, E. (1949) *Man For Himself*, London, Routledge and Kegan Paul
—— (1966) *Marx's Concept of Man*, New York, F. Unger
Gagné, R.M. (1977 — 3rd edn) *The Conditions of Learning*, New York, Holt, Rinehart and Winston
Giddens, A. (1979) *Central Problems in Social Theory: Action, Structure and Contradiction in Social Analysis*, London, Macmillan
Gladwin, T. (1973) 'Cultural and Logical Process' in Keddie (ed.) 1973
Goulet, L.R. and Baltes, P.B. (eds.) (1970) *Life-Span Developmental Psychology: Research and Theory*, New York, Academic Press
Habermas, J. (1971) *Towards a Rational Society*, London, Heinemann
—— (1972) *Knowledge and Human Interests*, London, Heinemann
Hall, C.S. (1954) *A Primer of Freudian Psychology*, New York, Mentor Books, The New American Library
Holmes, B. (1965) 'The Reflective Man; Dewey' in Nash *et al.* (eds.) 1965
Hilgard, E.R. and Atkinson, R.C. (1967 — 3rd edn) *Introduction to Psychology*, New York, Harcourt, Brace and World Inc.
Hilgard, E.R., Atkinson, R.L. and Atkinson, R.C. (1979 — 7th edn) *Introduction to Psychology*, New York, Harcourt Brace and Jovanovitch
Hollins, T.H.B. (ed.) (1964) *Aims in Education: The Philosophical Approach*, Manchester University Press
Holmes, B. (1965) 'The Reflective Man; Dewey' in Nash *et al.* (eds.) 1965
Horn, J.L. (1970) 'Organization of Data on Life-Span Development of Human Abilities' in Goulet, L. and Baltes, P. (eds.) 1970
Houle, C.O. (1972) *The Design of Education*, San Francisco, Jossey Bass
—— (1984) *Patterns of Learning*, San Francisco, Jossey Bass

Howe, M.J.A. (ed.) (1977) *Adult Learning*, Chichester, John Wiley and Sons

Ingham, R. and Nelson, R.M. (1984) 'How Does a Person Learn? Using Life History Method to Answer the Question', paper presented at American Association of Adult and Continuing Education, Louisville, Kentucky

Jarvis, P. (1983a) *Professional Education*, London, Croom Helm

—— (1983b) *Adult and Continuing Education; Theory and Practice*, London, Croom Helm

—— (1985) *The Sociology of Adult and Continuing Education*, London, Croom Helm

—— (1985a) 'Thinking Critically in an Information Society' in *Lifelong Learning: an Omnibus of Practice and Research*, vol. 8, no. 6

—— (1986) *Sociological Perspectives on Lifelong Education and Lifelong Learning*, University of Georgia, Dept of Adult Education

—— (1987) 'Meaningful and Meaningless Experience: Towards an Understanding of Learning from Life' in *Adult Education Quarterly*, Spring, vol. 37, no. 3

Jarvis, P. and Gibson, S. (1985) *The Teacher Practitioner in Nursing, Midwifery and Health Visiting*, London, Croom Helm

Jenkins, D. and Shipman, M.D. (1976) *Curriculum: An Introduction*, London, Open Books

Jenkins, J.J. (1969) 'Language and Thought' in Voss (ed.) 1969

Kagan, J. (1971) 'Developmental Studies in Reflection and Analysis' in Cashdan and Whitehead (eds.) 1971

Keddie, N. (ed.) (1973) *Tinker, Tailor . . . The Myth of Cultural Deprivation*, Harmondsworth, Penguin

Kelley, H.H. (1950) 'The Warm-Cold Variable in First Impressions of Persons' cited in Krech *et al.* (1962)

Kelly, G.A. (1963) *A Theory of Personality: The Psychology of Personal Constructs*, New York, W.W. Norton

Kemmis, S. (1985) 'Action Research and the Politics of Reflection' in Boud *et al.* (1985)

Kidd, J.R. (ed.) (1973) *How Adults Learn*, Chicago, Association Press

Knapper, C. and Cropley, A. (1985) *Life-long Learning and Higher Education*, London, Croom Helm

Knowles, M.S. (1970) *The Modern Practice of Adult Education: Andragogy versus Pedagogy*, Chicago, Association Press

—— (ed.) (1978) *The Adult Learner: a Neglected Species*, Houston, Gulf Publishing Co.

—— (1979) 'Andragogy Revisited II', in *Adult Education*, vol. 30, pp. 52–3

—— (ed.) (1980) *The Modern Practice of Adult Education; From Pedagogy to Andragogy*, Chicago, Association Press

Knowles, M.S. *et al.* (1984) *Andragogy in Action*, San Francisco, Jossey Bass

Knox, A.B. (1977) *Adult Development and Learning*, San Francisco, Jossey Bass

Kohlberg, L. (1973) 'Continuities in Childhood and Adult Moral Development Revisited' in Baltés and Schaie (eds.)

Kohn, M. (1969) *Class and Conformity*, Homewood Illinois, Dorsey Press

Kolb, D.A. (1984) *Experiential Learning*, New Jersey, Prentice Hall

Krech, D., Crutchfield, R.S. and Ballachey, E.L. (1962), *Individual in Society*, Berkeley, University of California

Kuhn, D. (ed.) (1979) *Intellectual Development Beyond Childhood*, San Francisco, Jossey Bass

LaBelle, T.J. (1982) 'Formal, Non-Formal and Informal Education: A Holistic Perspective on Lifelong Learning' in *International Review of Education*, vol. 28, no. 2

Labov, W. (1973) 'The Logic of Non Standard English' in Keddie (ed.) 1973

Lawton, D. (1973) *Social Change, Educational Theory and Curriculum Planning*, London, Hodder and Stoughton

Lovell, R.B. (1980) *Adult Learning*, London, Croom Helm

Luckmann, T. (1967) *The Invisible Religion*, London, Macmillan

Lukes, S. (1981) 'Fact and Theory in the Social Sciences' in Potter *et al.* (eds.) 1981

McKenzie, L. (1977) 'The Issue of Andragogy', in *Adult Education*, vol. 27, pp. 225–9

Mackie, R. (ed.) (1980) *Literacy and Revolution: the Pedagogy of Paulo Freire*, London, Pluto Press

Mallin. S.B. (1979) *Marleau-Ponty's Philosophy*, New Haven and London, Yale University Press

Mannheim, K. (1936) *Ideology and Utopia*, London, Routledge and Kegan Paul

Mannheim, K. and Stewart, W.A.C. (1962) *An Introduction to the Sociology of Education*, London, Routledge and Kegan Paul

Mannings, R. (1986 — no date given) *The Incidental Learning Research Project*, Bristol Folk House, Adult Education Centre

Marcuse, H. (1968) 'Industrialism and Capitalism in the Work of Max Weber' reprinted in Stammer (ed.) 1971

Marton, F. *et al.* (eds.) (1984) *The Experience of Learning*, Edinburgh, Scottish Academic Press.

Marton, F. and Saljo, R. (1984) 'Approaches to Learning' in Marton *et al.* (eds.) 1984

Maslow, A.H. (1968 ed) *Towards a Psychology of Being*, New York, D. van Nostrand

Merriam, S. (1986) 'Reviewing and Organizing the Literature on Adult Learning', unpublished paper, University of Georgia

Merton, R.K. (1968 ed.) *Social Theory and Social Structure*, New York, The Free Press

Mezirow, J. (1977) 'Perspective Transformation' in *Studies in Adult Education*, vol. 9, no. 2, Leicester NIAE

—— (1981) 'A Critical Theory of Adult Learning and Education' in *Adult Education*, vol. 32. no. 1, Fall pp. 3–24, Washington, D.C.

Midwinter, E. (ed.) (1984) *Mutual Aid Universities*, London, Croom Helm

Milgram, S. (1965) 'Some Conditions of Obedience and Disobedience to Authority' in Steiner, I.D. and Fishbein, M. (eds.) *op. cit.*

Miller, D.L. (1973) *George Herbert Mead — Self, Language and the World*, Austin and London, University of Texas Press

Miller, H.L. (1964) *Teaching and Learning in Adult Education*, New York, Macmillan

Mocker, D.W. and Spear, G.E. (1982) *Lifelong Learning: Formal, Non-Formal, Informal and Self-Directed*, Columbus, Ohio, The ERIC Clearinghouse on Adult Career and Vocational Education

Moshman, D. (1979) 'To Really Get Ahead, Get a Metatheory' in Kuhn, D. (ed.) 1979

Nash, P., Kazamias, A.M. and Perkinson, H.J. (1965) *The Educated Man: Studies in the History of Educated Thought*. Malabar, Florida, Robert E. Krieger

Neugarten, B.L. (1977) 'Adult Personality: Towards a Psychology of the Life Cycle' in Allman and Jaffe (1977–78) (eds.)

Niebuhr, H. Jr. (1984) *Revitalizing American Learning: a New Approach that Might Just Work*. Belmont Ca., Wadsworth Publishing

Passmore, J. (1967) 'On Teaching to be Critical' in Peters, R. (ed.) 1967

Paterson, R.W.K. (1979) *Values, Education and the Adult*, London, Routledge and Kegan Paul

Pavlov, I.P. (1927) *Conditional Reflexes*, New York, Oxford University Press

Peters, R. (ed.) (1967) *The Concept of Education*, London, Routledge and Kegan Paul

Piaget, J. (1929) *The Child's Conception of the World*, London, Routledge and Kegan Paul

Potter, D. *et al.* (eds.) (1981) *Society and the Social Sciences*, London, Routledge and Kegan Paul in association with the Open University Press

Rahman, M.A. (1984) 'Asian Rural Workers' Group Develop Own Grassroots Methodology' in *Convergence*, vol. XVII, no. 2

Reischmann, J. (1986) 'Learning "en passant": The Forgotten Dimension', unpublished paper, presented at the American Association of Adult and Continuing Education, Hollywood, Florida, October

Riegel, K. (1973) 'Dialectic Operations: The Final Period of Human Development' in *Human Development*, vol. 16, no. 3

Riesman, D. (1950) *The Lonely Crowd: a Study of Changing American Character*, New Haven, Yale University Press

Rogers, C.R. (1969) *Freedom to Learn*, Columbus, Charles E. Merrill

Rogers, J. (ed.) (1977) *Adults Learning*, Milton Keynes, Open University Press

Ryle, G. (1963) *The Concept of Mind*, Harmondsworth, Penguin Books

Scheffler, I. (1965) *Conditions of Knowledge*, Chicago, University of Chicago Press

Scheler, M. (1980) *Problems of the Sociology of Knowledge*, London, Routledge and Kegan Paul

Schon, D.A. (1983) *The Reflective Practitioner*, New York, Basic Books, Inc.

Schutz, A. (1970) *On Phenomenology and Social Relations*, Chicago, University of Chicago Press

Schutz, A. and Luckmann, T. (1974) *The Structures of the Life World*, London, Heinemann

Sherron, R.H. and Lumsden, D.B. (1985 ed.) *Introduction to Educational Gerontology*, Washington, Hemisphere Publishing

Simmel, G. (1903) 'The Metropolis and Mental Life' reprinted in Thompson and Tunstall (eds.) 1971

Skinner, B.F. (1953) *Science and Human Behavior*, New York, Macmillan
—— (1971) *Beyond Freedom and Dignity*, Harmondsworth, Pelican

Smith, M. (1977) 'Adult Learning and Industrial Training' in Howe (ed.) 1977

Snook, I.A. (ed.) (1972) *Concepts of Indoctrination*, London, Routledge and Kegan Paul

Stammer, O. (ed.) (1971) *Max Weber and Sociology Today*, Oxford, Basil Blackwell

Steiner, I.D. and Fishbein, M. (eds.) (1965) *Current Studies in Social Psychology*, New York, Holt, Rinehart and Winston

Strauss, A. (ed.) (1964) *George Herbert Mead on Social Psychology*, Chicago and London, University of Chicago Press

Thompson, K. and Tunstall, J. (eds.) (1971) *Sociological Perspectives*, Harmondsworth, Penguin in association with the Open University Press

Thorson, J.A. and Waskel, S.A. (1985) 'Future Trends in Education for Elder Adults' in Sherron, R.H. and Lumsden, D.B. (eds.) 1985

Tough, A. (1979) 2nd edition. *The Adult's Learning Projects*, Ontario, The Ontario Institute for Studies in Education

Usher, R. (1985) 'Beyond the Anecdotal: Adult Learning and the Use of Experience' in *Studies in the Education of Adults*, vol. 17, no. 1

—— (1986) 'Adult Students and Their Experience' in *Studies in the Education of Adults*, vol. 18, no. 1

Voss, J.F. (ed.7 1969) *Approaches to Thought,* Columbus, Ohio, Charles E. Merrill

Williams, R. (1976) 'Base and Superstructure in Marxist Cultural Theory' in Dale, R. *et al.* (eds.) 1976

Willis, P. (1977) *Learning to Labour*, Farnborough, Saxon House

Wlodkowski, R.J. (1985) *Enhancing Adult Motivation to Learn*, San Francisco, Jossey Bass

Woodruff, A.D. (1968) 'Learning — from a Workshop in the Analysis of Teaching in *Theory into Practice*, vol. 7, no. 5, Ohio State University

Wrong, D.H. (1961) 'The Over-Socialized Conception of Man' reprinted in Wrong (1976)

—— (1976) *Skeptical Sociology*, London, Heinemann

Yonge, G.D. (1985) 'Andragogy and Pedagogy: Two Ways of Accompaniment' in *Adult Education Quarterly*, vol. 35, no. 3

Young, M.F.D. (1971) 'Curricula as Socially Organized Knowledge' in Young (ed.) 1971

—— (ed.) (1971) *Knowledge and Control*, London, Collier Macmillan

Index

135, 137-8, 139-40, 142-3,
145
non-learning 26, 27, 28-31, 61,
83, 133-46, 169, 186, 188,
189, 199

objectivity 121
Open University 22, 129

Passeron, J.C. 147
Passmore, J. 111
Paterson, R.W.K. 37-9, 114-15,
127-8, 194
patriarchy 107
Pavlov, I. 4-5
pedagogy 5, 9-11, 33, 48, 147,
161
peer group 3
perception 14, 17, 72, 73, 74,
75, 78, 86, 91, 102, 105,
124, 126, 150
person 24, 37-62, 127-30, 148,
192-5, 206
more experienced 24-5,
127-30
personhood 37, 46
perspective transformation 79,
91, 92, 99, 168
phenomenology 6, 16
Piaget, J. 2, 56, 108
play 51-2
political dimension 98
power 43, 80, 89, 108, 140,
144, 145, 147, 154, 155,
161, 162, 163-6, 184, 188
powerless 82
practical 17, 113
practice 113-18, 172, 177, 200,
205
praxis 90, 184
presumption 26, 28-30, 133,
134-5, 137, 139, 141-2, 144
pio-action 64, 65-6, 67, 133,
136-7, 149, 151, 152, 153,
156, 157, 159, 160, 161,
162, 166, 169, 170, 171,
174, 178, 179, 180, 181,
191, 198
problem solving 87, 93, 100,
169, 171, 178, 179, 187

professional practice 95-6,
117-18, 139, 172, 178, 181,
185, 200, 204
psycho-motor domain 118

quality circle 181
questioning 202

Rahman, H.A. 177
rationality 97, 103, 106-7, 111,
117, 122
technical 172, 200
reaction 64, 65-6, 133, 135,
149, 151, 152, 153, 156,
157, 158, 159, 160, 169,
170, 171, 1782-3, 174, 178,
179, 180, 191
reality social 70-4, 89, 105, 110,
154, 171, 174, 186
reasoning 11, 87, 93
reflection 6, 11, 17-18, 19, 20,
81, 82, 83, 86-112, 113,
116-17, 117-18, 122, 124,
150-1, 156, 168, 172-4,
201-5
unconscious 100-2
Reischmann, J. 31-2, 149
Reisman, D. 49
rejection 26, 30-1, 133, 134,
135-7, 138, 140-1, 143,
145-6
relationship
teacher-learner 5, 138-9, 156,
161, 176-7, 197-8
relevance 75, 124, 195, 198,
199
religion 53-4, 56, 66
research methodology 20-4
revolutionary 89, 185, 186, 187,
188
Riegel, K. 108
ritualist 142
Rogers, C. 37, 47-8, 196
Rogers, J. 100-1
Rubel, M. 43
Ryle, G. 39, 40-6, 54

Saljo, R. 7, 27
Scheffler, M. 193
Scheler, M. 83